Local Knowledge

LOCAL KNOWLEDGE

FURTHER ESSAYS
IN INTERPRETIVE
ANTHROPOLOGY
BY
Clifford Geertz

Basic Books, Inc., Publishers

NEW YORK

Library of Congress Cataloging in Publication Data

Geertz, Clifford.
  Local knowledge.

  Includes bibliographical references and index.
  1. Ethnology—Addresses, essays, lectures. I. Title.
GN316.G43 1983   306   83–70754
ISBN 0–465–04158–2

Contents

PART III

"Je demande dans quel genre est cette pièce? Dans le genre comique? il n'y a pas le mot pour rire. Dans le genre tragique? la terreur, la commisération et les autres grandes passions n'y sont point excitées. Cependant il y a de l'intérêt; et il y en aura, sans ridicule que fasse rire, sans danger que fasse frémir, dans toute composition dramatique où le sujet sera important, où le poète prendra le ton que nous avons dans les affaires sérieuses, et où l'action s'avancera par le perplexité et par les embarras. Or, il me semble que ces actions étant les plus communes de la vie, le genre que les aura pour objet doit être le plus utile et le plus étendu. J'appellerai ce genre *le genre sérieux.*"

Diderot, *Théâtre*

Local Knowledge

Introduction

When, a decade ago, I collected a number of my essays and rereleased them under the title, half genuflection, half talisman, *The Interpretation of Cultures,* I thought I was summing things up; saying, as I said there, what it was I had been saying. But, as a matter of fact, I was imposing upon myself a charge. In anthropology, too, it so turns out, he who says A must say B, and I have spent much of my time since trying to say it. The essays below are the result; but I am now altogether aware how much closer they stand to the origins of a thought-line than they do to the outcomes of it.

I am more aware, too, than I was then, of how widely spread this thought-line—a sort of cross between a connoisseur's weakness for nuance and an exegete's for comparison—has become in the social sciences. In part, this is simple history. Ten years ago, the proposal that cultural phenomena should be treated as significative systems posing expositive questions was a much more alarming one for social scientists—allergic, as they tend to be, to anything literary or inexact—than it is now. In part, it is a result of the growing recognition that the established approach to treating such phenomena, laws-and-causes social physics, was not producing the triumphs of prediction, control, and testability that had for so long been promised in its name. And in part, it is a result of intellectual deprovincialization. The broader currents of modern thought have finally begun to impinge upon what has been, and in some quarters still is, a snug and insular enterprise.

Of these developments, it is perhaps the last that is the most important. The penetration of the social sciences by the views of such philosophers as Heidegger, Wittgenstein, Gadamer, or Ricoeur, such critics as Burke, Frye, Jameson, or Fish, and such all-purpose subversives as Foucault, Habermas, Barthes, or Kuhn makes any simple return to a technological conception of those sciences highly improbable. Of course, the turning away from such a conception is not completely new—Weber's name has always to be called up here, and Freud's and Collingwood's as well. But the sweep of it is. Caught up in some of the more shaking originalities of the twentieth century, the study of society seems on the way to becoming seriously irregular.

It is certainly becoming more pluralistic. Though those with what they take to be one big idea are still among us, calls for "a general theory" of just about anything social sound increasingly hollow, and claims to have one megalomanic. Whether this is because it is too soon to hope for unified science or too late to believe in it is, I suppose, debatable. But it has never seemed further away, harder to imagine, or less certainly desirable than it does right now. The Sociology is not About to Begin, as Talcott Parsons once half-facetiously announced. It is scattering into frameworks.

As frameworks are the very stuff of cultural anthropology, which is mostly engaged in trying to determine what this people or that take to be the point of what they are doing, all this is very congenial to it. Even in its most universalist moods—evolutionary, diffusionist, functionalist, most recently structuralist or sociobiological—it has always had a keen sense of the dependence of what is seen upon where it is seen from and what it is seen with. To an ethnographer, sorting through the machinery of distant ideas, the shapes of knowledge are always ineluctably local, indivisible from their instruments and their encasements. One may veil this fact with ecumenical rhetoric or blur it with strenuous theory, but one cannot really make it go away.

Long one of the most homespun of disciplines, hostile to anything smacking of intellectual pretension and unnaturally proud of an outdoorsman image, anthropology has turned out, oddly enough, to have been preadapted to some of the most advanced varieties of modern opinion. The contextualist, antiformalist, relativizing tendencies of the bulk of that opinion, its turn toward examining the ways in which the world is talked about—depicted, charted, represented—rather than the way it intrinsically is, have been rather easily absorbed by adventurer scholars used to dealing with strange perceptions and stranger stories. They have, wonder of wonders, been speaking Wittgenstein all along. Contrariwise, anthropology, once read mostly for amusement, curiosity, or moral broadening, plus, in colonial situations, for administrative convenience, has now become a primary arena of speculative debate. Since Evans-Pritchard and his ineffable chicken oracles and Lévi-Strauss and his knowing *bricoleurs,* some of the central issues of, as I put it below, "the way we think now," have been joined in terms of anthropological materials, anthropological methods, and anthropological ideas.

My own work, insofar as it is more than archival (a function of anthropology much underrated), represents an effort to edge my way into odd corners of this discussion. All the essays below are ethnographically informed (or, God knows, misinformed) reflections on general topics, the sort of matters philosophers might address from more conjectural foundations, critics from more textual ones, or historians from more inductive ones. The figurative nature of social theory, the moral interplay of contrasting mentalities, the practical difficulties in seeing things as others see them, the epistemological status of common sense, the revelatory power of art, the symbolic construction of authority, the clattering variousness of modern intellectual life, and the relationship between what people take as fact and what they regard as justice are treated, one after the other, in an attempt somehow to understand how it is we understand understandings not our own.

This enterprise, "the understanding of understanding," is nowadays usually referred to as hermeneutics, and in that sense what I am doing fits well enough under such a rubric, particularly if the word "cultural" is affixed. But one will not find very much in the way of "the theory and methodology of interpretation" (to give the dictionary definition of the term) in what follows, for I do not believe that what "hermeneutics" needs is to be reified into a para-science, as epistemology was, and there are enough general principles in the world already. What one will find is a number of actual interpretations of something, anthropologizing formulations of what I take to be some of the broader implications of those interpretations, and a recurring cycle of terms—symbol, meaning, conception, form, text . . . culture—designed to suggest there is system in persistence, that all these so variously aimed inquiries are driven by a settled view of how one should go about constructing an account of the imaginative make-up of a society.

But if the view is settled, the way to bring it to practical existence and make it work surely is not. The stuttering quality of not only my own efforts along these lines but of interpretive social science generally is a result not (as is often enough suggested by those who like their statements flat) of a desire to disguise evasion as some new form of depth or to turn one's back on the claims of reason. It is a result of not knowing, in so uncertain an undertaking, quite where to begin, or, having anyhow begun, which way to move. Argument grows oblique, and language with it, because the more orderly and straightforward a particular course looks the more it seems ill-advised.

To turn from trying to explain social phenomena by weaving them into grand textures of cause and effect to trying to explain them by placing them in local frames of awareness is to exchange a set of well-charted difficulties for a set of largely uncharted ones. Dispassion, generality, and empirical grounding are earmarks of any science worth the name, as is logical force. Those who take the determinative approach seek these elusive virtues by positing a radical distinction between description and evaluation and then confining themselves to the descriptive side of it; but those who take the hermeneutic, denying the distinction is radical or finding themselves somehow astride it, are barred from so brisk a strategy. If, as I have, you construct accounts of how somebody or other—Moroccan poets, Elizabethan politicians, Balinese peasants, or American lawyers—glosses experience and then draw from those accounts of those glosses some conclusions about expression, power, identity, or justice, you feel at each stage fairly well away from the standard styles of demonstration. One makes detours, goes by side roads, as I quote Wittgenstein below; one sees the straight highway before one, "but of course . . . cannot use it, because it is permanently closed."

For making detours and going by sideroads, nothing is more convenient than the essay form. One can take off in almost any direction, certain that if the thing does not work out one can turn back and start over in some other with only moderate cost in time and disappointment. Midcourse corrections are rather easy, for one does not have a hundred pages of previous argument to sustain, as one does in a monograph or a treatise. Wanderings into yet smaller sideroads and wider detours does little harm, for progress is not expected to be relentlessly forward anyway, but winding and improvisational, coming out where it comes out. And when there is nothing more to say on the subject at the moment, or perhaps altogether, the matter can simply be dropped. "Works are not finished," as Valéry said, "they are abandoned."

Another advantage of the essay form is that it is very adaptable to occasions. The ability to sustain a coherent line of thought through a flurry of wildly assorted invitations, to talk here, to contribute there, to honor someone's memory or celebrate someone's career, to advance the cause of this journal or that organization, or simply to repay similar favors one has oneself asked of others, is, though rarely mentioned, one of the defining conditions of contemporary scholarly life. One can struggle against it, and, to avoid measuring out one's life with coffee spoons, to some extent must. But one must also, if one is not to become a lectern acrobat, doing, over and over again, the anthropological number ("culture is learned"; "customs vary"; "it takes all kinds to make a world"), turn it to one's account and build, particular response by particular response, a gathering progress of analysis. All the essays below are such particular responses to such unconnected and, it so happens, extramural invitations. But all are, too, steps in a perseverant attempt to push forward, or anyway somewhere, a general program. Whatever these various audiences—lawyers, literary critics, philosophers, sociologists, or the miscellaneous savants of the American Academy of Arts and Sciences (to which two of these essays were addressed)—asked for, what they got was "interpretive anthropology," my way.

The opening essay, "Blurred Genres," was originally delivered, appropriately enough, as a lecture to the Humanities Council of the State of Nevada at Reno. The charge was to say something or other reasonably coherent about the relation of "The Humanities" and "The Social Sciences," a matter anthropologists, considered amphibious between the two, are continually being asked to address, and to which (following the examination-room maxim—if you don't know the answer, discuss the question) I responded by attempting to cast doubt upon the force of the distinction in the first place. Grand rubrics like "Natural Science," "Biological Science," "Social Science," and "The Humanities" have their uses in organizing curricula, in sorting scholars into cliques and professional communities, and in distinguishing broad traditions of intellectual style. And, of course, the sorts of work conducted under any one of them do show some general resemblances to one another and some genuine differences from the sorts that are conducted under the others. There is, so far anyway, no historiography of motion; and inertia in a novel means something else. But when these rubrics are taken to be a borders-and-territories map of modern intellectual life, or, worse, a Linnaean catalogue into which to classify scholarly species, they merely block from view what is really going on out there where men and women are thinking about things and writing down what it is they think.

So far as the social sciences are concerned, any attempt to define them in some essence-and-accidents, natural-kind way and locate them at some definite latitude and longitude in scholarly space is bound to fail as soon as one looks from labels to cases. No one can put what Lévi-Strauss does together with what B. F. Skinner does in anything but the most vacuous of categories. In "Blurred Genres," I argue, first, that this seemingly anomalous state of affairs has become the natural condition of things and, second, that it is leading to significant realignments in scholarly affinities—who borrows what from whom. Most particularly, it has brought it about that a growing number of people trying to understand insurrections, hospitals, or why it is that jokes are prized have turned to linguistics, aesthétics, cultural history, law, or literary criticism for illumination rather than, as they used to do, to mechanics or physiology. Whether this is making the social sciences less scientific or humanistic study more so (or, as I believe, altering our view, never very stable anyway, of what counts as science) is not altogether clear and perhaps not altogether important. But that it is changing the character of both is clear and important—and discomposing.

It is discomposing not only because who knows where it all will end, but because as the idiom of social explanation, its inflections and its imagery, changes, our sense of what constitutes such explanation, why we want it, and how it relates to other sorts of things we value changes as well. It is not just theory or method or subject matter that alters, but the whole point of the enterprise.

The second essay, "Found in Translation," originally delivered to the Lionel Trilling Memorial Seminar at Columbia University, seeks to make this proposition a bit more concrete by comparing the sort of thing an ethnographer of my stripe does with the sort of thing a critic of Trilling's does and finding them not all that different. Putting Balinese representations of how things stand in the world into interpretive tension with our own, as a kind of commentary on them, and assessing the significance for practical conduct of literary portrayals—Austen's or Hardy's or Faulkner's—of what life is like, are not just cognate activities. They are the same activity differently pursued.

I called this activity, for purposes rather broader than those immediate to the essay, "the social history of the moral imagination," meaning by that the tracing out of the way in which our sense of ourselves and others—ourselves amidst others—is affected not only by our traffic with our own cultural forms but to a significant extent by the characterization of forms not immediately ours by anthropologists, critics, historians, and so on, who make them, reworked and redirected, derivatively ours. Particularly in the modern world, where very little that is distant, past, or esoteric that someone can find something out about goes undescribed and we live immersed in meta-commentary (what Trilling thinks about what Geertz thinks about what the Balinese think, and what Geertz thinks about that), our consciousness is shaped at least as much by how things supposedly look to others, somewhere else in the lifeline of the world, as by how they look here, where we are, now to us. The instability this introduces into our moral lives (to say nothing of what it does to our epistemological self-confidence) accounts, I think, for much of the sense of believing too many things at once that seems to haunt us, as well as for our intense concern with whether we are in any position, or can somehow get ourselves into one, to judge other ways of life at all. And it is the claim to be able to help us in this that links, whatever their differences in view or method, those such as Trilling, trying to find out how to talk to contemporaries about Jane Austen, and those such as myself, trying to find out how to talk to them about imaginative constructions—widow burnings and the like—that contemporaries are even further away from in assumption and sensibility than they are from Austen.

I referred to this conception of what culture explainers of all sorts claim they can do for us as "translation"—a trope current in my own field since Evans-Pritchard, at least—and, invoking a line of James Merrill's, argued that though obviously much is lost in this, much also, if ambiguous and troubling, is found. But just what it involves, how it is in fact effected, was left unexamined. In "From the Native's Point of View," the piece to which Trilling had in fact originally reacted, I did examine it, and with some particularity, at least for anthropology.

Or at least for my own anthropology. The occasion this time was an address to the American Academy of Arts and Sciences in which, as they were giving me an award for my work, I thought I might try to tell them what sort of work it was. The publication of Malinowski's *A Diary in the Strict Sense of the Term* several years before had fairly well exploded the notion that anthropologists obtained their results through some special ability, usually called "empathy," to "get inside the skins" of savages. It is not clear how widely this was ever believed ("The more anthropologists write about the United States," Bernard DeVoto growled when Mead's *And Keep Your Powder Dry* came out, "the less we believe what they say about Samoa");

but with the *Diary* and its revelation of a man so deeply self-engrossed as to suggest he might have been better employed as a romantic poet, the question of how they did obtain them (as Malinowski and, DeVoto notwithstanding, Mead as well so clearly did) demanded to be addressed in less subjectivist terms.

The peoples I have worked among—various sorts of Moroccans and Indonesians; Muslims, Hindus, and one disguised as the other—can hardly be called savages by anybody's definition; but their approach to things differs enough from one another to put the issue into general focus. To demonstrate this, I first described, rather telegraphically, the concepts of selfhood I had found current in central Java, south Bali, and mid-Atlas Morocco and, even more telegraphically, the broader frames of thought and action in which those conceptions flourished. I then argued that what the anthropologist has to do to bring this kind of thing off is tack between the two sorts of descriptions—between increasingly fine-comb observations (of how Javanese distinguish feelings, Balinese name children, Moroccans refer to acquaintances) and increasingly synoptic characterizations ("quietism," "dramatism," "contextualism")—in such a way that, held in the mind together, they present a credible, fleshed-out picture of a human form of life. "Translation," here, is not a simple recasting of others' ways of putting things in terms of our own ways of putting them (that is the kind in which things get lost), but displaying the logic of their ways of putting them in the locutions of ours; a conception which again brings it rather closer to what a critic does to illumine a poem than what an astronomer does to account for a star.

However that may be, it is, this catching of "their" views in "our" vocabularies, one of those things like riding a bicycle that is easier done than said. And in the following two essays I attempt to do a bit of it, in a rather more organized way, for what under some descriptions, though not under mine, would be the antipodal extremes of culture: common sense and art.

Indeed, for many people and most especially for its champions, common sense is not cultural at all, but the simple truth of things artlessly apprehended; plain fact acknowledged by plain men. Thus, I began "Common Sense as a Cultural System," first given as a John Dewey Lecture at Antioch College in the middle of a sixties uprising, by arguing, contrary to this (commonsensical) idea, that common sense *was* a cultural system; a loosely connected body of belief and judgment, rather than just what anybody properly put together cannot help but think. There may be things that anybody prop-

erly put together cannot help but think—that rocks are hard and death inevitable. And there certainly are some—that rocks are insentient and death
disagreeable—that, though Wordsworth gave a moral life to stones and Fas-
cist thugs shouted *viva la muerte* at Unamuno, no one much doubts. But
common sense has more to do with how to deal with a world in which such
things obtain than with the mere recognition that they do so. Common
sense is not a fortunate faculty, like perfect pitch; it is a special frame of
mind, like piety or legalism. And like piety or legalism (or ethics or cosmology), it both differs from one place to the next and takes, nevertheless, a
characteristic form.

The rest of the essay then seeks to illustrate all this, first with some examples taken from the anthropological literature (Evans-Pritchard on witchcraft, Edgerton on hermaphroditism) to display the variation, and then with
some features seen as distinctive of common sense in whatever clime (distrust of subtlety, exaltation of the practical, and so forth) to expose the form.
The oscillation between looking particularly at particular views and defining globally the attitude that permeates them thus governs again the progress of analysis. Only here there is an attempt to push things on to broader
issues: the construction of anthropological categories, the generality of their
reference, and the conditions of their use.

When one turns to art these issues become, if anything, even more pointed, for the debate over whether it is an applicable category in
"non-Western" or "pre-Modern" contexts has, even when compared to
similar debates concerning "religion," "science," "ideology," or "law,"
been peculiarly unrelenting. It has also been peculiarly unproductive. Whatever you want to call a cave wall crowded with overlapping images of trans-
fixed animals, a temple tower shaped to a phallus, a feathered shield, a calli-
graphic scroll, or a tattooed face, you still have the phenomenon to deal
with, as well as perhaps the sense that to add kula exchange or the Domes-
day Book would be to spoil the series. The question is not whether art (or
anything else) is universal; it is whether one can talk about West African
carving, New Guinea palm-leaf painting, quattrocento picture making, and
Moroccan versifying in such a way as to cause them to shed some sort of
light on one another.

The essay in which I tried to do exactly this, "Art as a Cultural System,"
was delivered at Johns Hopkins University as part of a wildly multidiscipli-
nary symposium—Maurice Mandlebaum, Paul de Man, and Alan Dundes
to Umberto Eco, Thomas Sebeok, and Roman Jakobson—on "semiotics"

(the occasion being a commemoration of Charles Peirce, whom the University had at one time fired), with the result that I was almost as much concerned with how *not* to talk about such things—in terms of some sort of mechanical formalism—as I was with developing my own approach. In particular, the identification of semiotics, in the general sense of the science of signs, with structuralism seemed to me important to resist. (Structuralism, as a sort of high-tech rationalism, seems to me important to resist in general.) And so I employed my cases—Robert Faris Thompson's analysis of Yoruba line, Anthony Forge's of Abelam color, Michael Baxandall's of Renaissance composition, and my own of Moroccan rhetoric—to suggest that the social contextualization of such "signifiers" is a more useful way to comprehend how they signify, and what, than is forcing them into schematic paradigms or stripping them down to abstract rule systems that supposedly "generate" them. What enables us to talk about them usefully together is that they all inscribe a communal sensibility, present locally to locals a local turn of mind.

Like common sense—or religion or law or even, though it is, given our predilections, a touchier matter, science—art is neither some transcendent phenomenon variously disguised in different cultures nor a notion so thoroughly culture-bound as to be useless beyond Europe. Not only Sweeney's Law ("I gotta use words when I talk to ya") but the simple fact that thinking of Noh plays and operas, or Shalako and *L'Oiseau de feu,* in relation to one another seems a more profitable thing to do than to think of any of them in relation to canoe building or the *Code Civil* (though, remembering Zen and motorcycle maintenance, one ought not to be too sure) suggest that radical culturalism will get us nowhere. And the impossibility of collapsing these so very different things into one another at any but the most abstract, and vacuous, levels—"objects of beauty," "affective presences," "expressive forms"—suggests that a universalist tack is hardly more promising. The reshaping of categories (ours and other people's—think of "taboo") so that they can reach beyond the contexts in which they originally arose and took their meaning so as to locate affinities and mark differences is a great part of what "translation" comes to in anthropology. It is—think of what it has done to "family," "caste," "market," or "state"—a great part of what anthropology comes to.

The following essay, "Centers, Kings, and Charisma," written for a volume honoring the theoretical sociologist Edward Shils, focuses on one such usefully tortured category—along with "alienation," "ego," "anomie," and, of course, "culture," among the most useful and the most tortured in all social science—namely, "charisma." Originally charisma was a Christian theological term having to do with a God-given capacity to perform miracles; later it was adapted by Max Weber as a label for the I-Am-The-Man type of leadership grown all too familiar in our century. Most recently, however, an excessive currency has obscured its genealogy and taken the political edge off it almost altogether, transforming it into an up-market synonym for celebrity, popularity, glamour, or sex appeal. In "Centers" I attempt to restore both the genealogy and the edge by comparing royal progresses in more or less Protestant late-Tudor England, more or less Hindu late-Majapahit Java, and more or less Muslim late-Alawite Morocco.

The juxtaposition of Elizabeth's tours through her realm as an allegorical representation of Chastity, Peace, or Safety at Sea, Hayam Wuruk's parades through his as the incarnation of the Sun and the Moon Shining Over the Earth-Circle, and Mulay Hasan's expeditions through his as the material expression of Divine Will seeks, like the similarly eccentric juxtapositions in the earlier essays, to attain what generality it can by orchestrating contrasts rather than isolating regularities or abstracting types. It is analogy that informs, or is supposed to, in this sort of anthropologizing, and it is upon the capacity of theoretical ideas to set up effective analogies that their value depends. And it is this kind of analogy between, here, the cult of a Virgin Queen, of a God King, and of a Commander of the Faithful, that the concept of charisma, training our attention on the witchery of power, enables us to construct.

All this is perhaps acceptable enough for traditional monarchies, where the symbolics of domination are so elaborate and egregious; whether extending the comparison to modern states, as I do in a rather hurried and anecdotal conclusion, strains the analogy beyond reasonable bounds is a more difficult question. One may doubt that high politics have been completely demystified in such states, even that they ever will be. But the general issue that is raised by considering the matter against so panoramic a comparative background—how far a mode of analysis designed to apply to the long ago or far away can be applied to ourselves—nevertheless remains. The DeVoto Problem is all too real: what, save impressionism and self-parody, plus a certain amount of ideological axe grinding, might come from anthropological discussions of modern culture?

In the final two essays—or, more accurately, an essay and a three-part mini-treatise—I turn to this problem. "The Way We Think Now" was originally given as a bicentennial address to the American Academy of Arts and Sciences under the general theme "Unity and Diversity: The Life of the Mind," as a sort of dialectical counterpoint to one given by the artificial intelligencer Herbert Simon. Taking the charge to heart this time, and thinking about what Simon would be likely to say, I distinguished between two reasonably different approaches to the study of human "thought" currently in vogue: a unific one, which conceives of it as a psychological process, person-bounded and law governed, and a pluralistic one, which conceives of it as a collective product, culturally coded and historically constructed—thought in the head, thought in the world. Rather than trying to adjudicate between them (in their radical forms—Chomsky and Whorf—neither seems especially plausible), I first traced the tension between them as it developed in anthropology—"primitive thought," "conceptual relativism," and all that—to become a driving, and often enough a distorting, force in ethnological theory. Then, turning again to notions of interpretation, translation, disarrayed genres, and analogic comparison, I sought to show that the enormous diversity of modern thought as we in fact find it around us in every form from poems to equations must be acknowledged if we are to understand anything at all about the Life of the Mind, and that this can be accomplished without prejudice to the idea that human thinking has its own constraints and its own constancies.

To do this, to produce a description of modern thought that can account for the fact that such assorted enterprises as herpetology, kinship theory, fiction writing, psychoanalysis, differential topology, fluid dynamics, iconology, and econometrics can form for us any category at all, it is necessary to see them as social activities in a social world. The various disciplines and quasi-disciplines that make up the arts and sciences are, for those caught up in them, far more than a set of technical tasks and vocational obligations; they are cultural frames in terms of which attitudes are formed and lives conducted. Physics and haruspicy, sculpture and scarification are alike at least in this: for their practitioners they support particular modes of engagement with life, and for the rest of us they illustrate them. Where they differ is that, though we know at least something by now about the sorts of engagements haruspicy and scarification tend to support, physics and sculpture, and all the other grand departments of the Life of the Mind, remain for the most part ethnographically opaque, mere recognized ways of doing recognizable things.

The remainder of the essay then consists of some reflections on the specters ("subjectivism," "idealism," "relativism," and the like) that academics conjure up to scare us away from an ethnographic approach to their thought; on some methods already at work in anthropology by means of which such an approach, dismissing the specters for the concoctions they are, might be practically pursued; and on the usefulness, if it is pursued, of such an approach for the construction of a more realistic model of liberal education than the Athenian gentleman one that, however disguised at either Cambridge, still predominates. But it is only in the final three essays, devoted to a particular Life of the Mind subject, namely law, and to a particular issue within that subject, namely the relation between fact finding and rule applying in adjudicative processes, that the program—seeing thoughts as *choses sociales*—is empirically tried out.

These essays, collectively titled "Local Knowledge: Fact and Law in Comparative Perspective," were given as the Storrs Lectures for 1981 at the Yale Law School, and they are the only essays of those assembled here that have not been previously published. Faced with trying to imagine something properly anthropological that would be of interest to lawyers, apprentice lawyers, law teachers, and perhaps even the odd judge, I thought to discuss a topic central to both Anglo-American jurisprudence and to common law adjudication, the is/ought, what-happened/was-it-lawful distinction, and to trace its half-parallels in three other legal traditions I had encountered in the course of my own researches: the Islamic, the Indic, and the Malayo-Indonesian. The notion was, first, to examine the issue as it appears in the contemporary United States; second, to describe the quite different forms it takes in these other traditions—so different as to demand a fairly thoroughgoing reformulation of it; and then, third, to say something about the implications of such differences for the evolution of orderly adjudication in a world where, no longer confined to their classical terrains, contrasting legal traditions are being forced into the most direct and practical sorts of confrontation.

Accordingly, the lectures describe, once again, a rather dialectical movement, tacking between looking at things in lawyers' terms and looking at them in anthropologists' terms; between modern Western prepossessions and classical Middle Eastern and Asian ones; between law as a structure of normative ideas and law as a set of decision procedures; between pervading sensibilities and instant cases; between legal traditions as autonomous systems and legal traditions as contending ideologies; between, finally, the small imaginings of local knowledge and the large ones of cosmopolitan intent. It all looks almost experimental: an effort to assay the fact-law formula by seeing what remains of it after it has been rung through the changes of headlong comparative analysis. That much does and much does not is hardly surprising; that is how all such experiments without metrics come out. But what does remain (an accommodation of a language of general coherence and a language of practical consequence) and what does not (a social-echo view of legal process) are of perhaps a bit more interest.

In the last analysis, then, as in the first, the interpretive study of culture represents an attempt to come to terms with the diversity of the ways human beings construct their lives in the act of leading them. In the more standard sorts of science the trick is to steer between what statisticians call type-one and type-two errors—accepting hypotheses one would be better advised to reject and rejecting ones one would be wiser to accept; here it is to steer between overinterpretation and underinterpretation, reading more into things than reason permits and less into them than it demands. Where the first sort of mistake, telling stories about people only a professor can believe, has been much noted and more than a bit exaggerated, the second, reducing people to ordinary chaps out, like the rest of us, for money, sex, status, and power, never mind a few peculiar ideas that don't mean much anyway when push comes to shove, has been much less so. But the one is as mischievous as the other. We are surrounded (and we are surrounded) neither by Martians nor by less well got-up editions of ourselves; a proposition that holds no matter what "we"—American ethnographers, Moroccan judges, Javanese metaphysicians, or Balinese dancers—we start from.

To see ourselves as others see us can be eye-opening. To see others as sharing a nature with ourselves is the merest decency. But it is from the far more difficult achievement of seeing ourselves amongst others, as a local example of the forms human life has locally taken, a case among cases, a world among worlds, that the largeness of mind, without which objectivity is self-congratulation and tolerance a sham, comes. If interpretive anthropology has any general office in the world it is to keep reteaching this fugitive truth.

PART I

Chapter 1 / Blurred Genres:

The Refiguration of

Social Thought

✿
────────────

I

A number of things, I think, are true. One is that there has been an enormous amount of genre mixing in intellectual life in recent years, and it is, such blurring of kinds, continuing apace. Another is that many social scientists have turned away from a laws and instances ideal of explanation toward a cases and interpretations one, looking less for the sort of thing that connects planets and pendulums and more for the sort that connects chrysanthemums and swords. Yet another is that analogies drawn from the humanities are coming to play the kind of role in sociological understanding that analogies drawn from the crafts and technology have long played in physical understanding. Further, I not only think these things are true, I think they are true together; and it is the culture shift that makes them so that is my subject: the refiguration of social thought.

This genre blurring is more than just a matter of Harry Houdini or Richard Nixon turning up as characters in novels or of midwestern murder sprees described as though a gothic romancer had imagined them. It is

philosophical inquiries looking like literary criticism (think of Stanley Ca-
vell on Beckett or Thoreau, Sartre on Flaubert), scientific discussions looking like belles lettres *morceaux* (Lewis Thomas, Loren Eiseley), baroque
fantasies presented as deadpan empirical observations (Borges, Barthelme),
histories that consist of equations and tables or law court testimony (Fogel
and Engerman, Le Roi Ladurie), documentaries that read like true confes-
sions (Mailer), parables posing as ethnographies (Castenada), theoretical
treatises set out as travelogues (Lévi-Strauss), ideological arguments cast
as historiographical inquiries (Edward Said), epistemological studies constructed like political tracts (Paul Feyerabend), methodological polemics
got up as personal memoirs (James Watson). Nabokov's *Pale Fire,* that impossible object made of poetry and fiction, footnotes and images from the
clinic, seems very much of the time; one waits only for quantum theory
in verse or biography in algebra.

Of course, to a certain extent this sort of thing has always gone
on—Lucretius, Mandeville, and Erasmus Darwin all made their theories
rhyme. But the present jumbling of varieties of discourse has grown to the
point where it is becoming difficult either to label authors (What *is* Foucault—historian, philosopher, political theorist? What Thomas
Kuhn—historian, philosopher, sociologist of knowledge?) or to classify
works (What is George Steiner's *After Babel*—linguistics, criticism, culture
history? What William Gass's *On Being Blue*—treatise, causerie, apologet-
ic?). And thus it is more than a matter of odd sports and occasional curiosities, or of the admitted fact that the innovative is, by definition, hard to
categorize. It is a phenomenon general enough and distinctive enough to
suggest that what we are seeing is not just another redrawing of the cultural
map—the moving of a few disputed borders, the marking of some more
picturesque mountain lakes—but an alteration of the principles of mapping.
Something is happening to the way we think about the way we think.

We need not accept hermetic views of *écriture* as so many signs signing
signs, or give ourselves so wholly to the pleasure of the text that its meaning
disappears into our responses, to see that there has come into our view of
what we read and what we write a distinctly democratical temper. The
properties connecting texts with one another, that put them, ontologically
anyway, on the same level, are coming to seem as important in characteriz-
ing them as those dividing them; and rather than face an array of natural
kinds, fixed types divided by sharp qualitative differences, we more and
more see ourselves surrounded by a vast, almost continuous field of vari-

ously intended and diversely constructed works we can order only practically, relationally, and as our purposes prompt us. It is not that we no longer have conventions of interpretation; we have more than ever, built—often enough jerry-built—to accommodate a situation at once fluid, plural, uncentered, and ineradicably untidy.

So far as the social sciences are concerned, all this means that their oft-lamented lack of character no longer sets them apart. It is even more difficult than it always has been to regard them as underdeveloped natural sciences, awaiting only time and aid from more advanced quarters to harden them, or as ignorant and pretentious usurpers of the mission of the humanities, promising certainties where none can be, or as comprising a clearly distinctive enterprise, a third culture between Snow's canonical two. But that is all to the good: freed from having to become taxonomically upstanding, because nobody else is, individuals thinking of themselves as social (or behavioral or human or cultural) scientists have become free to shape their work in terms of its necessities rather than according to received ideas as to what they ought or ought not to be doing. What Clyde Kluckhohn once said about anthropology—that it's an intellectual poaching license—not only seems more true now than when he said it, but true of a lot more than anthropology. Born omniform, the social sciences prosper as the condition I have been describing becomes general.

It has thus dawned on social scientists that they did not need to be mimic physicists or closet humanists or to invent some new realm of being to serve as the object of their investigations. Instead they could proceed with their vocation, trying to discover order in collective life, and decide how what they were doing was connected to related enterprises when they managed to get some of it done; and many of them have taken an essentially hermeneutic—or, if that word frightens, conjuring up images of biblical zealots, literary humbugs, and Teutonic professors, an "interpretive"—approach to their task. Given the new genre dispersion, many have taken other approaches: structuralism, neo-positivism, neo-Marxism, micro-micro descriptivism, macro-macro system building, and that curious combination of common sense and common nonsense, sociobiology. But the move toward conceiving of social life as organized in terms of symbols (signs, representations, *signifiants, Darstellungen*... the terminology varies), whose meaning (sense, import, *signification, Bedeutung*...) we must grasp if we are to understand that organization and formulate its principles, has grown by now to formidable proportions. The woods are full of eager interpreters.

Interpretive explanation—and it is a form of explanation, not just exalted glossography—trains its attention on what institutions, actions, images, utterances, events, customs, all the usual objects of social-scientific interest, mean to those whose institutions, actions, customs, and so on they are. As a result, it issues not in laws like Boyle's, or forces like Volta's, or mechanisms like Darwin's, but in constructions like Burckhardt's, Weber's, or Freud's: systematic unpackings of the conceptual world in which *condottiere,* Calvinists, or paranoids live.

The manner of these constructions itself varies: Burckhardt portrays, Weber models, Freud diagnoses. But they all represent attempts to formulate how this people or that, this period or that, this person or that makes sense to itself and, understanding that, what we understand about social order, historical change, or psychic functioning in general. Inquiry is directed toward cases or sets of cases, and toward the particular features that mark them off; but its aims are as far-reaching as those of mechanics or physiology: to distinguish the materials of human experience.

With such aims and such a manner of pursuing them come as well some novelties in analytical rhetoric, the tropes and imageries of explanation. Because theory, scientific or otherwise, moves mainly by analogy, a "seeing-as" comprehension of the less intelligible by the more (the earth is a magnet, the heart is a pump, light is a wave, the brain is a computer, and space is a balloon), when its course shifts, the conceits in which it expresses itself shift with it. In the earlier stages of the natural sciences, before the analogies became so heavily intramural—and in those (cybernetics, neurology) in which they still have not—it has been the world of the crafts and, later, of industry that have for the most part provided the well-understood realities (well-understood because, *certum quod factum,* as Vico said, man had made them) with which the ill-understood ones (ill-understood because he had not) could be brought into the circle of the known. Science owes more to the steam engine than the steam engine owes to science; without the dyer's art there would be no chemistry; metallurgy is mining theorized. In the social sciences, or at least in those that have abandoned a reductionist conception of what they are about, the analogies are coming more and more from the contrivances of cultural performance than from those of physical manipulation—from theater, painting, grammar, literature, law, play. What the lever did for physics, the chess move promises to do for sociology.

Promises are not always kept, of course, and when they are, they often turn out to have been threats; but the casting of social theory in terms more familiar to gamesters and aestheticians than to plumbers and engineers is clearly well under way. The recourse to the humanities for explanatory analogies in the social sciences is at once evidence of the destabilization of genres and of the rise of "the interpretive turn," and their most visible outcome is a revised style of discourse in social studies. The instruments of reasoning are changing and society is less and less represented as an elaborate machine or a quasi-organism and more as a serious game, a sidewalk drama, or a behavioral text.

II

All this fiddling around with the proprieties of composition, inquiry, and explanation represents, of course, a radical alteration in the sociological imagination, propelling it in directions both difficult and unfamiliar. And like all such changes in fashions of the mind, it is about as likely to lead to obscurity and illusion as it is to precision and truth. If the result is not to be elaborate chatter or the higher nonsense, a critical consciousness will have to be developed; and as so much more of the imagery, method, theory, and style is to be drawn from the humanities than previously, it will mostly have to come from humanists and their apologists rather than from natural scientists and theirs. That humanists, after years of regarding social scientists as technologists or interlopers, are ill equipped to do this is something of an understatement.

Social scientists, having just freed themselves, and then only partially, from dreams of social physics—covering laws, unified science, operationalism, and all that—are hardly any better equipped. For them, the general muddling of vocational identities could not have come at a better time. If they are going to develop systems of analysis in which such conceptions as following a rule, constructing a representation, expressing an attitude, or forming an intention are going to play central roles—rather than such conceptions as isolating a cause, determining a variable, measuring a force, or defining a function—they are going to need all the help they can get from people who are more at home among such notions than they are. It is not interdisciplinary brotherhood that is needed, nor even less highbrow eclecticism. It is recognition on all sides that the lines grouping scholars together into intellecutal communities, or (what is the same thing) sorting them out into different ones, are these days running at some highly eccentric angles.

The point at which the reflections of humanists on the practices of social scientists seems most urgent is with respect to the deployment in social analysis of models drawn from humanist domains—that "wary reasoning from analogy," as Locke called it, that "leads us often into the discovery of truths and useful productions, which would otherwise lie concealed." (Locke was talking about rubbing two sticks together to produce fire and the atomic-friction theory of heat, though business partnership and the social contract would have served him as well.) Keeping the reasoning wary, thus useful, thus true, is, as we say, the name of the game.

The game analogy is both increasingly popular in contemporary social theory and increasingly in need of critical examination. The impetus for seeing one or another sort of social behavior as one or another sort of game has come from a number of sources (not excluding, perhaps, the prominence of spectator sports in mass society). But the most important are Wittgenstein's conception of forms of life as language games, Huizinga's ludic view of culture, and the new strategics of von Neumann's and Morgenstern's *Theory of Games and Economic Behavior.* From Wittgenstein has come the notion of intentional action as "following a rule"; from Huizinga, of play as the paradigm form of collective life; from von Neumann and Morgenstern, of social behavior as a reciprocative maneuvering toward distributive payoffs. Taken together they conduce to a nervous and nervous-making style of interpretation in the social sciences that mixes a strong sense of the formal orderliness of things with an equally strong sense of the radical arbitrariness of that order: chessboard inevitability that could as well have been otherwise.

The writings of Erving Goffman—perhaps the most celebrated American sociologist right now, and certainly the most ingenious—rest, for example, almost entirely on the game analogy. (Goffman also employs the language of the stage quite extensively, but as his view of the theater is that it is an oddly mannered kind of interaction game—ping-pong in masks—his work is not, at base, really dramaturgical.) Goffman applies game imagery to just about everything he can lay his hands on, which, as he is no respecter of property rights, is a very great deal. The to-and-fro of lies, meta-lies, unbelievable truths, threats, tortures, bribes, and blackmail that comprises the world of espionage is construed as an "expression game"; a carnival of deceptions rather like life in general, because, in a phrase that could have come from Conrad or Le Carré, "agents [are] a little like us all and all of us [are] a little like agents." Etiquette, diplomacy, crime, finance, advertising, law, seduction, and the everyday "realm of bantering decorum" are seen as "information games"—mazy structures of players, teams, moves, positions, signals, information states, gambles, and outcomes, in which only the "gameworthy"—those willing and able "to dissemble about anything"—prosper.

What goes on in a psychiatric hospital, or any hospital or prison or even a boarding school in Goffman's work, is a "ritual game of having a self," where the staff holds most of the face cards and all of the trumps. A tête-à-tête, a jury deliberation, "a task jointly pursued by persons physically close to one another," a couple dancing, lovemaking, or boxing—indeed, all face-to-face encounters—are games in which, "as every psychotic and comic ought to know, any accurately improper move can poke through the thin sleeve of immediate reality." Social conflict, deviance, entrepreneurship, sex roles, religious rites, status ranking, and the simple need for human acceptance get the same treatment. Life is just a bowl of strategies.

Or, perhaps better, as Damon Runyon once remarked, it is three-to-two against. For the image of society that emerges from Goffman's work, and from that of the swarm of scholars who in one way or another follow or depend on him, is of an unbroken stream of gambits, ploys, artifices, bluffs, disguises, conspiracies, and outright impostures as individuals and coalitions of individuals struggle—sometimes cleverly, more often comically—to play enigmatical games whose structure is clear but whose point is not. Goffman's is a radically unromantic vision of things, acrid and bleakly knowing, and one that sits rather poorly with traditional humanistic pieties. But it is no less powerful for that. Nor, with its uncomplaining play-it-as-it-lays ethic, is it all that inhumane.

However that may be, not all gamelike conceptions of social life are quite so grim, and some are positively frolicsome. What connects them all is the view that human beings are less driven by forces than submissive to rules, that the rules are such as to suggest strategies, the strategies are such as to inspire actions, and the actions are such as to be self-rewarding—*pour le sport*. As literal games—baseball or poker or Parcheesi—create little universes of meaning, in which some things can be done and some cannot (you can't castle in dominoes), so too do the analogical ones of worship, government, or sexual courtship (you can't mutiny in a bank). Seeing society as a collection of games means seeing it as a grand plurality of accepted conventions and appropriate procedures—tight, airless worlds of move and countermove, life *en règle.* "I wonder," Prince Metternich is supposed to have said when an aide whispered into his ear at a royal ball that the czar of all the Russians was dead, "I wonder what his motive could have been."

The game analogy is not a view of things that is likely to commend itself to humanists, who like to think of people not as obeying the rules and angling for advantage but as acting freely and realizing their finer capacities. But that it seems to explain a great deal about a great many aspects of modern life, and in many ways to catch its tone, is hardly deniable. ("If you can't stand the Machiavellianism," as a recent *New Yorker* cartoon said, "get out of the cabal.") Thus if the game analogy is to be countered it cannot be by mere disdain, refusing to look through the telescope, or by passioned restatements of hallowed truths, quoting scripture against the sun. It is necessary to get down to the details of the matter, to examine the studies and to critique the interpretations—whether Goffman's of crime as character gambling, Harold Garfinkel's of sex change as identity play, Gregory Bateson's of schizophrenia as rule confusion, or my own of the complicated goings-on in a mideastern bazaar as an information contest. As social theory turns from propulsive metaphors (the language of pistons) toward ludic ones (the language of pastimes), the humanities are connected to its arguments not in the fashion of skeptical bystanders but, as the source of its imagery, chargeable accomplices.

III

The drama analogy for social life has of course been around in a casual sort of way—all the world's a stage and we but poor players who strut and so on—for a very long time. And terms from the stage, most notably "role," have been staples of sociological discourse since at least the 1930s. What is relatively new—new, not unprecedented—are two things. First, the full weight of the analogy is coming to be applied extensively and systematically, rather than being deployed piecemeal fashion—a few allusions here, a few tropes there. And second, it is coming to be applied less in the depreciatory "mere show," masks and mummery mode that has tended to characterize its general use, and more in a constructional, genuinely dramaturgical one—making, not faking, as the anthropologist Victor Turner has put it.

The two developments are linked, of course. A constructionalist view of what theater is—that is, poiesis—implies that a dramatistic perspective in the social sciences needs to involve more than pointing out that we all have our entrances and exits, we all play parts, miss cues, and love pretense. It may or may not be a Barnum and Bailey world and we may or may not be walking shadows, but to take the drama analogy seriously is to probe behind such familiar ironies to the expressive devices that make collective life seem anything at all. The trouble with analogies—it is also their glory—is that they connect what they compare in both directions. Having trifled with theater's idiom, some social scientists find themselves drawn into the rather tangled coils of its aesthetic.

Such a more thoroughgoing exploitation of the drama analogy in social theory—as an analogy, not an incidental metaphor—has grown out of sources in the humanities not altogether commensurable. On the one hand, there has been the so-called ritual theory of drama associated with such diverse figures as Jane Harrison, Francis Fergusson, T. S. Eliot, and Antonin Artaud. On the other, there is the symbolic action—"dramatism," as he calls it—of the American literary theorist and philosopher Kenneth Burke, whose influence is, in the United States anyway, at once enormous and—because almost no one actually uses his baroque vocabulary, with its reductions, ratios, and so on—elusive. The trouble is, these approaches pull in rather opposite directions: the ritual theory toward the affinities of theater and religion—drama as communion, the temple as stage; the symbolic action theory toward those of theater and rhetoric—drama as persuasion, the platform as stage. And this leaves the basis of the analogy—just what in the theatron is like what in the agora—hard to focus. That liturgy and ideology are histrionic is obvious enough, as it is that etiquette and advertising are. But just what that means is a good deal less so.

Probably the foremost proponent of the ritual theory approach in the social sciences right now is Victor Turner. A British formed, American re-formed anthropologist, Turner, in a remarkable series of works trained on the ceremonial life of a Central African tribe, has developed a conception of "social drama" as a regenerative process that, rather like Goffman's of "social gaming" as strategic interaction, has drawn to it such a large number of able researchers as to produce a distinct and powerful interpretive school.

For Turner, social dramas occur "on all levels of social organization from state to family." They arise out of conflict situations—a village falls into factions, a husband beats a wife, a region rises against the state—and proceed to their denouements through publicly performed conventionalized behavior. As the conflict swells to crisis and the excited fluidity of heightened emotion, where people feel at once more enclosed in a common mood and loosened from their social moorings, ritualized forms of authority—litigation, feud, sacrifice, prayer—are invoked to contain it and render it orderly. If they succeed, the breach is healed and the status quo, or something resembling it, is restored; if they do not, it is accepted as incapable of remedy and things fall apart into various sorts of unhappy endings: migrations, divorces, or murders in the cathedral. With differing degrees of strictness and detail, Turner and his followers have applied this schema to tribal passage rites, curing ceremonies, and judicial processes; to Mexican insurrections, Icelandic sagas, and Thomas Becket's difficulties with Henry II; to picaresque narrative, millenarian movements, Caribbean carnivals, and Indian peyote hunts; and to the political upheaval of the sixties. A form for all seasons.

This hospitableness in the face of cases is at once the major strength of the ritual theory version of the drama analogy and its most prominent weakness. It can expose some of the profoundest features of social process, but at the expense of making vividly disparate matters look drably homogeneous.

Rooted as it is in the repetitive performance dimensions of social action—the reenactment and thus the reexperiencing of known form—the ritual theory not only brings out the temporal and collective dimensions of such action and its inherently public nature with particular sharpness; it brings out also its power to transmute not just opinions but, as the British critic Charles Morgan has said with respect to drama proper, the people who hold them. "The great impact [of the theater]," Morgan writes, "is neither a persuasion of the intellect nor a beguiling of the senses. . . . It is the enveloping movement of the whole drama on the soul of man. We surrender and are changed." Or at least we are when the magic works. What Morgan, in another fine phrase, calls "the suspense of form . . . the incompleteness of a known completion," is the source of the power of this "enveloping movement," a power, as the ritual theorists have shown, that is hardly less forceful (and hardly less likely to be seen as otherworldly) when the movement appears in a female initiation rite, a peasant revolution, a national epic, or a star chamber.

Yet these formally similar processes have different content. They say, as we might put it, rather different things, and thus have rather different implications for social life. And though ritual theorists are hardly incognizant of that fact, they are, precisely because they are so concerned with the general movement of things, ill-equipped to deal with it. The great dramatic rhythms, the commanding forms of theater, are perceived in social processes of all sorts, shapes, and significances (though ritual theorists in fact do much better with the cyclical, restorative periodicities of comedy than the linear, consuming progressions of tragedy, whose ends tend to be seen as misfires rather than fulfillments). Yet the individuating details, the sort of thing that makes *A Winter's Tale* different from *Measure for Measure, Macbeth* from *Hamlet,* are left to encyclopedic empiricism: massive documentation of a single proposition—*plus ça change, plus c'est le même changement.* If dramas are, to adapt a phrase of Susanne Langer's, poems in the mode of action, something is being missed: what exactly, socially, the poems say.

This unpacking of performed meaning is what the symbolic action approaches are designed to accomplish. Here there is no single name to cite, just a growing catalogue of particular studies, some dependent on Kenneth Burke, some on Ernst Cassirer, Northrop Frye, Michel Foucault, or Emile Durkheim, concerned to say what some bit of acted saying—a coronation, a sermon, a riot, an execution—says. If ritual theorists, their eye on experience, tend to be hedgehogs, symbolic action theorists, their eye on expression, tend to be foxes.

Given the dialectical nature of things, we all need our opponents, and both sorts of approach are essential. What we are most in want of right now is some way of synthesizing them. In my own analysis of the traditional Indic polity in Bali as a "theater state"—cited here not because it is exemplary, but because it is mine—I have tried to address this problem. In this analysis I am concerned, on the one hand (the Burkean one), to show how everything from kin group organization, trade, customary law, and water control to mythology, architecture, iconography, and cremation combines to a dramatized statement of a distinct form of political theory, a particular conception of what status, power, authority, and government are and should be: namely, a replication of the world of the gods that is at the same time a template for that of men. The state enacts an image of order that—a model for its beholders, in and of itself—orders society. On the other hand (the Turner one), as the populace at large does not merely view the state's expressions as so many gaping spectators but is caught up bodily in them, and especially in the great, mass ceremonies—political operas of Burgundian dimensions—that form their heart, the sort of "we surrender and are changed" power of drama to shape experience is the strong force that holds the polity together. Reiterated form, staged and acted by its own audience, makes (to a degree, for no theater ever wholly works) theory fact.

But my point is that some of those fit to judge work of this kind ought to be humanists who reputedly know something about what theater and mimesis and rhetoric are, and not just with respect to my work but to that of the whole steadily broadening stream of social analyses in which the drama analogy is, in one form or another, governing. At a time when social scientists are chattering about actors, scenes, plots, performances, and personae, and humanists are mumbling about motives, authority, persuasion, exchange, and hierarchy, the line between the two, however comforting to the puritan on the one side and the cavalier on the other, seems uncertain indeed.

IV

The text analogy now taken up by social scientists is, in some ways, the broadest of the recent refigurations of social theory, the most venturesome, and the least well developed. Even more than "game" or "drama," "text" is a dangerously unfocused term, and its application to social action, to people's behavior toward other people, involves a thoroughgoing conceptual wrench, a particularly outlandish bit of "seeing-as." Describing human conduct in the analogy of player and counterplayer, or of actor and audience, seems, whatever the pitfalls, rather more natural than describing it in that of writer and reader. Prima facie, the suggestion that the activities of spies, lovers, witch doctors, kings, or mental patients are moves or performances is surely a good deal more plausible than the notion that they are sentences.

But prima facie is a dubious guide when it comes to analogizing; were it not, we should still be thinking of the heart as a furnace and the lungs as bellows. The text analogy has some unapparent advantages still insufficiently exploited, and the surface dissimilarity of the here-we-are-and-there-we-are of social interaction to the solid composure of lines on a page is what gives it—or can when the disaccordance is rightly aligned—its interpretive force.

The key to the transition from text to text analogue, from writing as discourse to action as discourse, is, as Paul Ricoeur has pointed out, the concept of "inscription": the fixation of meaning. When we speak, our utterances fly by as events like any other behavior; unless what we say is inscribed in writing (or some other established recording process), it is as evanescent as what we do. If it is so inscribed, it of course passes, like Dorian Gray's youth, anyway; but at least its meaning—the *said,* not the *saying*—to a degree and for a while remains. This too is not different for action in general: its meaning can persist in a way its actuality cannot.

The great virtue of the extension of the notion of text beyond things written on paper or carved into stone is that it trains attention on precisely this phenomenon: on how the inscription of action is brought about, what its vehicles are and how they work, and on what the fixation of meaning from the flow of events—history from what happened, thought from thinking, culture from behavior—implies for sociological interpretation. To see social institutions, social customs, social changes as in some sense "readable" is to alter our whole sense of what such interpretation is and shift it toward modes of thought rather more familiar to the translator, the exegete, or the iconographer than to the test giver, the factor analyst, or the pollster.

All this comes out with exemplary vividness in the work of Alton Becker, a comparative linguist, on Javanese shadow puppetry, or the *wayang* as it is called. Wayang-ing (there is no other suitable verb) is, Becker says, a mode of text building, a way of putting symbols together to construct an expression. To construe it, to understand not just what it means but how it does so, one needs, he says, a new philology.

Philology, the text-centered study of language, as contrasted to linguistics, which is speech-centered, has of course traditionally been concerned with making ancient or foreign or esoteric documents accessible to those for whom they are ancient or foreign or esoteric. Terms are glossed, notes appended, commentaries written, and, where necessary, transcriptions made and translations effected—all toward the end of producing an annotated edition as readable as the philologist can make it. Meaning is fixed at a meta-level; essentially what a philologist, a kind of secondary author, does is reinscribe: interpret a text with a text.

Left at this, matters are straightforward enough, however difficult they may turn out to be in practice. But when philological concern goes beyond routinized craft procedures (authentication, reconstruction, annotation) to address itself to conceptual questions concerning the nature of texts as such—that is, to questions about their principles of construction—simplicity flees. The result, Becker notes, has been the shattering of philology, itself by now a near obsolescent term, into disjunct and rivalrous specialties, and most particularly the growth of a division between those who study individual texts (historians, editors, critics—who like to call themselves humanists), and those who study the activity of creating texts in general (linguists, psychologists, ethnographers—who like to call themselves scientists). The study of inscriptions is severed from the study of inscribing, the study of fixed meaning is severed from the study of the social processes that fix it. The result is a double narrowness. Not only is the extension of text analysis to nonwritten materials blocked, but so is the application of sociological analysis to written ones.

The repair of this split and the integration of the study of how texts are built, how the said is rescued from its saying, into the study of social phenomena—Apache jokes, English meals, African cult sermons, American high schools, Indian caste, or Balinese widow burning, to mention some recent attempts aside from Becker's—are what the "new philology," or whatever else it eventually comes to be called, is all about. "In a multicultured world," Becker writes, "a world of multiple epistemologies, there is need for a new philologist—a specialist in contextual relations—in all areas of knowledge in which text-building . . . is a central activity: literature, history, law, music, politics, psychology, trade, even war and peace."

Becker sees four main orders of semiotic connection in a social text for his new philologist to investigate: the relation of its parts to one another; the relation of it to others culturally or historically associated with it; the relation of it to those who in some sense construct it; and the relation of it to realities conceived as lying outside of it. Certainly there are others—its relation to its *materia,* for one; and, more certainly yet, even these raise profound methodological issues so far only hesitantly addressed. "Coherence," "inter-textuality," "intention," and "reference"—which are what Becker's four relations more or less come down to—all become most elusive notions when one leaves the paragraph or page for the act or institution.

Indeed, as Nelson Goodman has shown, they are not all that well defined for the paragraph or page, to say nothing of the picture, the melody, the statue, or the dance. Insofar as the theory of meaning implied by this multiple contextualization of cultural phenomena (some sort of symbolic constructivism) exists at all, it does so as a catalogue of wavering intimations and half-joined ideas.

How far this sort of analysis can go beyond such specifically expressive matters as puppetry, and what adjustments it will have to make in doing so, is, of course, quite unclear. As "life is a game" proponents tend to gravitate toward face-to-face interaction, courtship and cocktail parties, as the most fertile ground for their sort of analysis, and "life is a stage" proponents are attracted toward collective intensities, carnivals and insurrections, for the same reason, so "life is a text" proponents incline toward the examination of imaginative forms: jokes, proverbs, popular arts. There is nothing either surprising or reprehensible in this; one naturally tries one's analogies out where they seem most likely to work. But their long-run fates surely rest on their capacity to move beyond their easier initial successes to harder and less predictable ones—of the game idea to make sense of worship, the drama idea to explicate humor, or the text idea to clarify war. Most of these triumphs, if they are to occur at all, are, in the text case even more than the others, still to come. For the moment, all the apologist can do is what I have done here: offer up some instances of application, some symptoms of trouble, and some pleas for help.

V

So much, anyway, for examples. Not only do these particular three analogies obviously spill over into one another as individual writers tack back and forth between ludic, dramatistic, and textualist idioms, but there are other humanistic analogies on the social science scene at least as prominent as they: speech act analyses following Austin and Searle; discourse models as different as those of Habermas's "communicative competence" and Foucault's "archaeology of knowledge"; representationalist approaches taking their lead from the cognitive aesthetics of Cassirer, Langer, Gombrich, or Goodman; and of course Lévi-Strauss's higher cryptology. Nor are they as yet internally settled and homogeneous: the divisions between the play-minded and the strategy-minded to which I alluded in connection with the game approach, and between the ritualists and the rhetoricians in connection with the drama approach, are more than matched in the text approach by the collisions between the against-interpretation mandarins of deconstructionism and the symbolic-domination tribunes of neo-Marxism. Matters are neither stable nor consensual, and they are not likely soon to become so. The interesting question is not how all this muddle is going to come magnificently together, but what does all this ferment mean.

One thing it means is that, however raggedly, a challenge is being mounted to some of the central assumptions of mainstream social science. The strict separation of theory and data, the "brute fact" idea; the effort to create a formal vocabulary of analysis purged of all subjective reference, the "ideal language" idea; and the claim to moral neutrality and the Olympian view, the "God's truth" idea—none of these can prosper when explanation comes to be regarded as a matter of connecting action to its sense rather than behavior to its determinants. The refiguration of social theory represents, or will if it continues, a sea change in our notion not so much of what knowledge is but of what it is we want to know. Social events do have causes and social institutions effects; but it just may be that the road to discovering what we assert in asserting this lies less through postulating forces and measuring them than through noting expressions and inspecting them.

The turn taken by an important segment of social scientists, from physical process analogies to symbolic form ones, has introduced a fundamental debate into the social science community concerning not just its methods but its aims. It is a debate that grows daily in intensity. The golden age (or perhaps it was only the brass) of the social sciences when, whatever the differences in theoretical positions and empirical claims, the basic goal of the enterprise was universally agreed upon—to find out the dynamics of collective life and alter them in desired directions—has clearly passed. There are too many social scientists at work today for whom the anatomization of thought is wanted, not the manipulation of behavior.

But it is not only for the social sciences that this alteration in how we think about how we think has disequilibrating implications. The rising interest of sociologists, anthropologists, psychologists, political scientists, and even now and then a rogue economist in the analysis of symbol systems poses—implicitly anyway, explicitly sometimes—the question of the relationship of such systems to what goes on in the world; and it does so in a way both rather different from what humanists are used to and rather less evadable—with homilies about spiritual values and the examined life—than many of them, so it seems, would at all like.

If the social technologist notion of what a social scientist is is brought into question by all this concern with sense and signification, even more so is the cultural watchdog notion of what a humanist is. The specialist without spirit dispensing policy nostrums goes, but the lectern sage dispensing approved judgments does as well. The relation between thought and action in social life can no more be conceived of in terms of wisdom than it can in terms of expertise. How it is to be conceived, how the games, dramas, or texts that we do not just invent or witness but live have the consequence they do remains very far from clear. It will take the wariest of wary reasonings, on all sides of all divides, to get it clearer.

Chapter 2 / Found in Translation: On the Social History of the Moral Imagination

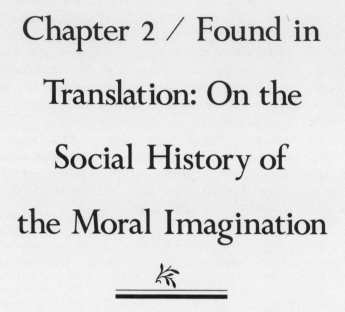

Anthropologists have a number of advantages when addressing the general public, one of them being that hardly anyone in their audience has much in the way of independent knowledge of the supposed facts being retailed. This allows one to get away with a good deal. But it is, as most such things, also something of a disadvantage. If a literary critic discourses on *King Lear,* a philosopher on Kant, or an historian on Gibbon, he can begin more or less directly with the presentation of his views, quoting only here and there to drive matters home. The context can be assumed to be shared between himself and those he is addressing. He need not inform them who Gloucester is, what epistemology is about, or where and when the Roman Empire was. This is usually not the case for the anthropologist, who is faced with the unattractive choice of boring his audience with a great deal of exotic information or attempting to make his argument in an empirical vacuum.

I want to avoid this choice, to the degree that I can, by beginning with a rather long, but I think most vivid quotation from a nineteenth-century Western writer on what is probably Bali's most famous, or notorious, custom. It will serve as my text—my jumping-off point into a variety of assertions which, with it as base and background, I hope to have accepted as relating in some responsible way to a certain peculiar social reality I have had some access to but most of my readers will have not.

While I was at Bali one of these shocking sacrifices took place. The Rajah of the neighbouring State died on the 20th of December 1847; his body was burned with great pomp, three of his concubines sacrificing themselves in the flames. It was a great day for the Balinese. It was some years since they had had the chance of witnessing one of these awful spectacles, a spectacle that meant for them a holiday with an odour of sanctity about it; and all the reigning Rajahs of Bali made a point of being present . . . and brought large followings.

It was a lovely day, and along the soft and slippery paths by the embankments which divide the lawn-like terraces of an endless succession of paddy-fields, groups of Balinese in festive attire, could be seen wending their way to the place of burning. Their gay dresses stood out in bright relief against the tender green of the ground over which they passed. They looked little enough like savages, but rather like a kindly festive crowd bent upon some pleasant excursion. The whole surroundings bore an impress of plenty, peace, and happiness, and, in a measure, of civilization. It was hard to believe that within a few miles of such a scene, three women, guiltless of any crime, were, for their affection's sake, and in the name of religion, to suffer the most horrible of deaths, while thousands of their countrymen looked on.

But already the walls which surround the palace of the King of Gianjar are in sight. Straight avenues, up the sides of a terraced hill, lead to the . . . palace; and, higher still, on the center of an open space, surrounded by a wooden rail, a gaudy structure with gilded roof, rising on crimson pillers, arrests the attention. It is the spot where the burning of the dead man's body is to take place. Upon closer inspection the structure is seen to rest upon a platform of brick-work four feet high, upon which is a second floor, covered with sand. In the centre stands the wooden image of a lion, gorgeous with purple and gold trappings. The back is made to open, and is destined to receive the body of the king for burning. The entire building is gaudily decorated with mirrors, china plates, and gilding.

Immediately adjoining this structure is a square surrounded by a wall four feet high, the whole of which space was filled with a fierce, bright fire, the fatal fire which was to consume the victims. At an elevation of twenty feet a light bamboo platform is connected with this place, a covering of green plantain stems protecting it against fire. The center of this bridge supports a small pavilion, intended to receive the victims while preparing for the fatal leap.

The spectators, who, possibly, did not number less than 40,000 or 50,000, [which, incidentally, would be about 5 percent of the total population of the island at the time] occupied the space between these structures and the outer wall, inside which a number of small pavilions had been erected for the use of women. This space was now rapidly filling, and all eyes were directed toward the [palace] whence the funeral procession was to come. Strange to say, the dead king did not leave his palace for the last time by the ordinary means. A corpse is considered impure, and nothing impure may pass the gateway. Hence, a contrivance resembling a bridge had been constructed across the walls, and over it the body was lifted. This bridge led to the uppermost storey of an immense tower of a pagoda shape, upon which the body was placed.

This tower . . . was carried by five hundred men. It consisted of eleven storeys, besides three lower platforms, the whole being gorgeously ornamented. Upon the upper storey rested the body, covered with white linen, and guarded by men carrying fans.

The procession marching before the [tower] consisted first of strong bodies of lancebearers, with [gamelan orchestra] music at intervals; then a great number of men and women carrying the offerings, which consisted of weapons, clothing, ornaments, gold and silver vessels containing holy water, [betelnut] boxes, fruit, meat-dishes, boiled rice of many colours, and, finally, the horse of the deceased, gaily caparisoned; then more lancebearers and some musicians. These were followed by the young [newly installed] king, the Dewa Pahang, with a large suite of princes and nobles. After them came the . . . high priest, carried upon an open chair, round which was wrapped one end of a coil of cloth, made to represent a huge serpent, painted in white, black, and gilt stripes, the huge head of the monster resting under the [priest's] seat, while the tail was fastened to the [tower], which came immediately after it, implying that the deceased was dragged to the place of burning by the serpent.

Following the large [tower] of the dead king, came three minor and less gorgeous ones, each containing a young woman about to become a sacrifice. . . . The victims of this cruel superstition showed no sign of fear at the terrible doom now so near. Dressed in white, their long black hair partly concealing them, with a mirror in one hand and a comb in the other, they appeared intent only upon adorning themselves as though for some gay festival. The courage which sustained them in a position so awful was indeed extraordinary, but it was born of the hope of happiness in a future world. From being bondswomen here, they believed they were to become the favourite wives and queens of their late master in another world. They were assured that readiness to follow him to a future world, with cheerfulness and amid pomp and splendour, would please the unseen powers, and induce the great god Siva to admit them without delay to Swerga Surya, the heaven of Indra.

Round the deluded women stood their relatives and friends. Even these did not view the ghastly preparations with dismay, or try to save their unhappy daughters and sisters from the terrible death awaiting them. Their duty was not to save but to act as executioners; for they were entrusted with the last horrible preparations, and finally sent the victims to their doom.

Meanwhile the procession moved slowly on, but before reaching its destination a strange act in the great drama had to be performed. The serpent had to be killed, and burned with the corpse. The high priest descended from his chair, seized a bow, and from the four corners of the compass discharged four wooden arrows at the serpent's head. It was not the arrow, however, but a flower, the champaka, that struck the serpent. The flower had been inserted at the feathered end of the arrow, from which, in its flight it detached itself, and by some strange dexterity the priest so managed that the flower, on each occasion hit its mark, viz. the serpent's head. The beast was then supposed to have been killed, and its body having been carried hitherto by men, was now wound round the priest's chair and eventually round the wooden image of the lion in which the corpse was burned.

The procession having arrived near the place of cremation, the [tower] was thrice turned, always having the priest at its head. Finally it was placed against the bridge which, meeting the eleventh story, connected it with the place of cremation. The body was now placed in the wooden image of the lion; five small plates of gold, silver, copper, iron and lead, inscribed with mystic words, were placed in the mouth of the corpse; the high priest read the Vedas, and emptied the jars containing holy water over the body. This done, the faggots, sticks striped in gold, black, and white, were placed under the lion, which was soon enveloped in flames. This part of the strange scene over, the more terrible one began.

The women were carried in procession three times round the place, and then lifted on to the fatal bridge. There, in the pavilion which has been already mentioned, they waited until the flames had consumed the image and its contents. Still they showed no fear, still their chief care seemed to be the adornment of the body, as though making ready for life rather than for death. Meanwhile, the attendant friends prepared for the horrible climax. The rail at the further end of the bridge was opened, and a plank was pushed over the flames, and attendants below poured quantities of oil on the fire, causing bright, lurid flames to shoot up to a great height. The supreme moment had arrived. With firm and measured steps the victims trod the fatal plank; three times they brought their hands together over their heads, on each of which a small dove was placed, and then, with body erect, they leaped into the flaming sea below, while the doves flew up, symbolizing the escaping spirits.

Two of the women showed, even at the very last, no sign of fear; they looked at each other, to see whether both were prepared, and then, without stopping, took the plunge. The third appeared to hesitate, and to take the leap with less resolution; she faltered for a moment, and then followed, all three disappearing without uttering a sound.

This terrible spectacle did not appear to produce any emotion upon the vast crowd, and the scene closed with barbaric music and firing of guns. It was a sight never to be forgotten by those who witnessed it, and brought to one's heart a strange feeling of thankfulness that one belonged to a civilization which, with all its faults, is merciful, and tends more and more to emancipate women from deception and cruelty. To the British rule it is due that this foul plague of suttee is extirpated in India, and doubtless the Dutch have, ere now, done as much for Bali. Works like these are the credentials by which the Western civilization makes good its right to conquer and humanize barbarous races and to replace ancient civilizations.

I have little more that is interesting to tell of Bali. . . .

I

This powerful, beautiful, and (not to neglect my own métier, which is supposed to be some sort of science) superbly observed passage was written in the 1880s by a Dane, L. V. Helms.[1] As a very young man Helms had apprenticed himself to a white rajah type merchant-adventurer straight out of *The Heart of Darkness* named Mads Lange—he played the violin, dashed about on half-broken horses cutting down enemies, had various complexions of native wives, and died suddenly, quite likely poisoned, in his late forties—who ran a port-of-trade enclave in South Bali between 1839 and 1856, a time when he and his staff were the only Europeans on the island. I quote Helms at such length not because I intend to go into Balinese ethnography here, or even, very much, into cremation rites. I quote this passage because I want to unpack it, or, better (because it is a bit hermetic and my interests a bit diffuse) to circle around it as a way into what I take to be some of the central concerns of Lionel Trilling as a literary critic, if one can confine so various a man in so cramped a category. These are concerns which, from a somewhat different perspective, but no less cramped a category, I share with him.

If Trilling was obsessed with anything it was with the relation of culture to the moral imagination; and so am I. He came at it from the side of literature; I come at it from the side of custom. But in Helms's text, portraying a custom which possesses that mysterious conjunction of beauty when it is taken as a work of art, horror when it is taken as actually lived life, and power when it is taken as a moral vision—a conjunction which we associate with such a great part of modern literature, and over which Trilling, in his cadenced way, so conscientiously agonized—I think we can meet. It does not really matter much in the end whether one trains one's attention on Joseph Conrad or on suttee: the social history of the moral imagination is a single subject.

Single, but of course vast. As any particular work of literature brings out certain aspects of the general problem—How does collective fantasy color collective life?—so any particular ritual dramatizes certain issues and mutes others. This is, indeed, the particular virtue of attending to such exotic mat-

[1] *Pioneering in the Far East and Journeys to California in 1849 and to the White Sea in 1848* (London, 1882), pp. 59–66.

ters as the splendid incineration of illustrious corpses and dutiful widows on a remote island some years ago. What is thereby brought to immediate notice is so different from what is brought to immediate notice by attending to what Trilling once called the shockingly personal literature of the talkative and attitudinizing present, that whatever deeper perceptions emerge to connect the two experiences have a peculiar force.

My task in sufficiently focusing matters so that something circumstantial can be said is powerfully assisted by the fact that Professor Trilling's last published piece—on the problems of teaching Jane Austen to Columbia students in the seventies, a heroic enterprise apparently—addressed itself to what is surely the central issue here.[2] It has always been, he says there, "the basic assumption of humanistic literary pedagogy" that the similarities between ourselves and others removed in place or period are so much more profound than are the surface differences separating us from them that, given the necessary scholarship and historical care, their imaginative products can be put at the service of our moral life. Referring to some recent discussions of my own (having to do, among other things, with the Balinese sense of self, which has—as I think you can gather from my text—a certain high peculiarity about it), he wondered how far this basic assumption was in fact valid. On the one hand, he seemed shaken in his confidence that the culturally distant was so readily available and doubted even whether he had, after all, really been able simply to understand, much less put to use, an Icelandic saga about a countryman's gift of a bear to one king which another king coveted, through the customary device of putting himself in the countryman's shoes. But, on the other, he seemed resolute, stubborn even, in his faith that however alien another people's modes of thought and feeling might be, they were somehow connectible to the way we live now. He remained convinced that he could bring those Columbia students at least somewhat closer to Jane Austen, or perhaps more exactly, could expose to them how close, in some things anyway, they already were.

Though this is not precisely the most comfortable position, nor even a wholly coherent one, it is, I think, the only one that can be effectively defended. The differences *do* go far deeper than an easy men-are-men humanism permits itself to see, and the similarities *are* far too substantial for an easy other-beasts, other-mores relativism to dissolve. Both literary critics and anthropologists—at least literary critics such as Trilling, still possessed,

[2]Lionel Trilling, "Why We Read Jane Austen," *Times Literary Supplement,* 5 March 1976, pp. 250–52.

as he says, of the primitive belief that there is such a thing as life itself; and anthropologists such as myself, who think that society comes to more than behavior—pursue their vocations haunted by a riddle quite as irresolvable as it is fundamental: namely, that the significant works of the human imagination (Icelandic saga, Austen novel, or Balinese cremation) speak with equal power to the consoling piety that we are all like to one another and to the worrying suspicion that we are not.

If we turn back to the Helms text, as well as to the sorts of "life itself" it in some way refracts—the indigenous one toward which it reaches, the intrusive one out of which it arises, and the separated one from which we apprehend it—this deep equivocality emerges in virtually every line. As we read it, a series of instabilities—instabilities of perspective, of meaning, of judgment—is set up, the one pressing hard upon the next, leaving us, in the end, not quite sure where we stand, what position we wish to take up toward what is being said to us, and indeed uncertain about just what has been said.

Some of these instabilities are, so to speak, intra-Balinese; they inhere in the structure of the ritual as such, form its theme and comprise its meaning. The conjunction (to which I have already alluded, and Helms, in struck wonder, keeps dazedly remarking) of an extravagant intensification of sensuous drama, an explosion of florid symbols and cabalic images, and a no less extravagant celebration of the quieter beauties of personal obliteration, a chaste hymn to annihilation, is, of course, only the most prominent of these. On the one hand, eleven-storey spangled towers, flowered arrows shot into fabric snakes, purple and gold coffins shaped as lions, incense, metallaphones, spices, flames; on the other, charred bones, entranced priests, somnambulant widows, affectless attendants, dissociate crowds, eerie in their picnic calm. Cocteau's aesthetic coupled with Beckett's.

But beyond the instabilities the rite in itself contains (narrowly contains, as a matter of fact—something, along with its gravedigger humor, our text rather fails to convey), there are also those set up in the collision between all this and the bundle of presumptions and predilections brought to it by an unusually broad-minded but hardly culture-free nineteenth-century Danish sea-clerk. He is, as countless intruders into the masque-world of Bali have been since, hopelessly bewitched by the soft loveliness of what he sees. Those virescent terraces, those slippery paths, those gay dresses, those cataracts of long black hair—all still seduce the coldest eye, and they addle the romantic one altogether. Yet his outrage at what this gorgeous ceremoniousness is actually producing in the real world, or, anyway, the real world as a Jutland apothecary's son conceives it—"three women, guiltless of any crime" suffering "the most horrible of deaths" for "affection's sake, and in the name of religion"—is not only unsuppressible, it disarranges his whole reaction.

The confusion of high artistry and high cruelty he thus confronts, a confusion Baudelaire would have relished and Artaud later on in fact did, is to him so shaking that it leaves him uncertain as to what sort of beings these gorgeously decorated pyrophiles marching about clanging gongs and waving pennants really are: "they looked little enough like savages"; "the surroundings bore an impress of plenty, peace and happiness, and, in a measure, of civilization." His aesthetic sensibility, an extremely powerful one, going one way, and his moral, more than its match, the other, he has great difficulty deciding what properly to feel: the women are deluded, their courage magnificent; the preparations are ghastly, the silent plunges breathtaking; the rite a cruel superstition, the spectacle one never to be forgotten; the crowd is kindly, gay, graceful, polite, and unmoved by the sight of three young women burned living to a crisp. All the familiar predicates seem to be getting in one another's way. Whatever relations beauty, truth, and goodness might have to one another in this cloud of smoke and sacrifice, they are, surely, not those of post-Napoleonic Scandinavia.

They are not those of post–World War II America either, or not at least those of the right-thinking part of it. In a twist any true connoisseur of the modern earnestness led in beyond its depth must surely savor, Helms (having both drawn us toward the ritual by dwelling on its grace and propelled us away from it by dwelling on its terror) turns it, via an outcry against the oppression of women, into an argument for imperialism. It is in extirpating such foul plagues—foul and splendid—as this that the West earns its credentials to conquer and transform the East. The English in India, the Dutch in Indonesia, and presumably the Belgians, the French, and the rest where they are, are right and justified in replacing ancient civilizations with their own, for they are on the side of mercy and emancipation, against deception and cruelty. In the space of a few paragraphs, we get some of the most thoroughly entrenched tropes of the liberal imagination (an imagination, I'd best confess, I more or less share)—the cultural integrity of "simpler" peoples, the sacredness of human life, the equality of the sexes, and the coercive character of imperial rule—struck off against one another in a way that can only leave us at least unsettled. To have moved from the magic garden of the dreaming Orient to the white man's burden, Gauguin's world to Kipling's, so rapidly and with such fine logic is but the last imbalancing blow the text delivers. It is not only the Balinese and Helms who seem morally elusive when we finish this remarkable account. So, unless we are willing to settle for a few embroidery mottoes of the eating-people-is-wrong variety, do we.

The case is general. For all the peculiarities here involved, the decentering of perception the Balinese cremation generates as it is worked through first, second, third, and nth order interpretations, coming from all sorts of directions and going all which ways, is characteristic of any imaginative construction powerful enough to interest anyone beyond its immediate audience. (And, indeed, if it is not powerful enough to do that it probably will not have an immediate audience.) Such a construction has a career, and one itself imaginative, for it consists of a set of encounters with other such constructions, or rather with consciousnesses informed by them. Whatever role it comes to play in the lives of individuals and groups removed in either space or time from the social matrix that brought it forth is an outcome of that career. The truth of the doctrine of cultural (or historical—it is the same thing) relativism is that we can never apprehend another people's or another period's imagination neatly, as though it were our own. The falsity of it is that we can therefore never genuinely apprehend it at all. We can apprehend it well enough, at least as well as we apprehend anything else not properly ours; but we do so not by looking *behind* the interfering glosses that connect us to it but *through* them. Professor Trilling's nervousness about the epistemological complacency of traditional humanism is not misplaced. The exactest reply to it is James Merrill's wrenching observation that life is translation, and we are all lost in it.

II

Whatever use the imaginative productions of other peoples—predecessors, ancestors, or distant cousins—can have for our moral lives, then, it cannot be to simplify them. The image of the past (or the primitive, or the classic, or the exotic) as a source of remedial wisdom, a prosthetic corrective for a damaged spiritual life—an image that has governed a good deal of humanist thought and education—is mischievous because it leads us to expect that our uncertainties will be reduced by access to thought-worlds constructed along lines alternative to our own, when in fact they will be multiplied. What Helms learned from Bali, and we learn from Helms, is that the growth in range a powerful sensibility gains from an encounter with another one, as powerful or more, comes only at the expense of its inward ease.

What I have called "the social history of the moral imagination," and announced to be the common enterprise of a critic of Trilling's ilk and an anthropologist of mine, turns out to be rather less straightforward than some current views in either of our disciplines take it to be. Neither the recovery of literary intentions ("what Austen wished to convey") nor the isolation of literary responses ("what Columbia students contrive to see in her"), neither the reconstruction of intra-cultural meaning ("Balinese cremation rites as caste drama") nor the establishment of cross-cultural uniformities ("the theophanous symbolism of mortuary fire") can by itself bring it to proper focus. Austen's precisian view of feminine honor, or the modernist delight in her reflexive fictionality; the Balinese conception of the indestructibility of hierarchy in the face of the most powerful leveling forces the world can muster, or the primordial seriousness of the death of kings: these things are but the raw materials of such a history. Its subject is what the sort of mentalities enthralled by some of them make of the sorts enthralled by others.

To write on it or to teach it—whether for Bali or Euro-America, and whether as a critic or an ethnographer—is to try to penetrate somewhat this tangle of hermeneutical involvements, to locate with some precision the instabilities of thought and sentiment it generates and set them in a social frame. Such an effort hardly dissolves the tangle or removes the instabilities. Indeed, as I have suggested, it rather brings them more disturbingly to notice. But it does at least (or can) place them in an intelligible context, and until some cliometrician, sociobiologist, or deep linguisticist really does contrive to solve the Riddle of the Sphinx, that will have to do.

For a literary example to parallel and interact with my developing anthropological one of what this sort of analysis comes to in the flesh, and to drive home the similarity of intellectual movement it requires (whether you are dealing with your own culture or somebody else's, with texts or events, poems or rituals, personal memories or collective dreams) one could do worse than to look for a moment at Paul Fussell's recent *The Great War*

and Modern Memory.[3] There are other possibilities, equally ger-
mane—Steven Marcus's investigations of the precarious intricacies of the
Victorian sexual imagination, or Quentin Anderson's of the development
of a plenary view of the self in American writing from Emerson forward,
for instance. But Fussell's work, justly acclaimed (by Trilling among others,
who must have felt a kinship between its intentions and his own), is especially useful, not only because it, too, centers on the clouds of imagery that
collect about impressive death, but because, set beside the Balinese case as
a sort of structural twin, it brings us further toward the question we are
struggling to find some researchable way to ask: how do the organs of distant sensibilities work in our own?

Fussell's book is concerned with the literary frames within which the
British experience on the Western Front was first perceived, later recol-
lected in intranquility, and finally expanded, by men whose encounters with
systematic social violence took place in other locales, into a total vision of
modern existence. His sacrifice scene is the trenches of Flanders and Picar-
dy; his off-balance chroniclers are the memoirists and poets—Sassoon,
Graves, Blunden, Owen—who turned it into a labyrinth of ironies; and his
latecomer heritors are the nightmare rhapsodists of endless war—Heller,
Mailer, Hughes, Vonnegut, Pynchon. There seems to be, he says, "One
dominating form of modern understanding; . . . it is essentially ironic; and
. . . it originates largely in the application of mind and memory to the events
of The Great War" (p. 35).

Whether or not one wants to accept this argument in so unvarnished a
form (just as there is more that is interesting to tell of Bali than immolation,
rather more has gone into the making of the contemporary imagination,
even the absurdist strain of it, than mustard gas and doomed athletes), its
logic is of the sort which, once sensed, seems blankly obvious.

Fussell begins by placing the factual iconography of trench war-
fare—mud, rats, barbed-wire, shell-holes, no-man's-land, three-on-
a-match, morning stand-to's, moving up, and over-the-top—against the
background of the largely literary one of Asquith's England—playing fields,
sunsets, nightingales, Country Life, *dulce et decorum est,* and *Shropshire
Lad* eroticism. The war thus becomes as much of a symbolic structure—or,
more exactly, comes to possess one—as Balinese cremation, though of a
rather different kind, with a rather different tone, engendering rather differ-

[3](New York, 1975).

ent reflections. It, too, arrives to us across a sequence of clashing imaginations and discomfited sensibilities, an interpretative career that makes it what it is—what, to us at least, it means. And setting the phases of that career in their social frames, bordering them with the tenor of the life around them, is not an exercise in sociological explaining away or historical explaining about: it is a way into the thing itself. What Fussell calls "the Curious Literariness of Real Life" is, if "literariness" be widened to accommodate all the forms of collective fantasy, a general phenomenon, embracing even Passchendaele or The Battle of the Somme.

The literariness of the real life of the men who went to France in the iron autumn after the gold summer of 1914 was largely late Romantic, a pastiche of pastoralism, elegy, earnestness, adventure, and high diction. "There was no *Waste Land,* with its rat's alleys, dull canals, and dead men who have lost their bones." Fussell writes, travestying (I presume intentionally) James's famous passage on Hawthorne's America, ". . . no *Ulysses,* no *Mauberly,* no *Cantos,* no Kafka, no Proust, no Waugh, no Huxley, no Cummings, no *Women in Love* or *Lady Chatterley's Lover.* There was no 'Valley of Ashes' in *The Great Gatsby.* One read Hardy and Kipling and Conrad and frequented the world of traditional moral action delineated in traditional moral language" (p. 23).

The inadequacy of such an imagination (though Hardy's wormwood and Housman's rue helped a little) to funk-holes and firing trenches was so vast as to be comic, and it shattered into a thousand pieces of sour irony; fragments of polished sentiment turned into hell-vignettes and horse-laughs. And it was these fragments—a world view in droplets—that the memoirists of the war tried, through the inversion of one received genre or another, to bring together into a once more graspable whole: Blunden in black pastoral, Sassoon in black romance, and Graves in black farce. And it was, in turn, that whole (half made and still trapped in traditional forms, traditional speech, and traditional imagery) upon which the later, more insurrectionary celebrants of dead men who have lost their bones afterward drew for what, by the time of *The Naked and the Dead, Catch-22, Slaughterhouse-Five,* and *Gravity's Rainbow,* Fussell can properly call, because it is settled, formal, and obsessively recurrent: the ritual of military memory.

This is how anything imaginational grows in our minds, is transformed, socially transformed, from something we merely know to exist or have existed, somewhere or other, to something which is properly ours, a working force in our common consciousness. In the Balinese case, it is not a matter (not for us at least) of the past recaptured, but of the strange construed. Yet this is only a genre detail—a fiction framed as ethnography rather than history; a complicating matter but not a decisive one. When major cultural lines are traversed in the process of interpretive reworking, a different sense of discovery is produced: one more of having come across something than of having remembered it, of an acquisition than of an inheritance. But the movement from some scene of singular experience (Flanders, 1915; Gianjar, 1847), through groping representations of what went on there raised to figurations of collective life is the same. Nor is the matter seriously otherwise when the originating scene is artefactual rather than, as we say, "real"— *Emma* or *Mansfield Park;* or, for that matter, suttee. That but alters vocabulary. The passage is still from the immediacies of one form of life to the metaphors of another.

In charting that passage, purist dogmas designed to keep supposed universes of learning properly distinct are more than obstructive, they are actively misleading. The notions of the self-interpreting text on the literary side or of the material determination of consciousness on the social science side may have their uses, or they may not; but so far as understanding how the constructions of other peoples' imaginations connect to those of our own, they head us off precisely in the wrong direction—toward an isolation of the meaning-form aspects of the matter from the practical contexts that give them life. The application of critical categories to social events and sociological categories to symbolic structures is not some primitive form of philosophic mistake, nor is it another mere confusion of art and life. It is the proper method for a study dedicated to getting straight how the massive fact of cultural and historical particularity comports with the equally massive fact of cross-cultural and cross-historical accessibility—how the deeply different can be deeply known without becoming any less different; the enormously distant enormously close without becoming any less far away.

Even unburdened by the cleverness that surpasseth all understanding of the more hermetic varieties of literary criticism or by the willed myopia, called realism, of the more hard-nosed varieties of social science, the thing is difficult enough. Faulkner, whose whole work was in some sense centered about it—about how particular imaginations are shadowed by others standing off in the cultural and temporal distance; how what happens, recountings of what happens, and metaphoric transfigurations of recountings of what happens into general visions, pile, one on top of the next, to produce a state of mind at once more knowing, more uncertain, and more disequili-brated—had as exact a sense for just how difficult it is as anyone who has written. In *Absalom, Absalom!*—that extraordinary interweaving of the manic narratives of various sorts of Sutpens, Coldfields, and Compsons over a century or so—he puts the matter with the sort of despair no one who engages in this sort of meaning chasing can ever entirely shake. Quentin Compson's father is telling Quentin (who has just come from hearing Rosa Coldfield's story about the Sutpen saga of miscegenation, near incest, fratri-cide, and murder) what his father, Quentin's grandfather, told him, Quen-tin's father, that old Sutpen a half-century earlier on told him, Quentin's grandfather, about it all, when he breaks off in frustration:

Yes, granted that, even to the unworldly Henry, let alone the more travelled father, the existence of the eighth part negro mistress and the sixteenth part negro son, granted even the morganatic ceremony—a situation which was as much a part of a wealthy young New Orleanian's social and fashionable equipment as his dancing slippers—was reason enough, which is drawing honor a little fine even for the shad-owy paragons which are our ancestors born in the South and come to man- and womanhood about eighteen sixty or sixty one. It's just incredible. It just does not explain. Or perhaps that's it: they don't explain and we are not supposed to know. We have a few old mouth-to-mouth tales; we exhume from old trunks and boxes and drawers letters without salutation or signature, in which men and women who once lived and breathed are now merely initials or nicknames out of some now in-comprehensible affection which sound to us like Sanskrit or Chocktaw; we see dimly people, the people in whose living blood and seed we ourselves lay dormant and waiting, in this shadowy attenuation of time possessing now heroic proportions, per-forming their acts of simple passion and simple violence, impervious to time and inexplicable—Yes, Judith, Bon, Henry, Sutpen: all of them. They are there, yet something is missing, they are like a chemical formula exhumed along with the let-ters from that forgotten chest, carefully, the paper old and faded and falling to pieces, the writing faded, almost indecipherable, yet meaningful, familiar in shape and sense, the name and presence of volatile and sentient forces; you bring them together in the proportions called for, but nothing happens; you re-read, tedious and intent, poring, making sure that you have forgotten nothing, made no miscalcu-lation; you bring them together again and again nothing happens: just the words, the symbols, the shapes themselves, shadowy inscrutable and serene, against that turgid background of a horrible and bloody mischancing of human affairs.[4]

But it is not all that desperate. Faulkner goes on bringing his volatile and sentient forces together again and again, adding the pieces, filling out the

[4]*Absalom, Absalom!* (New York, 1936), pp. 100–101.

narratives, not only through the couple hundred more pages of this novel, but through his whole work, rendering the history of this particular moral imagination (his, Oxford's, the inter-war South's) if not clear at least clearer, if not wholly decipherable at least not wholly inscrutable. One cannot expect more in this sort of effort, but one can expect that. Or to quote directly the lines from James Merrill (his piece, too, is about time, memory, puzzles, and cultural disconnections) I deliberately truncated earlier on:

> Lost, is it, buried? One more missing piece?
>
> But nothing's lost. Or else: all is translation
> And every bit of us is lost in it
>
> (Or found—I wander through the ruin of S
> Now and then, wondering at the peacefulness).[5]

III

Found in translation. Like the Great War, the Old South, that controversial Icelandic bear, and the equivocal picnic at Donwell Abbey, Balinese liturgical splendor continues to set off diverging commotions in our minds. Helms was only one of the earliest of its Western unriddlers, as I am only one of the latest. Between us come the soldiers, administrators, and technicians of Dutch colonialism; a multinational assortment of expatriate painters, musicians, dancers, novelists, poets, and photographers; an extraordinarily distinguished group of philologists and ethnographers, from V. E. Korn and Roelof Goris to Gregory Bateson and Margaret Mead; various sorts of missionaries, many of whom were also excellent scholars and all of whom had decided opinions; and, of course, one of the great tourist invasions of modern times, a swarm of eager experiencers the *New Yorker* cartoonist Peter Arno caught as well as anyone in his drawing of the man leaning breathlessly across the travel agency counter asking: "Is Bali . . . er . . . still Bali?"

Of course, it still is: what else could it be? And through all the changes

[5] "Lost in Translation," *Divine Comedies* (New York, 1976), p. 10.

that have occurred since 1847 (the population has tripled for one thing; the motor car has come for another; the breasts the gentleman coveted have been veiled for a third), the unnerving confusion of sensory beauty, dramatic cruelty, and moral impassivity Helms caught then has remained the marking character of its life. The Dutch suppressed widow-burning as he expected (though there seem to have been clandestine examples of it as late as the 1930s), but they could hardly suppress the sensibility of which it was an expression, at least not without transforming the society altogether, something its high gorgeousness inhibited them from even considering. The tension between the edenic image of Bali—"The Island of the Gods," "The Land of a Thousand Temples," "The Last Paradise," "The Morning of the World," and so on—and the ground bass of passionless horror that all but the most sentimental sojourners to the island sooner or later hear moving amid the loveliness persists. And I don't know that we are, we latecomers with our kincharts and cameras, much more comfortable with it than Helms was stumbling across it curious and unarmed one otherwise ordinary morning in Gianjar—just more conscious of the fascination it has come to have for us, how terribly intriguing, obsessing even, it has, in the meantime, somehow grown.

Since Bali's imaginative life has become seriously interconnected with that of the West, a phenomenon mainly of this century, it has been through our odd concern (odd in the sense that I know of no other people who share it) with the moral status of artistic genius—Where does it come from? How shall we deal with it? What will it do to us?—that, on our side, the connection has been made. (On their side it is otherwise: their daimon is rank, not creativity, and we disarrange them well enough on that score.) As a trope for our times, the island has functioned as a real-life image of a society in which the aesthetic impulse is allowed its true freedom, the unfettered expression of its inner nature. The trouble is that that image seems to serve equally well the perfection-of-humanity sort of view of art we associate with the German idealists and the flower-of-evil sort we associate with the French symbolists. And it is that Asian coincidence of European opposites, one advancing scholarship seems only to make less easy to ignore, that both unsteadies and absorbs us.

The idealist side is clear enough: the most prominent role the island has played in our imagination has been to serve as an aesthetic Arcady: a natural society of untutored artists and spontaneous artistry, actually existing in appropriate garb on a suitable landscape. The dancing, the music, the masks, the shadow plays, the carving, the breathtaking grace of posture, speech, and movement, the even more breathtaking intricacy of rite, myth, architecture, and politesse, and in the twenties and thirties, an astonishing burst of wildly original easel painting, have induced in us a vision of a profoundly creative popular culture in which art and life, at least, some place, genuinely are one. "Every Balinese," the most recent of a long line of French *livres des belles images* assures us, ". . . is an artist, but an anonymous artist whose creative talent is absorbed in that of the community and who has but a faint sense of his own creative power."[6] "The Balinese may be described as a nation of artists," the English anthropologist Geoffrey Gorer writes in a more school-mastery tone, in 1936, ". . . Balinese art is living, in a constant development."[7] And yet earlier, in 1922, the German art historian, Karl With, is moved to *jugendstil* by the miracle of it all:

The Balinese language has no word for art and no word for artist. And yet the life of this people overflows with a blossoming richness of festivals, temples, images, jewels, and decorations, gifts that are witness to an extravagant enjoyment in form-making and play. A flood of fantasy, a fullness of form, and a strength of expression wells up out of the hands, hearts, and bodies of this people and inundates everything. Full of immediacy, suffused with a blessed sensuousness, saturated with fecundity, a veritable life-frenzy grows out of the natural artistry of these peasants and continuously renews itself out of itself. . . .

   O, the artists of our time, martyrs and isolates who find neither response nor community. Life cripples who turn their solitude and poverty into their wealth; who consume themselves in the coldness of their environment; who all but mutilate themselves in the destructiveness of the life around them; who can find satisfaction and solace not through themselves but only through the object of their creation; who are forced to work, violated into self-expression, exclusively oriented toward a wrenching artistry; who wallow in themselves and lose thereby their strength, their selves, and reality.

   Compare to them, now, the fortunate and nameless artists of Bali, where the peasant carves his leisure evening into a figure; where children paint motley ornaments onto palm leaves; where a village family builds up an uncannily intricate multi-colored corpse tower; where women in honor of the gods and out of pure joy in their own persons decorate themselves like goddesses and make offerings into huge and flamboyant still lifes; where the peasant walking in his field is come upon by a god, and is thereupon inspired to chisel the god's image on the temple or to carve the god's spirit mask, while the neighbors take full care of his field and his family until he has finished his work and returns as peasant to his field; where out

[6] M. Boneff, *Bali* (Paris, 1974), pp. 69, 72; my translation.
[7] *Bali and Angkor* (Boston, 1936), pp. 54–55.

of the nothingness of the festal impulse a transported community arises through ceremony, dance, pageant, and temple building.[8]

And so on: the figure—Schiller's dream of a totally aestheticised existence—could be reproduced, in one form or another, from literally dozens of European and American works of all sorts of genres and all levels of seriousness. Bali, as Korn mordantly remarked, has had its reputation against it.

It is not so much that this reputation is a wholly false one (it has rather more truth in it than I, at least, professionally immunized against noble savageism, would have thought at all possible); it is that it is not the only one that it has. Drier looks at some of the products of all that creativity—not just cremation, but the witch and dragon dance, with its ravaging hag and tranced youths attacking their chests with daggers; sorcery, which is endemic in Bali and filled with images of perversion and wild brutality; the purified animal hatred of that popular enthusiasm, craze even, cockfighting—have conduced to a less genial view of things. So have similar looks at the social life out of which the creativity grows—pervasive factionalism, caste arrogance, collective ostracism, maternal inconstancy. And at some of the transforming events of recent history—the mass suicide with which the ruling classes greeted Dutch takeover in 1906 (they marched, blank and unseeing, dressed like cremation sacrifices, out of their palaces, directly into cannons, rifles, and swords); the mass murder, peasants killing peasants in a cry of "communism," after Sukarno's fall in 1965 (some estimates run to fifty thousand, which would be comparable to a half-million here; and in one of the villages I lived in a few years earlier, thirty households of a total seventy were incinerated all in a single night). Helms's flames still exist alongside his towers, his falling wives alongside his rising doves, his barbarous spectacles alongside his gay picnics. And they seem as inseparable from one another as ever.

Clearly, I cannot pursue this conjunction of Shangri-La and Pandaemonium any further here; what it does to conceptions, etherial or satanic, of the nature of artistic genius; what of ourselves we find in it in translation. Nor can I trace, beyond the glancing examples given, the role it has played in the history of our imagination. I merely want to insist that it has played

[8]G. Kraus and K. With, *Bali* (Hagen i W, 1922), p. 41; my translation.

one: minor surely in comparison to the ironies of World War I or the deliverances of such more consequential Asian cultures as China's or India's, but real nonetheless, not yet over, and in its own way telling. And that, therefore, the ethnographer of Bali, like the critic of Austen, is among other things absorbed in probing what Professor Trilling, in that last, winding, interrupted essay of his, called one of the significant mysteries of man's life in culture: how it is that other people's creations can be so utterly their own and so deeply part of us.

Chapter 3 / "From the Native's Point of View": On the Nature of Anthropological Understanding

I

Several years ago a minor scandal erupted in anthropology: one of its ancestral figures told the truth in a public place. As befits an ancestor, he did it posthumously, and through his widow's decision rather than his own, with the result that a number of the sort of right-thinking types who are with us always immediately rose to cry that she, an in-marrier anyway, had betrayed clan secrets, profaned an idol, and let down the side. What will the children think, to say nothing of the layman? But the disturbance was not much lessened by such ceremonial wringing of the hands; the damn thing was, after all, already printed. In much the same fashion as James Watson's *The Double Helix* exposed the way in which biophysics in fact gets done, Bronislaw Malinowski's *A Diary in the Strict Sense of the Term*

rendered established accounts of how anthropologists work fairly well implausible. The myth of the chameleon fieldworker, perfectly self-tuned to
his exotic surroundings, a walking miracle of empathy, tact, patience, and
cosmopolitanism, was demolished by the man who had perhaps done most
to create it.

The squabble that arose around the publication of the *Diary* concentrated, naturally, on inessentials and missed, as was only to be expected, the
point. Most of the shock seems to have arisen from the mere discovery that
Malinowski was not, to put it delicately, an unmitigated nice guy. He had
rude things to say about the natives he was living with, and rude words
to say it in. He spent a great deal of his time wishing he were elsewhere.
And he projected an image of a man about as little complaisant as the world
has seen. (He also projected an image of a man consecrated to a strange
vocation to the point of self-immolation, but that was less noted.) The discussion was made to come down to Malinowski's moral character or lack
of it, and the genuinely profound question his book raised was ignored;
namely, if it is not, as we had been taught to believe, through some sort
of extraordinary sensibility, an almost preternatural capacity to think, feel,
and perceive like a native (a word, I should hurry to say, I use here "in
the strict sense of the term"), how is anthropological knowledge of the way
natives think, feel, and perceive possible? The issue the *Diary* presents, with
a force perhaps only a working ethnographer can fully appreciate, is not
moral. (The moral idealization of fieldworkers is a mere sentimentality in
the first place, when it is not self-congratulation or a guild pretense.) The
issue is epistemological. If we are going to cling—as, in my opinion, we
must—to the injunction to see things from the native's point of view, where
are we when we can no longer claim some unique form of psychological
closeness, a sort of transcultural identification, with our subjects? What
happens to *verstehen* when *einfühlen* disappears?

As a matter of fact, this general problem has been exercising methodological discussion in anthropology for the last ten or fifteen years; Malinowski's
voice from the grave merely dramatizes it as a human dilemma over and
above a professional one. The formulations have been various: "inside" versus "outside," or "first person" versus "third person" descriptions; "phenomenological" versus "objectivist," or "cognitive" versus "behavioral"
theories; or, perhaps most commonly "emic" versus "etic" analyses, this
last deriving from the distinction in linguistics between phonemics and pho-

netics, phonemics classifying sounds according to their internal function in language, phonetics classifying them according to their acoustic properties as such. But perhaps the simplest and most directly appreciable way to put the matter is in terms of a distinction formulated, for his own purposes, by the psychoanalyst Heinz Kohut, between what he calls "experience-near" and "experience-distant" concepts.

An experience-near concept is, roughly, one that someone—a patient, a subject, in our case an informant—might himself naturally and effortlessly use to define what he or his fellows see, feel, think, imagine, and so on, and which he would readily understand when similarly applied by others. An experience-distant concept is one that specialists of one sort or another—an analyst, an experimenter, an ethnographer, even a priest or an ideologist—employ to forward their scientific, philosophical, or practical aims. "Love" is an experience-near concept, "object cathexis" is an experience-distant one. "Social stratification" and perhaps for most peoples in the world even "religion" (and certainly "religious system") are experience-distant; "caste" and "nirvana" are experience-near, at least for Hindus and Buddhists.

Clearly, the matter is one of degree, not polar opposition—"fear" is experience-nearer than "phobia," and "phobia" experience-nearer than "ego dyssyntonic." And the difference is not, at least so far as anthropology is concerned (the matter is otherwise in poetry and physics), a normative one, in the sense that one sort of concept is to be preferred as such over the other. Confinement to experience-near concepts leaves an ethnographer awash in immediacies, as well as entangled in vernacular. Confinement to experience-distant ones leaves him stranded in abstractions and smothered in jargon. The real question, and the one Malinowski raised by demonstrating that, in the case of "natives," you don't have to be one to know one, is what roles the two sorts of concepts play in anthropological analysis. Or, more exactly, how, in each case, ought one to deploy them so as to produce an interpretation of the way a people lives which is neither imprisoned within their mental horizons, an ethnography of witchcraft as written by a witch, nor systematically deaf to the distinctive tonalities of their existence, an ethnography of witchcraft as written by a geometer.

Putting the matter this way—in terms of how anthropological analysis is to be conducted and its results framed, rather than what psychic constitution anthropologists need to have—reduces the mystery of what "seeing things from the native's point of view" means. But it does not make it any easier, nor does it lessen the demand for perceptiveness on the part of the fieldworker. To grasp concepts that, for another people, are experience-near, and to do so well enough to place them in illuminating connection with experience-distant concepts theorists have fashioned to capture the general features of social life, is clearly a task at least as delicate, if a bit less magical, as putting oneself into someone else's skin. The trick is not to get yourself into some inner correspondence of spirit with your informants. Preferring, like the rest of us, to call their souls their own, they are not going to be altogether keen about such an effort anyhow. The trick is to figure out what the devil they think they are up to.

In one sense, of course, no one knows this better than they do themselves; hence the passion to swim in the stream of their experience, and the illusion afterward that one somehow has. But in another sense, that simple truism is simply not true. People use experience-near concepts spontaneously, un-self-consciously, as it were colloquially; they do not, except fleetingly and on occasion, recognize that there are any "concepts" involved at all. That is what experience-near means—that ideas and the realities they inform are naturally and indissolubly bound up together. What else could you call a hippopotamus? Of course the gods are powerful, why else would we fear them? The ethnographer does not, and, in my opinion, largely cannot, perceive what his informants perceive. What he perceives, and that uncertainly enough, is what they perceive "with"—or "by means of," or "through" . . . or whatever the word should be. In the country of the blind, who are not as unobservant as they look, the one-eyed is not king, he is spectator.

Now, to make all this a bit more concrete, I want to turn for a moment to my own work, which, whatever its other faults, has at least the virtue of being mine—in discussions of this sort a distinct advantage. In all three of the societies I have studied intensively, Javanese, Balinese, and Moroccan, I have been concerned, among other things, with attempting to determine how the people who live there define themselves as persons, what goes into the idea they have (but, as I say, only half-realize they have) of what a self, Javanese, Balinese, or Moroccan style, is. And in each case, I have tried to get at this most intimate of notions not by imagining myself someone else, a rice peasant or a tribal sheikh, and then seeing what I thought, but by searching out and analyzing the symbolic forms—words, images, institutions, behaviors—in terms of which, in each place, people actually represented themselves to themselves and to one another.

The concept of person is, in fact, an excellent vehicle by means of which to examine this whole question of how to go about poking into another people's turn of mind. In the first place, some sort of concept of this kind, one feels reasonably safe in saying, exists in recognizable form among all social groups. The notions of what persons are may be, from our point of view, sometimes more than a little odd. They may be conceived to dart about nervously at night shaped like fireflies. Essential elements of their psyches, like hatred, may be thought to be lodged in granular black bodies within their livers, discoverable upon autopsy. They may share their fates with *doppelgänger* beasts, so that when the beast sickens or dies they sicken or die too. But at least some conception of what a human individual is, as opposed to a rock, an animal, a rainstorm, or a god, is, so far as I can see, universal. Yet, at the same time, as these offhand examples suggest, the actual conceptions involved vary from one group to the next, and often quite sharply. The Western conception of the person as a bounded, unique, more or less integrated motivational and cognitive universe, a dynamic center of awareness, emotion, judgment, and action organized into a distinctive whole and set contrastively both against other such wholes and against its social and natural background, is, however incorrigible it may seem to us, a rather peculiar idea within the context of the world's cultures. Rather than attempting to place the experience of others within the framework of such a conception, which is what the extolled "empathy" in fact usually comes down to, understanding them demands setting that conception aside and seeing their experiences within the framework of their own idea of what selfhood is. And for Java, Bali, and Morocco, at least, that idea differs markedly not only from our own but, no less dramatically and no less instructively, from one to the other.

II

In Java, where I worked in the fifties, I studied a small, shabby inland county-seat sort of place; two shadeless streets of whitewashed wooden shops and offices, and even less substantial bamboo shacks crammed in helter-skelter behind them, the whole surrounded by a great half-circle of densely packed rice-bowl villages. Land was short, jobs were scarce, politics was unstable, health was poor, prices were rising, and life was altogether far from promising, a kind of agitated stagnancy in which, as I once put it, thinking of the curious mixture of borrowed fragments of modernity and exhausted relics of tradition that characterized the place, the future seemed about as remote as the past. Yet in the midst of this depressing scene there was an absolutely astonishing intellectual vitality, a philosophical passion really, and a popular one besides, to track the riddles of existence right down to the ground. Destitute peasants would discuss questions of freedom of the will, illiterate tradesmen discoursed on the properties of God, common laborers had theories about the relations between reason and passion, the nature of time, or the reliability of the senses. And, perhaps most importantly, the problem of the self—its nature, function, and mode of operation—was pursued with the sort of reflective intensity one could find among ourselves in only the most recherché settings indeed.

The central ideas in terms of which this reflection proceeded, and which thus defined its boundaries and the Javanese sense of what a person is, were arranged into two sets of contrasts, at base religious, one between "inside" and "outside," and one between "refined" and "vulgar." These glosses are, of course, crude and imprecise; determining exactly what the terms involved signified, sorting out their shades of meaning, was what all the discussion was about. But together they formed a distinctive conception of the self which, far from being merely theoretical, was the one in terms of which Javanese in fact perceived one another and, of course, themselves.

The "inside"/"outside" words, *batin* and *lair* (terms borrowed, as a matter of fact, from the Sufi tradition of Muslim mysticism, but locally reworked) refer on the one hand to the felt realm of human experience and on the other to the observed realm of human behavior. These have, one hastens to say, nothing to do with "soul" and "body" in our sense, for which there are in fact quite other words with quite other implications. *Batin,* the "inside" word, does not refer to a separate seat of encapsulated spirituality detached or detachable from the body, or indeed to a bounded unit at all, but to the emotional life of human beings taken generally. It consists of the fuzzy, shifting flow of subjective feeling perceived directly in all its phenomenological immediacy but considered to be, at its roots at least, identical across all individuals, whose individuality it thus effaces. And similarly, *lair,* the "outside" word, has nothing to do with the body as an object, even an experienced object. Rather, it refers to that part of human life which, in our culture, strict behaviorists limit themselves to studying—external actions, movements, postures, speech—again conceived as in its essence invariant from one individual to the next. These two sets of phenomena—inward feelings and outward actions—are then regarded not as functions of one another but as independent realms of being to be put in proper order independently.

It is in connection with this "proper ordering" that the contrast between *alus,* the word meaning "pure," "refined," "polished," "exquisite," "ethereal," "subtle," "civilized," "smooth," and *kasar,* the word meaning "impolite," "rough," "uncivilized," "coarse," "insensitive," "vulgar," comes into play. The goal is to be *alus* in both the separated realms of the self. In the inner realm this is to be achieved through religious discipline, much but not all of it mystical. In the outer realm, it is to be achieved through etiquette, the rules of which here are not only extraordinarily elaborate but have something of the force of law. Through meditation the civilized man thins out his emotional life to a kind of constant hum; through etiquette, he both shields that life from external disruptions and regularizes his outer behavior in such a way that it appears to others as a predictable, undisturbing, elegant, and rather vacant set of choreographed motions and settled forms of speech.

There is much more to all this, because it connects up to both an ontology and an aesthetic. But so far as our problem is concerned, the result is a bifurcate conception of the self, half ungestured feeling and half unfelt gesture. An inner world of stilled emotion and an outer world of shaped behavior confront one another as sharply distinguished realms unto themselves, any particular person being but the momentary locus, so to speak, of that confrontation, a passing expression of their permanent existence, their permanent separation, and their permanent need to be kept in their own order. Only when you have seen, as I have, a young man whose wife—a woman he had in fact raised from childhood and who had been the center of his life—has suddenly and inexplicably died, greeting everyone with a set smile and formal apologies for his wife's absence and trying, by mystical techniques, to flatten out, as he himself put it, the hills and valleys of his emotion into an even, level plain ("That is what you have to do," he said to me, "be smooth inside and out") can you come, in the face of our own notions of the intrinsic honesty of deep feeling and the moral importance of personal sincerity, to take the possibility of such a conception of selfhood seriously and appreciate, however inaccessible it is to you, its own sort of force.

III

Bali, where I worked both in another small provincial town, though one rather less drifting and dispirited, and, later, in an upland village of highly skilled musical instruments makers, is of course in many ways similar to Java, with which it shared a common culture to the fifteenth century. But at a deeper level, having continued Hindu while Java was, nominally at least, Islamized, it is quite different. The intricate, obsessive ritual life—Hindu, Buddhist, and Polynesian in about equal proportions—whose development was more or less cut off in Java, leaving its Indic spirit to turn reflective and phenomenological, even quietistic, in the way I have just described, flourished in Bali to reach levels of scale and flamboyance that have startled the world and made the Balinese a much more dramaturgical people with a self to match. What is philosophy in Java is theater in Bali.

As a result, there is in Bali a persistent and systematic attempt to stylize all aspects of personal expression to the point where anything idiosyncratic, anything characteristic of the individual merely because he is who he is physically, psychologically, or biographically, is muted in favor of his assigned place in the continuing and, so it is thought, never-changing pageant that is Balinese life. It is dramatis personae, not actors, that endure; indeed, it is dramatis personae, not actors, that in the proper sense really exist. Physically men come and go, mere incidents in a happenstance history, of no genuine importance even to themselves. But the masks they wear, the stage they occupy, the parts they play, and, most important, the spectacle they mount remain, and comprise not the façade but the substance of things, not least the self. Shakespeare's old-trouper view of the vanity of action in the face of mortality—all the world's a stage and we but poor players, content to strut our hour, and so on—makes no sense here. There is no make-believe; of course players perish, but the play does not, and it is the latter, the performed rather than the performer, that really matters.

Again, all this is realized not in terms of some general mood the anthropologist in his spiritual versatility somehow captures, but through a set of readily observable symbolic forms: an elaborate repertoire of designations and titles. The Balinese have at least a half-dozen major sorts of labels, ascriptive, fixed, and absolute, which one person can apply to another (or, of course, to himself) to place him among his fellows. There are birth-order markers, kinship terms, caste titles, sex indicators, teknonyms, and so on and so forth, each of which consists not of a mere collection of useful tags but a distinct and bounded, internally very complex, terminological system. When one applies one of these designations or titles (or, as is more common, several at once) to someone, one therefore defines him as a determinate point in a fixed pattern, as the temporary occupant of a particular, quite untemporary, cultural locus. To identify someone, yourself or somebody else, in Bali is thus to locate him within the familiar cast of characters—"king," "grandmother," "third-born," "Brahman"—of which the social drama is, like some stock company roadshow piece—*Charley's Aunt* or *Springtime for Henry*—inevitably composed.

The drama is of course not farce, and especially not transvestite farce, though there are such elements in it. It is an enactment of hierarchy, a theater of status. But that, though critical, is unpursuable here. The immediate point is that, in both their structure and their mode of operation, the terminological systems conduce to a view of the human person as an appropriate representative of a generic type, not a unique creature with a private fate. To see how they do this, how they tend to obscure the mere materialities—biological, psychological, historical—of individual existence in favor of standardized status qualities would involve an extended analysis. But perhaps a single example, the simplest further simplified, will suffice to suggest the pattern.

All Balinese receive what might be called birth-order names. There are four of these, "first-born," "second-born," "third-born," "fourth-born," after which they recycle, so that the fifth-born child is called again "first-born," the sixth "second-born," and so on. Further, these names are bestowed independently of the fates of the children. Dead children, even stillborn ones, count, so that in fact, in this still high-birthrate, high-mortality society, the names do not really tell you anything very reliable about the birth-order relations of concrete individuals. Within a set of living siblings, someone called "first-born" may actually be first, fifth, or ninth-born, or, if somebody is missing, almost anything in between, and someone called "second-born" may in fact be older. The birth-order naming system does not identify individuals as individuals, nor is it intended to; what it does is to suggest that, for all procreating couples, births form a circular succession of "firsts," "seconds," "thirds," and "fourths," an endless four-stage replication of an imperishable form. Physically men appear and disappear as the ephemerae they are, but socially the acting figures remain eternally the same as new "firsts," "seconds," and so on emerge from the timeless world of the gods to replace those who, dying, dissolve once more into it. All the designation and title systems, so I would argue, function in the same way: they represent the most time-saturated aspects of the human condition as but ingredients in an eternal, footlight present.

Nor is this sense the Balinese have of always being on stage a vague and ineffable one either. It is, in fact, exactly summed up in what is surely one of their experience-nearest concepts: *lek*. *Lek* has been variously translated or mistranslated ("shame" is the most common attempt); but what it really means is close to what we call stage fright. Stage fright consists, of course, in the fear that, for want of skill or self-control, or perhaps by mere accident, an aesthetic illusion will not be maintained, that the actor will show through his part. Aesthetic distance collapses, the audience (and the actor) lose sight of Hamlet and gain it, uncomfortably for all concerned, of bumbling John Smith painfully miscast as the Prince of Denmark. In Bali, the case is the same: what is feared is that the public performance to which one's cultural location commits one will be botched and that the personality—as we would call it but the Balinese, of course, not believing in such a thing, would not—of the individual will break through to dissolve his standardized public identity. When this occurs, as it sometimes does, the immediacy of the moment is felt with excruciating intensity and men become suddenly and unwillingly creatural, locked in mutual embarrassment, as though they had happened upon each other's nakedness. It is the fear of faux pas, rendered only that much more probable by the extraordinary ritualization of daily life, that keeps social intercourse on its deliberately narrowed rails and protects the dramatistical sense of self against the disruptive threat implicit in the immediacy and spontaneity even the most passionate ceremoniousness cannot fully eradicate from face-to-face encounters.

IV

Morocco, Middle Eastern and dry rather than East Asian and wet, extrovert, fluid, activist, masculine, informal to a fault, a Wild West sort of place without the barrooms and the cattle drives, is another kettle of selves altogether. My work there, which began in the mid-sixties, has been centered around a moderately large town or small city in the foothills of the Middle Atlas, about twenty miles south of Fez. It's an old place, probably founded in the tenth century, conceivably even earlier. It has the walls, the gates, the narrow minarets rising to prayer-call platforms of a classical Muslim town, and, from a distance anyway, it is a rather pretty place, an irregular oval of blinding white set in the deep-sea-green of an olive grove oasis, the mountains, bronze and stony here, slanting up immediately behind it. Close up, it is less prepossessing, though more exciting: a labyrinth of passages and alleyways, three quarters of them blind, pressed in by wall-like buildings and curbside shops and filled with a simply astounding variety of very emphatic human beings. Arabs, Berbers, and Jews; tailors, herdsmen, and soldiers; people out of offices, people out of markets, people out of tribes; rich, superrich, poor, superpoor; locals, immigrants, mimic Frenchmen, unbending medievalists, and somewhere, according to the official government census for 1960, an unemployed Jewish airplane pilot—the town houses one of the finest collections of rugged individuals I, at least, have ever come up against. Next to Sefrou (the name of the place), Manhattan seems almost monotonous.

Yet no society consists of anonymous eccentrics bouncing off one another like billiard balls, and Moroccans, too, have symbolic means by which to sort people out from one another and form an idea of what it is to be a person. The main such means—not the only one, but I think the most important and the one I want to talk about particularly here—is a peculiar linguistic form called in Arabic the *nisba*. The word derives from the triliteral root, *n-s-b,* for "ascription," "attribution," "imputation," "relationship," "affinity," "correlation," "connection," "kinship." *Nsīb* means "in-law"; *nsab* means "to attribute or impute to"; *munāsaba* means "a relation," "an analogy," "a correspondence"; *mansūb* means "belonging to," "pertaining to"; and so on to at least a dozen derivatives, from *nassāb* ("genealogist") to *nīsbīya* ("[physical] relativity").

Nisba itself, then, refers to a combination morphological, grammatical, and semantic process that consists in transforming a noun into what we would call a relative adjective but what for Arabs is just another sort of noun by adding *ī* (f., *īya*): *Ṣefrū*/Sefrou—*Ṣefrūwī*/native son of Sefrou; *Sūs*/region of southwestern Morocco—*Sūsī*/man coming from that region; *Beni Yaz̄ga*/a tribe near Sefrou—*Yazḡī*/a member of that tribe; *Yahūd*/the Jews as a people, Jewry—*Yahūdī*/a Jew; *ʿAdlun*/surname of a prominent Sefrou family—*ʿAdlūnī*/a member of that family. Nor is the procedure confined to this more or less straightforward "ethnicizing" use, but is employed in a wide range of domains to attribute relational properties to persons. For example, occupation (*hrār*/silk—*hrārī*/silk merchant); religious sect (*Darqāwā*/a mystical brotherhood—*Darqāwī*/an adept of that brotherhood or spiritual status), (*Ali*/The Prophet's son-in-law—*Alawī*/descendant of the Prophet's son-in-law, and thus of the Prophet).

Now, as once formed, nisbas tend to be incorporated into personal names—Umar Al-Buhadiwi/Umar of the Buhadu Tribe; Muhammed Al-Sussi/Muhammed from the Sus Region—this sort of adjectival attributive classification is quite publicly stamped onto an individual's identity. I was unable to find a single case where an individual was generally known, or known about, but his or her nisba was not. Indeed, Sefrouis are far more likely to be ignorant of how well-off a man is, how long he has been around, what his personal character is, or where exactly he lives, than they are of what his nisba is—Sussi or Sefroui, Buhadiwi or Adluni, Harari or Darqawi. (Of women to whom he is not related that is very likely to be all that he knows—or, more exactly, is permitted to know.) The selves that bump and jostle each other in the alleys of Sefrou gain their definition from associative relations they are imputed to have with the society that surrounds them. They are contextualized persons.

But the situation is even more radical than this; nisbas render men relative to their contexts, but as contexts themselves are relative, so too are nisbas, and the whole thing rises, so to speak, to the second power: relativism squared. Thus, at one level, everyone in Sefrou has the same nisba, or at least the potential of it—namely, Sefroui. However, within Sefrou such a nisba, precisely because it does not discriminate, will never be heard as part of an individual designation. It is only outside of Sefrou that the relationship to that particular context becomes identifying. Inside it, he is an Adluni, Alawi, Meghrawi, Ngadi, or whatever. And similarly within these categories: there are, for example, twelve different nisbas (Shakibis, Zuinis, and so forth) by means of which, among themselves, Sefrou Alawis distinguish one another.

The whole matter is far from regular: what level or sort of nisba is used and seems relevant and appropriate (to the users, that is) depends heavily on the situation. A man I knew who lived in Sefrou and worked in Fez but came from the Beni Yazgha tribe settled nearby—and from the Hima lineage of the Taghut subfraction of the Wulad Ben Ydir fraction within it—was known as a Sefroui to his work fellows in Fez, a Yazghi to all of us non-Yazghis in Sefrou, an Ydiri to other Beni Yazghas around, except for those who were themselves of the Wulad Ben Ydir fraction, who called him a Taghuti. As for the few other Taghutis, they called him a Himiwi. That is as far as things went here, but not as far as they can go, in either direction. Should, by chance, our friend journey to Egypt, he would become a Maghrebi, the nisba formed from the Arabic word for North Africa. The social contextualization of persons is pervasive and, in its curiously unmethodical way, systematic. Men do not float as bounded psychic entities, detached from their backgrounds and singularly named. As individualistic, even willful, as the Moroccans in fact are, their identity is an attribute they borrow from their setting.

Now as with the Javanese inside/outside, smooth/rough phenomenological sort of reality dividing, and the absolutizing Balinese title systems, the nisba way of looking at persons—as though they were outlines waiting to be filled in—is not an isolated custom, but part of a total pattern of social life. This pattern is, like the others, difficult to characterize succinctly, but surely one of its outstanding features is a promiscuous tumbling in public settings of varieties of men kept carefully segregated in private ones—all-out cosmopolitanism in the streets, strict communalism (of which the famous secluded woman is only the most striking index) in the home. This is, indeed, the so-called mosaic system of social organization so often held to be characteristic of the Middle East generally: differently shaped and colored chips jammed in irregularly together to generate an intricate overall design within which their individual distinctiveness remains nonetheless intact. Nothing if not diverse, Moroccan society does not cope with its diversity by sealing it into castes, isolating it into tribes, dividing it into ethnic groups, or covering it over with some common-denominator concept of nationality, though, fitfully, all have now and then been tried. It copes with it by distinguishing, with elaborate precision, the contexts—marriage, worship, and to an extent diet, law, and education—within which men are separated by their dissimilitudes, and those—work, friendship, politics, trade—where, however warily and however conditionally, they are connected by them.

To such a social pattern, a concept of selfhood which marks public identity contextually and relativistically, but yet does so in terms—tribal, territorial, linguistic, religious, familial—that grow out of the more private and settled arenas of life and have a deep and permanent resonance there, would seem particularly appropriate. Indeed, the social pattern would seem virtually to create this concept of selfhood, for it produces a situation where people interact with one another in terms of categories whose meaning is almost purely positional, location in the general mosaic, leaving the substantive content of the categories, what they mean subjectively as experienced forms of life, aside as something properly concealed in apartments, temples, and tents. Nisba discriminations can be more specific or less, indicate location within the mosaic roughly or finely, and they can be adapted to almost any changes in circumstance. But they cannot carry with them more than the most sketchy, outline implications concerning what men so named as a rule are like. Calling a man a Sefroui is like calling him a San Franciscan: it classifies him, but it does not type him; it places him without portraying him.

It is the nisba system's capacity to do this—to create a framework within which persons can be identified in terms of supposedly immanent characteristics (speech, blood, faith, provenance, and the rest)—and yet to minimize the impact of those characteristics in determining the practical relations among such persons in markets, shops, bureaus, fields, cafés, baths, and roadways that makes it so central to the Moroccan idea of the self. Nisba-type categorization leads, paradoxically, to a hyperindividualism in public relationships, because by providing only a vacant sketch, and that shifting, of who the actors are—Yazghis, Adlunis, Buhadiwis, or whatever—it leaves the rest, that is, almost everything, to be filled in by the process of interaction itself. What makes the mosaic work is the confidence that one can be as totally pragmatic, adaptive, opportunistic, and generally ad hoc in one's relations with others—a fox among foxes, a crocodile among crocodiles—as one wants without any risk of losing one's sense of who one is. Selfhood is never in danger because, outside the immediacies of procreation and prayer, only its coordinates are asserted.

V

Now, without trying to tie up the dozens of loose ends I have not only left dangling in these rather breathless accounts of the senses of selfhood of nearly ninety million people but have doubtless frazzled even more, let us return to the question of what all this can tell us, or could if it were done adequately, about "the native's point of view" in Java, Bali, and Morocco. Are we, in describing symbol uses, describing perceptions, sentiments, outlooks, experiences? And in what sense? What do we claim when we claim that we understand the semiotic means by which, in this case, persons are defined to one another? That we know words or that we know minds?

In answering this question, it is necessary, I think, first to notice the characteristic intellectual movement, the inward conceptual rhythm, in each of these analyses, and indeed in all similar analyses, including those of Malinowski—namely, a continuous dialectical tacking between the most local of local detail and the most global of global structure in such a way as to bring them into simultaneous view. In seeking to uncover the Javanese, Balinese, or Moroccan sense of self, one oscillates restlessly between the sort of exotic minutiae (lexical antitheses, categorical schemes, morphophonemic transformations) that make even the best ethnographies a trial to read and the sort of sweeping characterizations ("quietism," "dramatism," "contextualism") that make all but the most pedestrian of them somewhat implausible. Hopping back and forth between the whole conceived through the parts that actualize it and the parts conceived through the whole that motivates them, we seek to turn them, by a sort of intellectual perpetual motion, into explications of one another.

All this is, of course, but the now familiar trajectory of what Dilthey called the hermeneutic circle, and my argument here is merely that it is as central to ethnographic interpretation, and thus to the penetration of other people's modes of thought, as it is to literary, historical, philological, psychoanalytic, or biblical interpretation, or for that matter to the informal annotation of everyday experience we call common sense. In order to follow a baseball game one must understand what a bat, a hit, an inning, a left fielder, a squeeze play, a hanging curve, and a tightened infield are, and what the game in which these "things" are elements is all about. When an *explication de texte* critic like Leo Spitzer attempts to interpret Keats's "Ode on a Grecian Urn," he does so by repetitively asking himself the alternating question "What is the whole poem about?" and "What exactly has Keats seen (or chosen to show us) depicted on the urn he is describing?," emerging at the end of an advancing spiral of general observations and specific remarks with a reading of the poem as an assertion of the triumph of the aesthetic mode of perception over the historical. In the same way, when a meanings-and-symbols ethnographer like myself attempts to find out what some pack of natives conceive a person to be, he moves back and forth between asking himself, "What is the general form of their life?" and "What exactly are the vehicles in which that form is embodied?," emerging in the end of a similar sort of spiral with the notion that they see the self as a composite, a persona, or a point in a pattern. You can no more know what *lek* is if you do not know what Balinese dramatism is than you can know what a catcher's mitt is if you do not know what baseball is. And you can no more know what mosaic social organization is if you do not know what a nisba is than you can know what Keats's Platonism is if you are unable to grasp, to use Spitzer's own formulation, the "intellectual thread of thought" captured in such fragment phrases as "Attic shape," "silent form," "bride of quietness," "cold pastoral," "silence and slow time," "peaceful citadel," or "ditties of no tone."

In short, accounts of other peoples' subjectivities can be built up without recourse to pretensions to more-than-normal capacities for ego effacement and fellow feeling. Normal capacities in these respects are, of course, essential, as is their cultivation, if we expect people to tolerate our intrusions into their lives at all and accept us as persons worth talking to. I am certainly not arguing for insensitivity here, and hope I have not demonstrated it. But whatever accurate or half-accurate sense one gets of what one's informants are, as the phrase goes, really like does not come from the experience of that acceptance as such, which is part of one's own biography, not of theirs. It comes from the ability to construe their modes of expression, what I would call their symbol systems, which such an acceptance allows one to work toward developing. Understanding the form and pressure of, to use the dangerous word one more time, natives' inner lives is more like grasping a proverb, catching an allusion, seeing a joke—or, as I have suggested, reading a poem—than it is like achieving communion.

PART II

Chapter 4 / Common Sense

as a Cultural System

I

Very early on in that album of notional games and abrupt metaphors he called *Philosophical Investigations,* Wittgenstein compares language to a city:

Do not be troubled by the fact that [some reduced languages he has just invented for didactic purposes] consist only of imperatives. If you want to say that they are therefore incomplete, ask yourself whether our language is complete—whether it was before the symbolism of chemistry and the notation of the infinitestimal calculus were annexed to it, for these are, so to speak, the suburbs of our language. (And how many houses or streets does it take before a town begins to be a town?) Our language can be seen as an old city: a maze of little streets and squares, of old and new houses, and of houses with additions from various periods; and this surrounded by a multitude of modern sections with straight regular streets and uniform houses.[1]

If we extend this image to culture, we can say that anthropologists have traditionally taken the old city for their province, wandering about its haphazard alleys trying to work up some rough sort of map of it, and have only lately begun to wonder how the suburbs, which seem to be crowding in more closely all the time, got built, what connection they have to the

[1] L. Wittgenstein, *Philosophical Investigations,* trans. G. E. M. Anscombe (New York, 1953), p. 8; I have slightly altered the Anscombe translation.

old city (Did they grow out of it? Has their creation changed it? Will they finally swallow it up altogether?), and what life in such symmetrical places could possibly be like. The difference between the sorts of societies anthropologists have traditionally studied, traditional ones, and the sorts they normally inhabit, modern ones, has commonly been put in terms of primitivity. But it might rather be put in terms of the degree to which there has grown up around the ancient tangle of received practices, accepted beliefs, habitual judgments, and untaught emotions those squared off and straightened out systems of thought and action—physics, counterpoint, existentialism, Christianity, engineering, jurisprudence, Marxism—that are so prominent a feature of our own landscape that we cannot imagine a world in which they, or something resembling them, do not exist.

We know, of course, that there is little chemistry and less calculus in Tikopia or Timbuctoo, and that bolshevism, vanishing-point perspective, doctrines of hypostatic union, and disquisitions on the mind-body problem are not exactly universally distributed phenomena. Yet we are reluctant, and anthropologists are especially reluctant, to draw from such facts the conclusion that science, ideology, art, religion, or philosophy, or at least the impulses they serve, are not the common property of all mankind.

And out of that reluctance has grown a whole tradition of argument designed to prove that "simpler" peoples do so have a sense for the divine, a dispassionate interest in knowledge, a feel for legal form, or a for-itself-alone appreciation of beauty, even if these things are not immured in the neat, compartmentalized realms of culture so familiar to us. Thus Durkheim found elementary forms of religious life among the Australian aborigines, Boas a spontaneous sense of design on the Northwest Coast, Lévi-Strauss a "concrete" science in the Amazon, Griaule a symbolic ontology in a West African tribe, and Gluckman an implicit *jus commune* in an East African one. Nothing in the suburbs that was not first in the old city.

Yet, though all this has had a certain success, in that hardly anyone now conceives of primitives, insofar as they use the term at all any more, as simple pragmatists groping for physical well-being through a fog of superstition, it has not stilled the essential question: wherein lies the difference—for even the most passionate defenders of the proposition that every people has its own sort of depth (and I am one of them) admit that there is a difference—between the worked-up shapes of studied, and the rough-cast ones of colloquial, culture?

It is going to be part of my argument here that this whole discussion has been generally miscast, and that the issue is not whether there is an elementary form of science to be found in the Trobriands or an elementary form of law among the Barotse, or whether totemism is "really" a religion or the cargo cult "really" an ideology (questions which seem to me to turn so completely on definitions as to reduce without residue to matters of intellectual policy and rhetorical taste); but to what degree aspects of culture are systematized at all in such places, the degree to which there are any suburbs. And in attacking that problem, an effort more promising than searching for essentialist definitions of art or science or religion or law and then trying to decide whether the Bushmen have any, I want to turn to a dimension of culture not usually conceived as forming an ordered realm in the way these more familiar districts of the soul do. I mean "common sense."

There are a number of reasons why treating common sense as a relatively organized body of considered thought, rather than just what anyone clothed and in his right mind knows, should lead on to some useful conclusions; but perhaps the most important is that it is an inherent characteristic of common-sense thought precisely to deny this and to affirm that its tenets are immediate deliverances of experience, not deliberated reflections upon it. Knowing that rain wets and that one ought to come in out of it, or that fire burns and one ought not to play with it (to stick to our own culture for the moment) are conflated into comprising one large realm of the given and undeniable, a catalog of in-the-grain-of-nature realities so peremptory as to force themselves upon any mind sufficiently unclouded to receive them. Yet this is clearly not so. No one, or no one functioning very well, doubts that rain wets; but there may be some people around who question the proposition that one ought to come in out of it, holding that it is good for one's character to brave the elements—hatlessness is next to godliness. And the attractions of playing with fire often, with some people usually, override the full recognition of the pain that will result. Religion rests its case on revelation, science on method, ideology on moral passion; but common sense rests its on the assertion that it is not a case at all, just life in a nutshell. The world is its authority.

The analysis of common sense, as opposed to the exercise of it, must then begin by redrawing this erased distinction between the mere matter-of-fact apprehension of reality—or whatever it is you want to call what we apprehend merely and matter-of-factly—and down-to-earth, colloquial wisdom, judgments or assessments of it. When we say someone shows common sense we mean to suggest more than that he is just using his eyes and ears, but is, as we say, keeping them open, using them judiciously, intelligently, perceptively, reflectively, or trying to, and that he is capable of coping with everyday problems in an everyday way with some effectiveness. And when we say he lacks common sense we mean not that he is retarded, that he fails to grasp the fact that rain wets or fire burns, but that he bungles the everyday problems life throws up for him: he leaves his house on a cloudy day without an umbrella; his life is a series of scorchings he should have had the wit not merely to avoid but not to have stirred the flames for in the first place. The opposite of someone who is able to apprehend the sheer actualities of experience is, as I have suggested, a defective; the opposite of someone who is able to come to sensible conclusions on the basis of them is a fool. And this last has less to do with intellect, narrowly defined, than we generally imagine. As Saul Bellow, thinking of certain sorts of government advisors and certain sorts of radical writers, has remarked, the world is full of high-IQ morons.

This analytical dissolution of the unspoken premise from which common sense draws its authority—that it presents reality neat—is not intended to undermine that authority but to relocate it. If common sense is as much an interpretation of the immediacies of experience, a gloss on them, as are myth, painting, epistemology, or whatever, then it is, like them, historically constructed and, like them, subjected to historically defined standards of judgment. It can be questioned, disputed, affirmed, developed, formalized, contemplated, even taught, and it can vary dramatically from one people to the next. It is, in short, a cultural system, though not usually a very tightly integrated one, and it rests on the same basis that any other such system rests; the conviction by those whose possession it is of its value and validity. Here, as elsewhere, things are what you make of them.

The importance of all this for philosophy is, of course, that common sense, or some kindred conception, has become a central category, almost *the* central category, in a wide range of modern philosophical systems. It has always been an important category in such systems from the Platonic Socrates (where its function was to demonstrate its own inadequacy) forward. Both the Cartesian and Lockean traditions depended, in their different ways—indeed, their culturally different ways—upon doctrines about what was and what was not self-evident, if not exactly to the vernacular mind at least to the unencumbered one. But in this century the notion of (as it tends to be put) "untutored" common sense—what the plain man thinks when sheltered from the vain sophistications of schoolmen—has, with so much else disappearing into science and poetry, grown into almost the thematic subject of philosophy. The focus on ordinary language in Wittgenstein, Austin, Ryle; the development of the so-called phenomenology of everyday life by Husserl, Schutz, Merleau-Ponty; the glorification of personal, in-the-midst-of-life decision in continental existentialism; the taking of garden-variety problem solving as the paradigm of reason in American pragmatism—all reflect this tendency to look toward the structure of down-to-earth, humdrum, *brave type* thought for clues to the deeper mysteries of existence. G. E. Moore, proving the reality of the external world by holding up one hand and saying here is a physical object and then holding up the other and saying here is another, is, doctrinal details aside, the epitomizing image of a very large part of recent philosophy in the West.

Yet though it has thus emerged as a focus of so much intense attention, common sense remains more an assumed phenomenon than an analyzed one. Husserl, and following him Schutz, have dealt with the conceptual foundations of "everyday" experience, how we construe the world we biographically inhabit, but without much recognition of the distinction between that and what Dr. Johnson was doing when he kicked the stone to confute Berkeley, or Sherlock Holmes was doing when he reflected on the silent dog in the night; and Ryle has at least remarked in passing that one does not "exhibit common sense or the lack of it in using a knife and fork. [One does] in dealing with a plausible beggar or a mechanical breakdown when [one has] not got the proper tools." But generally, the notion of common sense has been rather commonsensical: what anyone with common sense knows.

Anthropology can be of use here in much the same way as it is generally: providing out-of-the-way cases, it sets nearby ones in an altered context. If we look at the views of people who draw conclusions different from our own by the mere living of their lives, learn different lessons in the school of hard knocks, we will rather quickly become aware that common sense is both a more problematical and a more profound affair than it seems from the perspective of a Parisian café or an Oxford Common Room. As one of the oldest suburbs of human culture—not very regular, not very uniform, but yet moving beyond the maze of little streets and squares toward some less casual shape—it displays in a particularly overt way the impulse upon which such developments are built: the desire to render the world distinct.

II

Consider, from this perspective rather than the one from which it is usually considered (the nature and function of magic), Evans-Pritchard's famous discussion of Azande witchcraft. He is, as he explicitly says but no one seems much to have noticed, concerned with common-sense thought—Zande common-sense thought—as the general background against which the notion of witchcraft is developed. It is the flouting of Zande notions of natural causation, what in the mere experience of the world leads to what, that suggests the operation of some other sort of causation—Evans-Pritchard calls it "mystical"—which an in fact rather materialistic concept of witchcraft (it involves a blackish substance located in an individual's belly, and so on) sums up.

Take a Zande boy, he says, who has stubbed his foot on a tree stump and developed an infection. The boy says it's witchcraft. Nonsense, says Evans-Pritchard, out of his own common-sense tradition: you were merely bloody careless; you should have looked where you were going. I did look where I was going; you have to with so many stumps about, says the boy—*and if I hadn't been witched I would have seen it.* Furthermore, all cuts do not take days to heal, but on the contrary, close quickly, for that is the nature of cuts. But this one festered, thus witchcraft must be involved.

Or take a Zande potter, a very skilled one, who, when now and again one of his pots cracks in the making, cries "witchcraft!" Nonsense! says Evans-Pritchard, who, like all good ethnographers, seems never to learn: of course sometimes pots crack in the making; it's the way of the world. But, says the potter, I chose the clay carefully, I took pains to remove all the pebbles and dirt, I built up the clay slowly and with care, and I abstained from sexual intercourse the night before. And *still* it broke. What else can it be but witchcraft? And yet another time, when he was ill—feeling unfit, as he puts it—Evans-Pritchard wondered aloud to some Zandes whether it may have been that he had eaten too many bananas, and they said, nonsense! bananas don't cause illness; it must have been witchcraft.

Thus, however "mystical" the content of Zande witchcraft beliefs may or may not be (and I have already suggested they seem so to me only in the sense that I do not myself hold them), they are actually employed by the Zande in a way anything but mysterious—as an elaboration and defense of the truth claims of colloquial reason. Behind all these reflections upon stubbed toes, botched pots, and sour stomachs lies a tissue of common-sense notions the Zande apparently regard as being true on their face: that minor cuts normally heal rapidly; that stones render baked clay liable to cracking; that abstention from sexual intercourse is prerequisite to success in pot making; that in walking about Zandeland it is unwise to daydream, for the place is full of stumps. And it is as part of this tissue of common-sense assumptions, not of some primitive metaphysics, that the concept of witchcraft takes on its meaning and has its force. For all the talk about its flying about in the night like a firefly, witchcraft does not celebrate an unseen order, it certifies a seen one.

It is when ordinary expectations fail to hold, when the Zande man-in-the-field is confronted with anomalies or contradictions, that the cry of witchcraft goes up. It is, in this respect at least, a kind of dummy variable in the system of common-sense thought. Rather than transcending that thought, it reinforces it by adding to it an all-purpose idea which acts to reassure the Zande that their fund of commonplaces is, momentary appearances to the contrary notwithstanding, dependable and adequate. Thus, if a man contracts leprosy it is attributed to witchcraft only if there is no incest in the family, for "everyone knows" that incest causes leprosy. Adultery, too, causes misfortune. A man may be killed in war or hunting as a result of his wife's infidelities. Before going to war or out to hunt, a man, as is only sensible, will often demand that his wife divulge the names of her lovers. If she says, truthfully, that she has none and he dies anyway, then it must have been witchcraft—unless, of course, he has done something else obviously foolish. Similarly, ignorance, stupidity, or incompetence, culturally defined, are quite sufficient causes of failure in Zande eyes. If, in examining his cracked pot, the potter does in fact find a stone, he stops muttering about witchcraft and starts muttering about his own negligence—instead, that is, of merely assuming that witchcraft was responsible for the stone's being there. And when an inexperienced potter's pot cracks it is put down, as seems only reasonable, to his inexperience, not to some ontological kink in reality.

In this context, at least, the cry of witchcraft functions for the Azande as the cry of *Insha Allah* functions for some Muslims or crossing oneself functions for some Christians, less to lead into more troubling questions—religious, philosophical, scientific, moral—about how the world is put together and what life comes to, than to block such questions from view; to seal up the common-sense view of the world—"everything is what it is and not another thing," as Joseph Butler put it—against the doubts its inevitable insufficiencies inevitably stimulate.

"From generation to generation," Evans-Pritchard writes, "Azande regulate their economic activities according to a transmitted body of knowledge, in their building and crafts no less than their agricultural and hunting pursuits. They have a sound working knowledge of nature in so far as it concerns their welfare. . . . It is true that their knowledge is empirical and incomplete and that it is not transmitted by any systematic teaching but is handed over from one generation to another slowly and casually during childhood and early manhood. Yet it suffices for their everyday tasks and seasonal pursuits." It is this conviction of the plain man that he is on top of things, and not only economic things, that makes action possible for him at all, and which—here through invoking witchcraft to blunt failures, with us by appealing to a long tradition of cracker-barrel philosophizing to commemorate successes—must therefore be protected at all costs. It has, of course, often been remarked that the maintenance of religious faith is a problematic matter in any society; and, theories of the supposed spontaneity of primitives' religious impulses aside, that is, I think, true. But it is at least as true, and very much less remarked, that maintaining faith in the reliability of the axioms and arguments of common sense is no less problematical. Dr. Johnson's famous device for silencing common-sense doubts—"and that's an end on the matter!"—is, when you get right down to it, not that much less desperate than Tertullian's for halting it of religious doubts—*"credo quia impossible"*—and "witchcraft!" is no worse than either of them. Men plug the dikes of their most needed beliefs with whatever mud they can find.

All this comes out rather more dramatically when, instead of confining oneself to a single culture looked at generally one views several at once with respect to a single-problem focus. An excellent example of such an approach can be found in an article in the *American Anthropologist* of a few years back by Robert Edgerton on what is now called intersexuality, but is perhaps more commonly known as hermaphroditism.

Surely if there is one thing that everyone takes to be part of the way in which the world is arranged it is that human beings are divided without remainder into two biological sexes. Of course, it is recognized everywhere that some people—homosexuals, transvestites, and so on—may not behave in terms of the role expectations ascribed to them on the basis of their biological sex, and more recently some people in our society have gone so far as to suggest that roles thus differentiated should not be assigned at all. But whether one wants to shout *"vive la différence!"* or *"à bas la différence!,"* the sheer existence of *la différence* is not subject to much discussion. The view of that legendary little girl—that people come in two kinds, plain and fancy—may have been lamentably unliberated; but that she noticed something anatomically real seems apparent enough.

Yet, as a matter of fact, she may not have inspected a large enough sample. Gender in human beings is not a purely dichotomous variable. It is not an evenly continuous one either, of course, or our love life would be even more complicated than it already is. But a fair number of human beings are markedly intersexual, a number of them to the point where both sorts of external genitalia appear, or where developed breasts occur in an individual with male genitalia, and so on. This raises certain problems for biological science, problems with respect to which a good deal of headway is right now being made. But it raises, also, certain problems for common sense, for the network of practical and moral conceptions woven about those supposedly most rooted of root realities: maleness and femaleness. Intersexuality is more than an empirical surprise; it is a cultural challenge.

It is a challenge that is met in diverse ways. The Romans, Edgerton reports, regarded intersexed infants as supernaturally cursed and put them to death. The Greeks, as was their habit, took a more relaxed view and, though they regarded such persons as peculiar, put it all down as just one of those things—after all, Hermaphroditus, the son of Hermes and Aphrodite who became united in one body with a nymph, provided precedent enough—and let them live out their lives without undue stigma. Edgerton's paper indeed pivots around a fascinating contrast among three quite variant responses to the phenomenon of intersexuality—that of the Americans, the Navaho, and the Pokot (the last a Kenyan tribe)—in terms of the common-sense views these people hold concerning human gender and its general place in nature. As he says, different people may react differently when confronted with individuals whose bodies are sexually anomalous, but they can hardly ignore them. If received ideas of "the normal and the natural" are to be kept intact, something must be said about these rather spectacular disaccordances with them.

Americans regard intersexuality with what can only be called horror. Individuals, Edgerton says, can be moved to nausea by the mere sight of intersexed genitalia or even by a discussion of the condition. "As a moral and legal enigma," he continues, "it knows few peers. Can such a person marry?

Is military service relevant? How is the sex on a birth certificate to be made out? Can it properly be changed? Is it psychologically advisable, or even possible, for someone raised as a girl, suddenly to become a boy? . . . How can an intersexed person behave in school shower rooms, in public bathrooms, in dating activities?" Clearly, common sense is at the end of its tether.

The reaction is to encourage, usually with great passion and sometimes with rather more than that, the intersexual to adopt either a male or female role. Many intersexuals do thus "pass" for the whole of their lives as "normal" men or women, something that involves a good deal of careful artifice. Others either seek or are forced into surgery to "correct," cosmetically anyway, the condition and become "legitimate" males or females. Outside of freak shows, we permit only one solution to the dilemma of intersexuality, a solution the person with the condition is obliged to adopt to soothe the sensibilities of the rest of us. "All concerned," Edgerton writes, "from parents to physicians are enjoined to discover which of the two natural sexes the intersexed person most appropriately is and then to help the ambiguous, incongruous, and upsetting 'it' to become at least a partially acceptable 'him' or 'her.' In short, if the facts don't measure up to your expectations, change the facts, or, if that's not feasible, disguise them."

So much for savages. Turning to the Navaho, among whom W. W. Hill made a systematic study of hermaphroditism as early as 1935, the picture is quite different. For them, too, of course, intersexuality is abnormal, but rather than evoking horror and disgust it evokes wonder and awe. The intersexual is considered to have been divinely blessed and to convey that blessing to others. Intersexuals are not only respected, they are practically revered. "They know everything," one of Hill's informants said, "they can do the work of both a man and a woman. I think when all the [intersexuals] are gone, that it will be the end of the Navaho." "If there were no [intersexuals]," another informant said, "the country would change. They are responsible for all the wealth in the country. If there were no more left, the horses, sheep, and Navaho would all go. They are leaders, just like President Roosevelt." Yet another said, "An [intersexual] around the hogan will bring good luck and riches. It does a great deal for the country if you have an [intersexual] around." And so on.

Navaho common sense thus places the anomaly of intersexuality—for, as I say, it seems no less an anomaly to them than it does to us, because it *is* no less an anomaly—in a quite different light than does ours. Interpreting it to be not a horror but a blessing leads on to notions that seem as peculiar to us as that adultery causes hunting accidents or incest leprosy, but that seem to the Navaho only what anyone with his head screwed on straight cannot help but think. For example, that rubbing the genitals of intersexed animals (which are also highly valued) on the tails of female sheep and goats and on the noses of male sheep and goats causes the flocks to prosper and more milk to be produced. Or, that intersexed persons should be made the heads of their families and given complete control over all the family property, because then that too will grow. Change a few interpretations of a few curious facts and you change, here anyway, a whole cast of mind. Not size-up-and-solve, but marvel-and-respect.

Finally, the East African tribe, the Pokot, adopt yet a third view. Like the Americans, they do not regard intersexuals highly; but, like the Navaho, they are not at all revolted or horrified by them. They regard them, quite matter of factly, as simple errors. They are, in what is apparently a popular African image, like a botched pot. "God made a mistake," they say, rather than, "the gods have produced a wonderous gift," or "we are faced with an unclassifiable monster."

Pokot regard the intersexed person as useless—"it" cannot reproduce or extend the patriline as can a proper man nor can it bring in bride-price as can a proper woman. Nor can "it" indulge in what the Pokot say "is the most pleasant thing of all," sex. Frequently, intersexed children are killed, in the offhand way one discards an ill-made pot (so, too, are microcephalics, infants without appendages, and so on; so, too, grossly deformed animals), but often they are allowed, in an equally offhand way, to live. The lives they live are miserable enough, but they are not pariahs—merely neglected, lonely, treated with indifference as though they were mere objects, and ill-made ones at that. Economically they tend to be better off than the average Pokot because they have neither the ordinary kinship drains on their wealth nor the distractions of family life to hinder their accumulation of it. They have, in this apparently typical segmentary lineage and bride-wealth sort of system, no place. Who needs them?

One of Edgerton's cases admits to great unhappiness. "I only sleep, eat, and work. What else can I do? God made a mistake." And another: "God made me this way. There was nothing I could do. All the others [are] able to live as Pokot. I [am] no real Pokot." In a society where common sense stamps even a normally equipped childless man as a forlorn figure and a childless woman is said to be "not even a person," an intersexual's life is the ultimate image of futility. He is "useless" in a society that values the "useful," as, in its cattle-wives-and-children way, it conceives it, very highly.

In short, given the given, not everything else follows. Common sense is not what the mind cleared of cant spontaneously apprehends; it is what the mind filled with presuppositions—that sex is a disorganizing force, that sex is a regenerative gift, that sex is a practical pleasure—concludes. God may have made the intersexuals, but man has made the rest.

III

But there is more to it than this. What man has made is an authoritative story. Like *Lear,* the New Testament, or quantum mechanics, common sense consists in an account of things which claims to strike at their heart. Indeed, it is something of a natural rival to such more sophisticated stories when they are present, and when they are not to the phantasmagoric narratives of dream and myth. As a frame for thought, and a species of it, common sense is as totalizing as any other: no religion is more dogmatic, no science more ambitious, no philosophy more general. Its tonalities are different, and so are the arguments to which it appeals, but like them—and like art and like ideology—it pretends to reach past illusion to truth, to, as we say, things as they are. "Whenever a philosopher says something is 'really real,' " to quote again that great modern celebrant of common sense, G. E. Moore, "you can be really sure that what he says is 'really real' isn't real, really." When a Moore, a Dr. Johnson, a Zande potter, or a Pokot hermaphrodite say something is real, they damn well mean it.

And what is more, you damn well know it. It is precisely in its "tonalities"—the temper its observations convey, the turn of mind its conclusions reflect—that the differentiae of common sense are properly to be sought. The concept as such, as a fixed and labeled category, an explicitly bounded semantic domain, is, of course, not universal, but, like religion, art, and the rest, part of our own more or less common-sense way of distinguishing the genres of cultural expression. And, as we have seen, its actual content, as with religion, art, and the rest, varies too radically from one place and time to the next for there to be much hope of finding a defining constancy within it, an ur-story always told. It is only in isolating what might be called its stylistic features, the marks of attitude that give it its peculiar stamp, that common sense (or indeed any of its sister genres) can be transculturally characterized. Like the voice of piety, the voice of sanity sounds pretty much the same whatever it says; what simple wisdom has everywhere in common is the maddening air of simple wisdom with which it is uttered.

Just how to formulate such stylistic features, marks of attitude, tonal shadings—whatever you want to call them—is something of a problem, because there is no ready vocabulary in which to do so. Short of simply inventing new terms, which, as the point is to characterize the familiar not to describe the unknown, would be self-defeating here, one can only stretch old ones in the way a mathematician does when he says a proof is deep, a critic does when he says a painting is chaste, or a wine connoisseur does when he says a Bordeaux is assertive. The terms I want to use in this way with respect to common sense, each with a "-ness" added on to substantivise it, are: natural, practical, thin, immethodical, accessible. "Naturalness," "practicalness," "thinness," "immethodicalness," and "accessibleness" are the somewhat unstandard properties I want to attribute to common sense generally, as an everywhere-found cultural form.

The first of these quasi-qualities, naturalness, is perhaps the most fundamental. Common sense represents matters—that is, certain matters and not others—as being what they are in the simple nature of the case. An air of "of-courseness," a sense of "it figures" is cast over things—again, some selected, underscored things. They are depicted as inherent in the situation, intrinsic aspects of reality, the way things go. This is true even with respect to an anomaly like intersexuality. What divides the American attitude from the other two is not that people with bisexual organs seem that much more peculiar to us, but that the peculiarity seems unnatural, a contradiction in the settled terms of existence. Navaho and Pokot take, in their different ways, the view that intersexuals are a product, if a somewhat unusual product, of the normal course of things—gifted prodigies, botched pots—where the Americans, to the degree their view is being properly portrayed, apparently regard femaleness and maleness as exhausting the natural categories in which persons can conceivably come: what falls between is a darkness, an offense against reason.

But naturalness as a characteristic of the sorts of stories about the real we call common sense can be more plainly seen in less sensational examples.

Among the Australian aborigines, to choose one more or less at random, a whole host of features of the physical landscape are considered as resulting from the activities of totemic ancestors—mostly kangaroos, emus, witchety grubs, and the like—performed in that time-out-of-time usually glossed in English as "the dreaming." As Nancy Munn has pointed out, this transformation of ancestral persons into natural features is conceived to have occurred in at least three ways: by actual metamorphosis, the body of the ancestor changing into some material object; by imprinting, the ancestor leaving the impression of his body or of some tool he uses; and by what she calls externalization, the ancestor taking some object out of his body and discarding it. Thus, a rocky hill or even a stone may be seen as a crystalized ancestor (he did not die, the informants say, he ceased moving about and "became the country"); a waterhole, or even a whole campsite, may be seen as the impress left by the buttocks of an ancestor who in his wanderings sat down to rest there; and various other sorts of material objects—string crosses and oval boards—are considered to have been drawn by some primordial kangaroo or snake out of his belly and "left behind" as he moved on. The details of all this (and they are enormously complicated) aside, the external world as the aborigines confront it is neither a blank reality nor some complicated sort of metaphysical object, but the natural outcome of trans-natural events.

What this particular example, here so elliptically given, demonstrates is that the naturalness, which as a modal property characterizes common sense, does not rest, or at least does not necessarily rest, on what we would call philosophical naturalism—the view that there are no things in heaven and earth undreamt of by the temporal mind. Indeed, for the aborigines, as for the Navaho, the naturalness of the everyday world is a direct expression, a resultant, of a realm of being to which a quite different complex of quasi-qualities—"grandeur," "seriousness," "mystery," "otherness"—is attributed. The fact that the natural phenomena of their physical world are the remains of actions of inviolable kangaroos or thaumaturgical snakes does not make those phenomena any less natural in aboriginal eyes. The fact that a particular creek was formed because Possum happened to drag his tail along the ground right there makes it no less a creek. It makes it, of course, something more, or at least something other, than a creek is to us; but water runs downhill in both of them.

The point is general. The development of modern science has had a profound effect—though perhaps not so profound as sometimes imagined—upon Western common-sense views. Whether, as I rather doubt, the plain man has become a genuine Copernican or not (to me, the sun still rises and shines upon the earth), he has surely been brought round, and quite recently, to a version of the germ theory of disease. The merest television commercial demonstrates that. But, as the merest television commercial also demonstrates, it is as a bit of common sense, not as an articulated scientific theory, that he believes it. He may have moved beyond "feed a cold and starve a fever," but only to "brush your teeth twice a day and see your dentist twice a year." A similar argument could be made for art—there was no fog in London until Whistler painted it, and so on. The naturalness common-sense conceptions give to . . . well, whatever they give it to—drinking from fast-running creeks in preference to slow-running ones, staying out of crowds in the influenza season . . . may be dependent on other sorts of quite unordinary stories about the way things are. (Or, of course, may not: "Man is born to trouble as the sparks fly upward" depends for its persuasiveness on one's merely having lived long enough to discover how terribly accurate it is.)

The second characteristic, "practicalness," is perhaps more obvious to the naked eye than the others on my list, for what we most often mean when we say an individual, an action, or a project displays a want of common sense is that they are impractical. The individual is in for some rude awakenings, the action is conducing toward its own defeat, the project won't float. But, simply because it seems so more readily apparent, it is also more susceptible to misconstruction. For it is not "practicalness" in the narrowly pragmatical sense of the useful but in the broader, folk-philosophical sense of sagacity that is involved. To tell someone, "be sensible," is less to tell him to cling to the utilitarian than to tell him, as we say, to wise up: to be prudent, levelheaded, keep his eye on the ball, not buy any wooden nickels, stay away from slow horses and fast women, let the dead bury the dead.

There has been, in fact, something of a debate—part of the larger discussion concerning the cultural inventories of "simpler" peoples, I mentioned earlier—as to whether "primitives" have any interest in matters of empirical fact which do not bear, and rather directly bear, on their immediate material interests. This is the view—that is, that they do not—to which Malinowski largely held and which Evans-Pritchard, in a passage I deliberately elided earlier, affirms concerning the Zande. "They have a sound working knowledge of nature insofar as it concerns their welfare. Beyond this point it has for them no scientific interest or sentimental appeal." Against this,

other anthropologists, of whom Lévi-Strauss is if not the first anyway the
most emphatic, have argued that "primitives," "savages," or whatever have
elaborated, and even systematized, bodies of empirical knowledge which
have no very clear practical import for them. Some Philippine tribes distinguish over six hundred types of named plants, most of these plants being
unused, unusable, and in fact but rarely encountered. American Indians
of the northeastern United States and Canada have an elaborate taxonomy
of reptiles they neither eat nor otherwise have very much traffic with. Some
Southwestern Indians—Pueblans—have names for every one of the types
of coniferous tree in their region, most of which barely differ from one another and certainly in no way of material concern to the Indians. Southeast
Asian Pygmies can distinguish the leaf-eating habits of more than fifteen
species of bats. Against Evans-Pritchard's primitive utilitarian sort of
view—know what it profits you to know and leave the rest to witchcraft—one has Lévi-Strauss's primitive intellectual one—know everything
your mind provokes you to know and range it into categories. "It may be
objected," he writes, "that science of this kind [that is, botanical classification, herpetological observation, and so forth] can scarcely be of much practical effect. The answer to this is that its main purpose is not a practical
one. It meets intellectual requirements rather than or instead of satisfying
[material] needs."

There is little doubt that the consensus in the field now supports the
Lévi-Strauss sort of view rather than the Evans-Pritchard sort—
"primitives" are interested in all kinds of things of use neither to their
schemes nor to their stomachs. But that is hardly all there is to the matter.
For they are not classifying all those plants, distinguishing all those snakes,
or sorting out all those bats out of some overwhelming cognitive passion
rising out of innate structures at the bottom of the mind either. In an environment populated with conifers, or snakes, or leaf-eating bats it is practical
to know a good deal about conifers, snakes, or leaf-eating bats, whether or
not what one knows is in any strict sense materially useful, because it is
of such knowledge that "practicalness" is there composed. Like its "naturalness," the "practicalness" of common sense is a quality it bestows upon
things, not one that things bestow upon it. If, to us, studying a racing form
seems a practical activity and chasing butterflies does not, that is not because the one is useful and the other is not; it is because the one is considered
an effort, however feckless, to know what's what and the other, however
charming, is not.

The third of the quasi-qualities common sense attributes to reality, "thinness," is, like modesty in cheese, rather hard to formulate in more explicit terms. "Simpleness," or even "literalness," might serve as well or better, for what is involved is the tendency for common-sense views of this matter or that to represent them as being precisely what they seem to be, neither more nor less. The Butler line I quoted earlier—"everything is what it is and not another thing"—expresses this quality perfectly. The world is what the wide-awake, uncomplicated person takes it to be. Sobriety, not subtlety, realism, not imagination, are the keys to wisdom; the really important facts of life lie scattered openly along its surface, not cunningly secreted in its depths. There is no need, indeed it is a fatal mistake, to deny, as poets, intellectuals, priests, and other professional complicators of the world so often do, the obviousness of the obvious. Truth is as plain, as the Dutch proverb has it, as a pikestaff over water.

Again, like Moore's oversubtle philosophers discoursing musefully on the real, anthropologists often spin notional complexities they then report as cultural facts through a failure to realize that much of what their informants are saying is, however strange it may sound to educated ears, meant literally. Some of the most crucial properties of the world are not regarded as concealed beneath a mask of deceptive appearances, things inferred from pale suggestions or riddled out of equivocal signs. They are conceived to be just there, where stones, hands, scoundrels, and erotic triangles are, invisible only to the clever. It takes a while (or, anyway, it took me a while) to absorb the fact that when the whole family of a Javanese boy tells me that the reason he has fallen out of a tree and broken his leg is that the spirit of his deceased grandfather pushed him out because some ritual duty toward the grandfather has been inadvertently overlooked, that, so far as they are concerned, is the beginning, the middle, and the end of the matter: it is precisely what they think has occurred, it is all that they think has occurred, and they are puzzled only at my puzzlement at their lack of puzzlement. And when, after listening to a long, complicated business from an old, illiterate, no-nonsense Javanese peasant woman—a classic type if ever there was one—about the role of "the snake of the day" in determining the wisdom of embarking on a journey, holding a feast, or contracting a marriage (the story was actually mostly loving accounts of the terrible things that happened—carriages overturning, tumors appearing, fortunes dissolving—when that role was ignored), I asked what this snake of the day looked like and was met with, "Don't be an idiot; you can't see Tuesday, can you?,"

I began to realize that patentness, too, is in the eye of the beholder. "The world divides into facts" may have its defects as a philosophical slogan or a scientific creed; as an epitomization of the "thinness"—"simpleness," "literalness"—that common sense stamps onto experience it is graphically exact.

As for "immethodicalness," another not too well named quality common-sense thought represents the world as possessing, it caters at once to the pleasures of inconsistency which are so very real to any but the most scholastical of men ("A foolish consistency is the hobgoblin of little minds," as Emerson said; "I contradict myself, so I contradict myself. I contain multitudes," as Whitman did); and also to the equal pleasures, felt by any but the most obsessional of men, of the intractable diversity of experience ("The world is full of a number of things"; "Life is one damn thing after another"; "If you think you understand the situation, that only proves you are misinformed"). Common-sense wisdom is shamelessly and unapologetically ad hoc. It comes in epigrams, proverbs, *obiter dicta,* jokes, anecdotes, *contes morals*—a clatter of gnomic utterances—not in formal doctrines, axiomized theories, or architectonic dogmas. Silone says somewhere that southern Italian peasants pass their lives exchanging proverbs with one another like so many precious gifts. Elsewhere the forms may be polished witicisms à la Wilde, didactic verses à la Pope, or animal fables à la La Fontaine; among the classical Chinese they seem to have been embalmed quotations. Whatever they are, it is not their interconsistency that recommends them but indeed virtually the opposite: "Look before you leap," but "He who hesitates is lost"; "A stitch in time saves nine," but "Seize the day." It is, indeed, in the sententious saying—in one sense, the paradigmatic form of vernacular wisdom—that the immethodicalness of common sense comes out most vividly. In witness of which, consider the following bundle of Ba-Ila proverbs I excerpt from Paul Radin (who excerpted them in turn from Smith and Dale):

Get grown up and then you will know the things of the earth.

Annoy your doctors and sicknesses will come laughing.

The prodigal cow threw away her own tail.

It is the prudent hyena that lives long.

The god that speaks up gets the meat.

You may cleanse yourself but it is not to say that you cease to be a slave.

When a chief's wife steals she puts the blame on the slaves.

Build rather with a witch than with a false-tongued person, for he destroys the community.

Better help a fighting man than a hungry man, for he has no gratitude.

And so on. It is this sort of potpourri of disparate notions—again not necessarily or even usually expressed proverbially—which not only characterizes systems of common sense generally but which in fact recommends them as capable of grasping the vast multifariousness of life in the world. The Ba-Ila even have a proverb expressing this: "Wisdom comes out of an ant heap."

The final quasi-quality—final here, surely not so in actuality—"accessibleness," more or less follows as a logical consequence once the others are acknowledged. Accessibleness is simply the assumption, in fact the insistence, that any person with faculties reasonably intact can grasp common-sense conclusions, and indeed, once they are unequivocally enough stated, will not only grasp but embrace them. Of course, some people—usually the old, sometimes the afflicted, occasionally the merely orotund—tend to be regarded as rather wiser in an "I've been through the mill" sort of way than others, while children, frequently enough women, and, depending upon the society, various sorts of underclasses are regarded as less wise, in an "they are emotional creatures" sort of way, than others. But, for all that, there are really no acknowledged specialists in common sense. Everyone thinks he's an expert. Being common, common sense is open to all, the general property of at least, as we would put it, all solid citizens.

Indeed, its tone is even anti-expert, if not anti-intellectual: we reject, and so, as far as I can see, do other peoples, any explicit claim to special powers in this regard. There is no esoteric knowledge, no special technique or peculiar giftedness, and little or no specialized training—only what we rather redundantly call experience and rather mysteriously call maturity—involved. Common sense, to put it another way, represents the world as a familiar world, one everyone can, and should, recognize, and within which everyone stands, or should, on his own feet. To live in the suburbs called physics, or Islam, or law, or music, or socialism, one must meet certain particular requirements, and the houses are not all of the same imposingness. To live in the semi-suburb called common sense, where all the houses are *sans façon,* one need only be, as the old phrase has it, sound of mind and practical of conscience, however those worthy virtues be defined in the particular city of thought and language whose citizen one is.

IV

As we began with an alley-and-avenue pictograph from Wittgenstein, it is only appropriate that we end with one, this one even more compressed: "In the actual use of expressions we make detours, we go by side roads. We see the straight highway before us, but of course we cannot use it, because it is permanently closed."[2]

If one wants to demonstrate, or even (which is all I have been able to do) to suggest, that common sense is a cultural system, that there is an ingenerate order to it capable of being empirically uncovered and conceptually formulated, one cannot do so by cataloguing its content, which is wildly heterogeneous, not only across societies but within them—ant-heap wisdom. One cannot do so, either, by sketching out some logical structure it always takes, for there is none. And one cannot do so by summing up the substantive conclusions it always draws, for there are, too, none of those. One has to proceed instead by the peculiar detour of evoking its generally recognized tone and temper, the untraveled side road that leads through constructing metaphorical predicates—near-notions like "thinness"—to remind people of what they already know. There is something (to change the image) of the purloined-letter effect in common sense; it lies so artlessly before our eyes it is almost impossible to see.

To us, science, art, ideology, law, religion, technology, mathematics, even nowadays ethics and epistemology, seem genuine enough genres of cultural expression to lead us to ask (and ask, and ask) to what degree other peoples possess them, and to the degree that they do possess them what form do they take, and given the form they take what light has that to shed on our own versions of them. But this is still not true of common sense. Common sense seems to us what is left over when all these more articulated sorts of symbol systems have exhausted their tasks, what remains of reason when its more sophisticated achievements are all set aside. But if this is not so,

[2]Wittgenstein, *Philosophical Investigations*, p. 127.

if knowing chalk from cheese, a hawk from a handsaw, or your ass from your elbow ("earthiness" might well have been adduced as another quasi-quality of common sense) is as positive an accomplishment, if perhaps not so lofty a one, as appreciating motets, following a logic proof, keeping the Covenant, or demolishing capitalism—as dependent as they are upon developed traditions of thought and sensibility—then the comparative investigation of "the ordinary ability to keep ourselves from being imposed upon by gross contradictions, palpable inconsistencies, and unmask'd impostures" (as a 1726 "Secret History of the University of Oxford" defined common sense) ought to be more deliberately cultivated.

Should this be done it should lead, for anthropology, to some new ways of looking at some old problems, most especially those concerning how culture is jointed and put together, and to a movement (one actually already well begun) away from functionalist accounts of the devices on which societies rest toward interpretive ones of the kinds of lives societies support. But for philosophy, the effects may be even graver, for it should lead to the disarrangement of a half-examined concept lying very near its heart. What for anthropology, that most foxlike of disciplines, would be but the most recent in a long series of shifts in attention, could be, for philosophy, that most hedgehoggish, a plenary jolt.

Chapter 5 / Art as a

Cultural System

I

Art is notoriously hard to talk about. It seems, even when made of words in the literary arts, all the more so when made of pigment, sound, stone, or whatever in the nonliterary ones, to exist in a world of its own, beyond the reach of discourse. It not only is hard to talk about it; it seems unnecessary to do so. It speaks, as we say, for itself: a poem must not mean but be; if you have to ask what jazz is you are never going to get to know.

Artists feel this especially. Most of them regard what is written and said about their work, or work they admire, as at best beside the point, at worst a distraction from it. "Everyone wants to understand art," Picasso wrote, "why not try to understand the song of a bird? . . . People who try to explain pictures are usually barking up the wrong tree."[1] Or if that seems too avant-garde, there is Millet, resisting the classification of himself as a Saint-Simoniste: "The gossip about my *Man With a Hoe* seems to me all very strange, and I am obliged to you for letting me know it, as it furnishes me with another opportunity to wonder at the ideas people attribute to me. . . . My critics are men of taste and education, but I can-

[1]Quoted in R. Goldwater and M. Treves, *Artists on Art* (New York, 1945), p. 421.

not put myself in their shoes, and as I have never seen anything but fields since I was born, I try to say as best I can what I saw and felt when I was at work."[2]

But anyone at all responsive to aesthetic forms feels it as well. Even those among us who are neither mystics nor sentimentalists, nor given to outbursts of aesthetic piety, feel uneasy when we have talked very long about a work of art in which we think we have seen something valuable. The excess of what we have seen, or imagine we have, over the stammerings we can manage to get out concerning it is so vast that our words seem hollow, flatulent, or false. After art talk, "whereof one cannot speak, thereof one must be silent" seems like very attractive doctrine.

But, of course, hardly anyone, save the truly indifferent, is thus silent, artists included. On the contrary, the perception of something important in either particular works or in the arts generally moves people to talk (and write) about them incessantly. Something that meaningful to us cannot be left just to sit there bathed in pure significance, and so we describe, analyze, compare, judge, classify; we erect theories about creativity, form, perception, social function; we characterize art as a language, a structure, a system, an act, a symbol, a pattern of feeling; we reach for scientific metaphors, spiritual ones, technological ones, political ones; and if all else fails we string dark sayings together and hope someone else will eludicate them for us. The surface bootlessness of talking about art seems matched by a depth necessity to talk about it endlessly. And it is this peculiar state of affairs that I want here to probe, in part to explain it, but even more to determine what difference it makes.

To some degree art is everywhere talked about in what may be called craft terms—in terms of tonal progressions, color relations, or prosodic shapes. This is especially true in the West where subjects like harmony or pictorial composition have been developed to the point of minor sciences, and the modern move toward aesthetic formalism, best represented right now by structuralism, and by those varieties of semiotics which seek to follow its lead, is but an attempt to generalize this approach into a comprehensive one, to create a technical language capable of representing the internal relations of myths, poems, dances, or melodies in abstract, transposable terms. But the craft approach to art talk is hardly confined to either the

[2]Quoted in ibid., pp. 292–93.

West or the modern age, as the elaborate theories of Indian musicology, Javanese choreography, Arabic versification, or Yoruba embossment remind us. Even the Australian aborigines, everybody's favorite example of primitive peoples, analyze their body designs and ground paintings into dozens of isolable and named formal elements, unit graphs in an iconic grammar of representation.[3]

But what is more interesting and I think more important is that it is perhaps only in the modern age and in the West that some people (still a minority, and destined, one suspects, to remain such) have managed to convince themselves that technical talk about art, however developed, is sufficient to a complete understanding of it; that the whole secret of aesthetic power is located in the formal relations among sounds, images, volumes, themes, or gestures. Everywhere else—and, as I say, among most of us as well—other sorts of talk, whose terms and conceptions derive from cultural concerns art may serve, or reflect, or challenge, or describe, but does not in itself create, collects about it to connect its specific energies to the general dynamic of human experience. "The purpose of a painter," Matisse, who can hardly be accused of undervaluing form, wrote, "must not be conceived as separate from his pictorial means, and these pictorial means must be more complete (I do not mean more complicated) the deeper his thought. I am unable to distinguish between the feeling I have for life and my way of expressing it."[4]

The feeling an individual, or what is more critical, because no man is an island but a part of the main, the feeling a people has for life appears, of course, in a great many other places than in their art. It appears in their religion, their morality, their science, their commerce, their technology, their politics, their amusements, their law, even in the way they organize their everyday practical existence. The talk about art that is not merely technical or a spiritualization of the technical—that is, most of it—is largely directed to placing it within the context of these other expressions of human purpose and the pattern of experience they collectively sustain. No more than sexual passion or contact with the sacred, two more matters it is difficult to talk about, but yet somehow necessary, can confrontation with aesthetic objects be left to float, opaque and hermetic, outside the general course of social life. They demand to be assimilated.

[3]See N. D. Munn, *Walbiri Iconography* (Ithaca, N.Y., 1973).
[4]Quoted in Goldwater and Treves, *Artists on Art*, p. 410.

What this implies, among other things, is that the definition of art in any society is never wholly intra-aesthetic, and indeed but rarely more than marginally so. The chief problem presented by the sheer phenomenon of aesthetic force, in whatever form and in result of whatever skill it may come, is how to place it within the other modes of social activity, how to incorporate it into the texture of a particular pattern of life. And such placing, the giving to art objects a cultural significance, is always a local matter; what art is in classical China or classical Islam, what it is in the Pueblo southwest or highland New Guinea, is just not the same thing, no matter how universal the intrinsic qualities that actualize its emotional power (and I have no desire to deny them) may be. The variety that anthropologists have come to expect in the spirit beliefs, the classification systems, or the kinship structures of different peoples, and not just in their immediate shapes but in the way of being-in-the-world they both promote and exemplify, extends as well to their drummings, carvings, chants, and dances.

It is the failure to realize this on the part of many students of non-Western art, and particularly of so-called "primitive art," that leads to the oft-heard comment that the peoples of such cultures don't talk, or not very much, about art—they just sculpt, sing, weave, or whatever, silent in their expertise. What is meant is that they don't talk about it the way the observer talks about it—or would like them to—in terms of its formal properties, its symbolic content, its affective values, or its stylistic features, except laconically, cryptically, and as though they had precious little hope of being understood.

But, of course, they do talk about it, as they talk about everything else striking, or suggestive, or moving, that passes through their lives—about how it is used, who owns it, when it is performed, who performs or makes it, what role it plays in this or that activity, what it may be exchanged for, what it is called, how it began, and so forth and so on. But this tends to be seen not as talk about art, but about something else—everyday life, myths, trade, or whatever. To the man who may not know what he likes but knows what art is, the Tiv, aimlessly sewing raffia onto cloth prior to resist dyeing it (he will not even look at how the piece is going until it is completely finished), who told Paul Bohannan, "if the design does not turn out well, I will sell it to the Ibo; if it does, I will keep it; if it comes out extraordinarily well, I shall give it to my mother-in-law," seems not to be discussing his work at all, but merely some of his social attitudes.[5] The approach to art from the side of Western aesthetics (which, as Kristeller has reminded us, only emerged in the mid-eighteenth century, along with our rather peculiar notion of the "fine arts"), and indeed from any sort of prior formalism, blinds us to the very existence of the data upon which a comparative understanding of it could be built. And we are left, as we used to be in studies of totemism, caste, or bride-wealth—and still are in structuralist ones—with an externalized conception of the phenomenon supposedly under intense inspection but actually not even in our line of sight.

For Matisse, as is no surprise, was right: the means of an art and the feeling for life that animates it are inseparable, and one can no more understand aesthetic objects as concatenations of pure form than one can understand speech as a parade of syntactic variations, or myth as a set of structural transformations. Take, as an example, a matter as apparently transcultural and abstract as line, and consider its meaning, as Robert Faris Thompson brilliantly describes it, in Yoruba sculpture.[6] Linear precision, Thompson says, the sheer clarity of line, is a major concern of Yoruba carvers, as it is of those who assess the carvers' work, and the vocabulary of linear qualities, which the Yoruba use colloquially and across a range of concerns far broader than sculpture, is nuanced and extensive. It is not just their statues, pots, and so on that Yoruba incise with lines: they do the same with their faces. Line, of varying depth, direction, and length, sliced into their cheeks and left to scar over, serves as a means of lineage identification, personal allure, and status expression; and the terminology of the sculptor and of the cicatrix specialist—"cuts" distinguished from "slashes," and "digs" or "claws" from "splittings open"—parallel one another in exact precision. But there is more to it than this. The Yoruba associate line with civilization: "This country has become civilized," literally means, in Yoruba, "this earth has lines upon its face." " 'Civilization' in Yoruba," Thompson goes on,

is ilàjú—face with lined marks. The same verb which civilizes the face with marks of membership in urban and town lineages civilizes the earth: Ó ṣá kẹ́kẹ́; Ó sáko (He slashes the [cicatrix] marks; he clears the bush). The same verb which opens Yoruba marks upon a face, opens roads, and boundaries in the forest: Ó lànọ̀n; Ò là ààlà; Ó lapa (He cut a new road; he marked out a new boundary; he cut a

[5]P. Bohannan, "Artist and Critic in an African Society," in *Anthropology and Art*, ed. C. M. Otten (New York, 1971), p. 178.
[6]R. F. Thompson, "Yoruba Artistic Criticism," in *The Traditional Artist in African Societies*, ed. W. L. d'Azaredo (Bloomington, Ind., 1973), pp. 19–61.

new path). In fact, the basic verb to cicatrize *(là)* has multiple associations of imposing of human pattern upon the disorder of nature: chunks of wood, the human face,
and the forest are all "opened" . . . allowing the inner quality of the substance to
shine forth.[7]

The intense concern of the Yoruba carver with line, and with particular
forms of line, stems therefore from rather more than a detached pleasure
in its intrinsic properties, the problems of sculptural technique, or even
some generalized cultural notion one could isolate as a native aesthetic. It
grows out of a distinctive sensibility the whole of life participates in forming—one in which the meanings of things are the scars that men leave on
them.

This realization, that to study an art form is to explore a sensibility, that
such a sensibility is essentially a collective formation, and that the foundations of such a formation are as wide as social existence and as deep, leads
away not only from the view that aesthetic power is a grandiloquence for
the pleasures of craft. It leads away also from the the so-called functionalist
view that has most often been opposed to it: that is, that works of art are
elaborate mechanisms for defining social relationships, sustaining social
rules, and strengthening social values. Nothing very measurable would happen to Yoruba society if carvers no longer concerned themselves with the
fineness of line, or, I daresay, even with carving. Certainly, it would not
fall apart. Just some things that were felt could not be said—and perhaps,
after awhile, might no longer even be felt—and life would be the greyer
for it. Anything may, of course, play a role in helping society work, painting
and sculpting included; just as anything may help it tear itself apart. But
the central connection between art and collective life does not lie on such
an instrumental plane, it lies on a semiotic one. Matisse's color jottings (the
word is his own) and the Yoruba's line arrangements do not, save glancing-
ly, celebrate social structure or forward useful doctrines. They materialize
a way of experiencing, bring a particular cast of mind out into the world
of objects, where men can look at it.

The signs or sign elements—Matisse's yellow, the Yoruba's slash—that
make up a semiotic system we want, for theoretical purposes, to call aesthetic are ideationally connected to the society in which they are found,
not mechanically. They are, in a phrase of Robert Goldwater's, primary
documents; not illustrations of conceptions already in force, but concep-

[7]Ibid., pp. 35–36.

tions themselves that seek—or for which people seek—a meaningful place in a repertoire of other documents, equally primary.[8]

To develop the point more concretely, and to dissipate any intellectualist or literary aura such words as "ideational" and "conception" may seem to carry with them, we can look for a moment at some aspects of one of the few other discussions of tribal art that manages to be sensitive to semiotic concerns without disappearing into a haze of formulas: Anthony Forge's analysis of the four-color flat painting of the Abelam people of New Guinea.[9] The group produces, in Forge's phrase, "acres of painting," on flat sheets of sago spathe, all done in cult situations of one sort or another. The details of all this are outlined in his studies. But what is of immediate interest is the fact that, although Abelam painting ranges from the obviously figurative to the totally abstract (a distinction which, as their painting is declamatory, not descriptive, has no meaning to them), it is mainly connected to the wider world of Abelam experience by means of an almost obsessively recurrent motif, a pointed oval, representing, and called, the belly of a woman. The representation is, of course, at least vaguely iconic. But the power of the connection for the Abelam lies less in that, hardly much of an achievement, than in the fact that they are able with it to address a burning preoccupation of theirs in terms of color-shapes (in itself, line here hardly exists as an aesthetic element; while paint has a magical force)—a preoccupation they address in somewhat different ways in work, in ritual, in domestic life: the natural creativity of the female.

The concern for the difference between female creativity, which the Abelam see as precultural, a product of woman's physical being, and therefore primary, and male creativity, which they see as cultural, dependent upon men's access to supernatural power through ritual, and therefore derivative, runs through the whole of their culture. Women created vegetation and discovered the yams that men eat. Women first encountered the supernaturals, whose lovers they became, until the men, grown suspicious, discovered what was going on and took the supernaturals, now turned into wood carvings, as the focus of their ceremonials. And, of course, women produce men from the swell of their bellies. Male power, dependent upon

[8] R. Goldwater, "Art and Anthropology: Some Comparisons of Methodology," in *Primitive Art and Society,* ed. A. Forge (London, 1973), p. 10.
[9] A. Forge, "Style and Meaning in Sepik Art," in *Primitive Art and Society,* ed. Forge, pp. 169–92. See also, A. Forge, "The Abelam Artist," in *Social Organization,* ed. M. Freedman (Chicago, 1967), pp. 65–84.

ritual, a matter now jealously kept secret from women, is thus encapsulated within female power, dependent upon biology; and it is this prodigious fact the paintings, packed with red, yellow, white, and black ovals (Forge found eleven of them in one small painting that was virtually composed of them), are, as we would say, "about."

But they are directly about it, not illustratively. One could as well argue that the rituals, or the myths, or the organization of family life, or the division of labor enact conceptions evolved in painting as that painting reflects the conceptions underlying social life. All these matters are marked by the apprehension of culture as generated in the womb of nature as man is in the belly of woman, and all of them give it a specific sort of voice. Like the incised lines on Yoruba statues, the color-ovals in Abelam paintings are meaningful because they connect to a sensibility they join in creating—here, one where, rather than scars signing civilization, pigment signs power:

In general colour (or strictly paint) words are applied only to things of ritual concern. This can be seen very clearly in the Abelam classification of nature. Tree species are subject to an elaborate classification, but . . . the criteria used are seed and leaf shapes. Whether the tree has flowers or not, and the colour of flowers or leaves are rarely mentioned as criteria. Broadly speaking, the Abelam had use only for the hibiscus and a yellow flower, both of which served as [ritual] decorations for men and yams. Small flowering plants of any colour were of no interest and were classified merely as grass or undergrowth. Similarly with insects: all those that bite or sting are carefully classified, but butterflies form one huge class regardless of size or colour. In the classification of bird species, however, colour is of vital importance . . . but then birds are totems, and unlike butterflies and flowers are central to the ritual sphere. . . . It would seem . . . that colour to be describable has to be of ritual interest. The words for the four colours are . . . really words for paints. Paint is an essentially powerful substance and it is perhaps not so surprising that the use of colour words is restricted to those parts of the natural environment that have been selected as ritually relevant. . . .

The association between colour and ritual significance can also be seen in Abelam reactions to European importations. Coloured magazines sometimes find their way into the village and occasionally pages are torn from them and attached to the matting at the base of the ceremonial house façade. . . . The pages selected were brightly coloured, usually food advertisements . . . [and] the Abelam had no idea of what was represented but thought that with their bright colours and incomprehensibility the selected pages were likely to be European [sacred designs] and therefore powerful.[10]

[10]A. Forge, "Learning to See in New Guinea," in *Socialization, the Approach from Social Anthropology,* ed. P. Mayer (London, 1970), pp. 184–86.

So in at least two places, two matters on the face of them as self-luminous as line and color draw their vitality from rather more than their intrinsic appeal, as real as that might be. Whatever the innate capacities for response to sculptile delicacy or chromatic drama, these responses are caught up in wider concerns, less generic and more content-full, and it is this encounter with the locally real that reveals their constructive power. The unity of form and content is, where it occurs and to the degree it occurs, a cultural achievement, not a philosophical tautology. If there is to be a semiotic science of art it is that achievement it will have to explain. And to do so it will have to give more attention to talk, and to other sorts of talk but the recognizably aesthetic, than it has usually been inclined to give.

II

A common response to this sort of argument, especially when it comes from the side of anthropologists, is to say, that may be all well and good for primitives, who confuse the realms of their experience into one large, unreflective whole, but it does not apply to more developed cultures where art emerges as a differentiated activity responsive mainly to its own necessities. And like most such easy contrasts between peoples on different sides of the literacy revolution, it is false, and in both directions: as much in underestimating the internal dynamic of art in—What shall I call them? Unlettered societies?—as in overestimating its autonomy in lettered ones. I will set aside the first sort of error here—the notion that Yoruba and Abelam type art traditions are without a kinetic of their own—perhaps to come back to it on a later occasion. For the moment I want to scotch the second by looking briefly at the matrix of sensibility in two quite developed, and quite different, aesthetic enterprises: quattrocento painting and Islamic poetry.

For Italian painting, I will mainly rely on Michael Baxandall's recent book, *Painting and Experience in Fifteenth Century Italy,* which takes precisely the sort of approach I here am advocating.[11] Baxandall is concerned with defining what he calls "the period eye"—that is, "the equipment that a fifteenth-century painter's public [that is, other painters and "the patron-

[11]M. Baxandall, *Painting and Experience in Fifteenth Century Italy* (London, 1972).

izing classes"] brought to complex visual stimulations like pictures."[12] A picture, he says, is sensitive to the kinds of interpretive skill—patterns, categories, inferences, analogies—the mind brings to it:

A man's capacity to distinguish a certain kind of form or relationship of forms will have consequences for the attention with which he addresses a picture. For instance, if he is skilled in noting proportional relationships, or if he is practiced in reducing complex forms to compounds of simple forms, or if he has a rich set of categories for different kinds of red and brown, these skills may well lead him to order his experience of Piero della Francesca's *Annunciation* differently from people without these skills, and much more sharply than people whose experience has not given them many skills relevant to the picture. For it is clear that some perceptual skills are more relevant to any one picture than others: a virtuosity in classifying the ductus of flexing lines—a skill many Germans, for instance, possessed in this period . . . would not find much scope on the *Annunciation*. Much of what we call "taste" lies in this, the conformity between discriminations demanded by a painting and skills of discrimination possessed by the beholder.[13]

But what is even more important, these appropriate skills, for both the beholder and the painter, are for the most part not built in like retinal sensitivity for focal length but are drawn from general experience, the experience in this case of living a quattrocento life and seeing things in a quattrocento way:

. . . some of the mental equipment a man orders his visual experience with is variable, and much of this variable equipment is culturally relative, in the sense of being determined by the society which has influenced his experience. Among these variables are categories with which he classifies his visual stimuli, the knowledge he will use to supplement what his immediate vision gives him, and the attitude he will adopt to the kind of artificial object seen. The beholder must use on the painting such visual skills as he has, very few of which are normally special to painting, and he is likely to use those skills his society esteems highly. The painter responds to this; his public's visual capacity must be his medium. Whatever his own specialized professional skills, he is himself a member of the society he works for and shares its visual experience and habit.[14]

The first fact (though, as in Abelam, only the first) to be attended to in these terms is, of course, that most fifteenth-century Italian paintings were religious paintings, and not just in subject matter but in the ends they were

[12]Ibid., p. 38.
[13]Ibid., p. 34.
[14]Ibid., p. 40.

designed to serve. Pictures were meant to deepen human awareness of the spiritual dimensions of existence; they were visual invitations to reflections on the truths of Christianity. Faced with an arresting image of the Annunciation, the Assumption of the Virgin, the Adoration of the Magi, the Charge to St. Peter, or the Passion, the beholder was to complete it by reflecting on the event as he knew it and on his personal relationship to the mysteries it recorded. "For it is one thing to adore a painting," as a Dominican preacher defending the virtuousness of art, put it, "but it is quite another to learn from a painted narrative what to adore."[15]

Yet the relation between religious ideas and pictorial images (and this I think is true for art generally) was not simply expositive; they were not Sunday school illustrations. The painter, or at least the religious painter, was concerned with inviting his public to concern themselves with first things and last, not with providing them with a recipe or a surrogate for such concern, nor with a transcription of it. His relation, or more exactly, the relations of his painting, to the wider culture was interactive or, as Baxandall puts it, complementary. Speaking of Giovanni Bellini's *Transfiguration,* a generalized, almost typological, but of course marvellously plastic, rendering of the scene, he calls it a relic of cooperation between Bellini and his public—"The fifteenth-century experience of the *Transfiguration* was an interaction between the painting, the configuration on the wall, and the visualizing activity of the public mind—a public mind with different furniture and dispositions from ours."[16] Bellini could count on a contribution from the other side and designed his panel so as to call that contribution out, not to depict it. His vocation was to construct an image to which a distinctive spirituality could forcibly react. The public does not need, as Baxandall remarks, what it has already got. What it needs is an object rich enough to see it in; rich enough, even, to, in seeing it, deepen it.

There were, of course, all sorts of cultural institutions active in forming the sensibility of quattrocento Italy which converged with painting to produce the "period eye," and not all of them were religious (as not all the paintings were religious). Among the religious ones, popular sermons, classifying and subclassifying the revelatory events and personages of the Christian myth and setting forth the types of attitude—disquiet, reflection, inquiry, humility, dignity, admiration—appropriate to each, as well as offering dicta as to how such matters were represented visually, were probably the

[15]Quoted in ibid., p. 41.
[16]Ibid., p. 48.

most important. "Popular preachers . . . drilled their congregations in a
set of interpretive skills right at the centre of the fifteenth-century response
to painting."[17] Gestures were classified, physiognomies typed, colors sym-
bologized, and the physical appearance of central figures discussed with
apologetical care. "You ask," another Dominican preacher announced,

Was the Virgin dark or fair? Albertus Magnus says that she was not simply dark,
nor simply red-haired, nor just fair-haired. For any one of these colours by itself
brings a certain imperfection to a person. This is why one says: "God save me from
a red-haired Lombard," or "God save me from a black-haired German," or "from
a fair-haired Spaniard," or "from a Belgian of whatever colour." Mary was a blend
of complexions, partaking of all of them, because a face partaking of all of them
is a beautiful one. It is for this reason medical authorities declare that a complexion
compounded of red and fair is best when a third colour is added: black. And yet
this, says Albertus, we must admit: she was a little on the dark side. There are three
reasons for thinking this—firstly by reason of complexion, since Jews tend to be
dark and she was a Jewess; secondly by reason of witness, since St. Luke made the
three pictures of her now at Rome, Loreto and Bologna, and these are
brown-complexioned; thirdly by reason of affinity. A son commonly takes after his
mother, and vice versa; Christ was dark, therefore . . .[18]

Of the other domains of Renaissance culture that contributed to the way
fifteenth-century Italians looked at paintings, two which Baxandall finds
to have been of particular importance were another art, though a lesser one,
social dancing, and a quite practical activity he calls gauging—that is, esti-
mating quantities, volumes, proportions, ratios, and so on for commercial
purposes.

Dancing had relevance to picture seeing because it was less a temporal
art allied to music, as with us, than a graphic one allied to spectacle—religious pageants, street masques, and so on; a matter of figural grouping not, or anyway not mainly, of rhythmic motion. As such, it both depended upon and sharpened the capacity to discern psychological interplay
among static figures grouped in subtle patterns, a kind of body arranging—a
capacity the painters shared and used to evoke their viewer's response. In
particular, the *bassa danza,* a slow paced, geometrized dance popular in
Italy at the time, presented patterns of figural grouping that painters such
as Botticelli, in his *Primavera* (which revolves, of course, around the dance
of the Graces) or his *Birth of Venus,* employed in organizing their work.

[17]Ibid.
[18]Quoted in ibid., p. 57.

The sensibility the *bassa danza* represented, Baxandall says, "involved a public skill at interpreting figure patterns, a general experience of semi-dramatic arrangement [of human bodies] that allowed Botticelli and other painters to assume a similar public readiness to interpret their own groups."[19] Given a widespread familiarity with highly stylized dance forms consisting essentially of discrete sequences of *tableaux vivants,* the painter could count on an immediate visual understanding of his own sort of figural tableaux in a way not very open in a culture such as ours where dance is a matter more of movement framed between poses than poses framed between movement and the general sense for tacit gesture is weak. "The transmutation of a vernacular social art of grouping into an art where a pattern of people—not gesticulating or lunging or grimacing people—can still stimulate a strong sense of . . . psychological interplay, is the problem: it is doubtful if we have the right predispositions to see such refined innuendo at all spontaneously."[20]

Beyond and behind this tendency to conceive of both dances and paintings as patterns of body arrangement carrying implicit meaning lies, of course, a wider tendency in the whole society, and particularly in its cultivated classes, to regard the way in which men grouped themselves with respect to one another, the postural orderings they fell into in one another's company, as not accidental but the result of the sorts of relationships they had to one another. But it is in the other matter Baxandall takes to have had a forming impact on how the people of the Renaissance saw paintings—gauging—that this deeper penetration of visual habit into the life of society, and the life of society into it, is apparent.

It is an important fact of art history, he notes, that commodities have come regularly in standard-size containers only since the nineteenth century (and even then, he might have added, only in the West). "Previously a container—barrel, sack, or bale—was unique, and calculating its volume quickly and accurately was a condition of business."[21] And the same was true of lengths, as in the cloth trade, proportions, as in brokerage, or ratios, as in surveying. One did not survive in commerce without such skills, and it was merchants who, for the most part, commissioned the paintings, and in some cases, like Piero della Francesca, who wrote a mathematical handbook on gauging, painted them.

[19]Ibid., p. 80.
[20]Ibid., p. 76.
[21]Ibid., p. 86.

In any case, both painters and their merchant patrons had a similar education in such matters—to be literate was at the same time to have command of the sorts of techniques available to judge the dimensions of things. So far as solid objects were concerned these skills involved the ability to break down irregular or unfamiliar masses into compounds of regular and familiar, and thus calculable, ones—cylinders, cones, cubes and so on; for two-dimensional ones, a similar ability to analyze ununiform surfaces into simple planes: squares, circles, triangles, hexagons. The heights to which this could rise is indicated in a passage Baxandall gives from Piero's handbook:

There is a barrel, each of its ends being 2 bracci in diameter; the diameter at its bung is $2\frac{1}{4}$ bracci and halfway between bung and end it is $2\frac{2}{9}$ bracci. The barrel is 2 bracci long. What is its cubic measure?

This is like a pair of truncated cones. Square the diameter at the ends: $2 \times 2 = 4$. Then square the median diameter $2\frac{2}{9} \times 2\frac{2}{9} = 4\frac{76}{81}$. Add them together [giving] $8\frac{76}{81}$. Multiply $2 \times \frac{2}{9} = 4\frac{4}{9}$. Add this to $8\frac{76}{81} = 13\frac{31}{81}$. Divide by $3 = 4\frac{112}{243}$. . . . Now square $2\frac{1}{4}$ [giving] $5\frac{1}{16}$. Add it to the square of the median diameter: $5\frac{1}{16} + 4\frac{76}{81} = 10\frac{1}{129}$. Multiply $2\frac{2}{9} \times 2\frac{1}{4} = 5$. Add this to the previous sum [getting] $15\frac{1}{129}$. Divide by 3 [which yields] 5 and $\frac{1}{3888}$. Add it to the first result . . . $= 9\frac{1792}{3888}$. Multiply this by 11 and then divide by 14 [that is, multiply by pi/4]: the final result is $7\frac{23600}{54432}$. This is the cubic measure of the barrel.[22]

This is, as Baxandall says, a special intellectual world; but it is one in which all of the educated classes in places like Venice and Florence lived. Its connection with painting, and the perception of painting, lay less in the calculational processes as such than in a disposition to attend to the structure of complex forms as combinations of simpler, more regular, and more comprehensible ones. Even the objects involved in paintings—cisterns, columns, brick towers, paved floors, and so on—were the same ones that handbooks used to practice students in the art of gauging. And so when Piero, in his other hat as painter, renders *The Annunciation* as set in a columned, multilevel, advancing and receding Perugian portico, or the Madonna in a domed, half-rounded cloth pavillion, a framing dress to her own, he is calling upon his public's ability to see such forms as compounds of others and thus to interpret—gauge, if you will—his paintings and grasp their meaning:

[22]Ibid.

To the commercial man almost anything was reducible to geometrical figures underlying surface irregularities—that pile of grain reduced to a cone, the barrel to a cylinder or a compound of truncated cones, the cloak to a circle of stuff allowed to lapse into a cone of stuff, the brick tower to a compound cubic body composed of a calculable number of smaller cubic bodies, and . . . this habit of analysis is very close to the painter's analysis of appearances. As a man gauged a bale, the painter surveyed a figure. In both cases there is a conscious reduction of irregular masses and voids to combinations of manageable geometric bodies. . . . Because they were practised in manipulating ratios and in analysing the volume or surface of compound bodies, [fifteenth-century Italians] were sensitive to pictures carrying the marks of similar processes.[23]

The famous lucid solidity of Renaissance painting had at least part of its origins in something else than the inherent properties of planar representation, mathematical law, and binocular vision.

Indeed, and this is the central point, all these broader cultural matters, and others I have not mentioned, interworked to produce the sensibility in which quattrocento art was formed and had its being. (In an earlier work, *Giotto and the Orators,* Baxandall connects the development of pictorial composition to the narrative forms, most especially the periodic sentence, of humanist rhetoric; the orator's hierarchy of period, clause, phrase, and word being consciously matched, by Alberti and others, to the painter's one of picture, body, member, and plane.)[24] Different painters played upon different aspects of that sensibility, but the moralism of religious preaching, the pageantry of social dancing, the shrewdness of commercial gauging, and the grandeur of Latin oratory all combined to provide what is indeed the painter's true medium: the capacity of his audience to see meanings in pictures. An old picture, Baxandall says, though he could have omitted the "old," is a record of visual activity that one has to learn to read, just as one has to learn to read a text from a different culture. "If we observe that Piero della Francesca tends to a gauged sort of painting, Fra Angelico to a preached sort of painting, and Botticelli to a danced sort of painting, we are observing something not only about them but about their society."[25]

The capacity, variable among peoples as it is among individuals, to perceive meaning in pictures (or poems, melodies, buildings, pots, dramas, statues) is, like all other fully human capacities, a product of collective experi-

[23]Ibid., pp. 87–89, 101.
[24]M. Baxandall, *Giotto and the Orators* (Oxford, 1971).
[25]Baxandall, *Painting and Experience,* p. 152.

ence which far transcends it, as is the far rarer capacity to put it there in
the first place. It is out of participation in the general system of symbolic
forms we call culture that participation in the particular we call art, which
is in fact but a sector of it, is possible. A theory of art is thus at the same
time a theory of culture, not an autonomous enterprise. And if it is a semiotic theory of art it must trace the life of signs in society, not in an invented
world of dualities, transformations, parallels, and equivalences.

III

There is hardly a better example of the fact that an artist works with signs
that have a place in semiotic systems extending far beyond the craft he
practices than the poet in Islam. A Muslim making verses faces a set of
cultural realities as objective to his intentions as rocks or rainfall, no less
substantial for being nonmaterial, and no less stubborn for being
man-made. He operates, and alway has operated, in a context where the
instrument of his art, language, has a peculiar, heightened kind of status,
as distinctive a significance, and as mysterious, as Abelam paint. Everything from metaphysics to morphology, scripture to calligraphy, the patterns of public recitation to the style of informal conversation conspires
to make of speech and speaking a matter charged with an import if not
unique in human history, certainly extraordinary. The man who takes up
the poet's role in Islam traffics, and not wholly legitimately, in the moral
substance of his culture.

In order even to begin to demonstrate this it is of course necessary first
to cut the subject down to size. It is not my intention to survey the whole
course of poetic development from the Prophecy forward, but just to make
a few general, and rather unsystematic, remarks about the place of poetry
in traditional Islamic society—most particularly Arabic poetry, most particularly in Morocco, most particularly on the popular, oral verse level. The
relationship between poetry and the central impulses of Muslim culture is,
I think, rather similar more or less everywhere, and more or less since the
beginning. But rather than trying to establish that, I shall merely assume
it and proceed, on the basis of somewhat special material, to suggest what
the terms of that relationship—an uncertain and difficult one—seem to be.

There are, from this perspective, three dimensions of the problem to review and interrelate. The first, as always in matters Islamic, is the peculiar nature and status of the Quran, "the only miracle in Islam." The second is the performance context of the poetry, which, as a living thing, is as much a musical and dramatic art as it is a literary one. And the third, and most difficult to delineate in a short space, is the general nature—agonistic, as I will call it—of interpersonal communication in Moroccan society. Together they make of poetry a kind of paradigmatic speech act, an archetype of talk, which it would take, were such a thing conceivable, a full analysis of Muslim culture to unpack.

But as I say, wherever the matter ends it starts with the Quran. The Quran (which means neither "testament" nor "teaching" nor "book," but "recitation") differs from the other major scriptures of the world in that it contains not reports about God by a prophet or his disciples, but His direct speech, the syllables, words, and sentences of Allah. Like Allah, it is eternal and uncreated, one of His attributes, like Mercy or Omnipotence, not one of his creatures, like man or the earth. The metaphysics are abstruse and not very consistently worked out, having to do with Allah's translation into Arabic rhymed prose of excerpts from an eternal text, the Well-Guarded Tablet, and the dictation of these, one by one and in no particular order over a period of years, by Gabriel to Muhammad, Muhammad in turn dictating them to followers, the so-called Quran-reciters, who memorized them and transmitted them to the community at large, which, rehearsing them daily, has continued them since. But the point is that he who chants Quranic verses—Gabriel, Muhammad, the Quran-reciters, or the ordinary Muslim, thirteen centuries further along the chain—chants not words about God, but of Him, and indeed, as those words are His essence, chants God himself. The Quran, as Marshall Hodgson has said, is not a treatise, a statement of facts and norms, it is an event, an act:

It was never designed to be read for information or even for inspiration, but to be recited as an act of commitment in worship. . . . What one did with the Qur'ân was not to peruse it but to worship by means of it; not to passively receive it but, in reciting it, to reaffirm it for oneself: the event of revelation was renewed every time one of the faithful, in the act of worship, relived [that is, respoke] the Qur'ânic affirmation.[26]

[26]M. G. S. Hodgson, *The Venture of Islam,* vol. 1 (Chicago, 1974), p. 367.

Now, there are a number of implications of this view of the Quran—among them that its nearest equivalent in Christianity is not the Bible but Christ—but for our purposes the critical one is that its language, seventh-century Meccan Arabic, is set apart as not just the vehicle of a divine message, like Greek, Pali, Aramaic, or Sanskrit, but as itself a holy object. Even an individual recitation of the Quran, or portions of it, is considered an uncreated entity, something that puzzles a faith centered on divine persons, but to an Islamic one, centered on divine rhetoric, signifies that speech is sacred to the degree that it resembles that of God. One result of this is the famous linguistic schizophrenia of Arabic-speaking peoples: the persistence of "classical" *(mudāri)* or "pure *(fuṣḥā)* written Arabic, contrived to look as Quranic as possible and rarely spoken outside of ritual contexts, alongside one or another unwritten vernacular, called "vulgar" *(ʿāmmīya)* or "common" *(dārija),* and considered incapable of conveying serious truths. Another is that the status of those who seek to create in words, and especially for secular purposes, is highly ambiguous. They turn the tongue of God to ends of their own, which if it not quite sacrilege, borders on it; but at the same time they display its incomparable power, which if not quite worship, approaches it. Poetry, rivaled only by architecture, became the cardinal fine art in Islamic civilization, and especially the Arabic-speaking part of it, while treading the edge of the gravest form of blasphemy.

This sense for Quranic Arabic as the model of what speech should be, and a constant reproof to the way people actually talk, is reinforced by the whole pattern of traditional Muslim life. Almost every boy (and more recently, many girls as well) goes to a drill-school where he learns to recite and memorize verses from the Quran. If he is adept and diligent he may get the whole 6200 or so by heart and become a *ḥafīẓ,* a "memorizer," and bring a certain celebrity to his parents; if, as is more likely, he is not, he will at least learn enough to conduct his prayers, butcher chickens, and follow sermons. If he is especially pious, he may even go to a higher school in some urban center like Fez or Marrakech and obtain a more exact sense of the meaning of what he has memorized. But whether a man comes away with a handful of half-understood verses or the entire collection reasonably comprehended, the main stress is always on recitation and on the rote learning necessary to it. What Hodgson has said of medieval Islam—that all statements were seen as either true or false; that the sum of all true statements, a fixed corpus radiating from the Quran, which at least implicitly contained them all, was knowledge; and that the way to obtain knowledge was to commit to memory the phrases it was stated in—could be said today for the greater part of Morocco, where whatever weakening faith has experienced it has yet to relax its passion for recitable truth.[27]

Such attitudes and such training lead to everyday life being punctuated by lines from the Quran and other classical tags. Aside from the specifically religious contexts—the daily prayers, the Friday worship, the mosque sermons, the bead-telling cantations in the mystical brotherhoods, the recital of the whole book on special occasions such as the Fast month, the offering of verses at funerals, weddings, and circumcisions—ordinary conversation is laced with Quranic formulae to the point where even the most mundane subjects seem set in a sacred frame. The most important public speeches—those from the throne, for example—are cast in an Arabic so classicized that most who hear them but vaguely understand them. Arabic newspapers, magazines, and books are written in a similar manner, with the result that the number of people who can read them is small. The cry of Arabization—the popular demand, swept forward by religious passions, for conducting education in classical Arabic and using it in government and administration—is a potent ideological force, leading to a great deal of linguistic hypocrisy on the part of the political elite and to a certain amount of public disturbance when the hypocrisy grows too apparent. It is this sort of world, one in which language is as much symbol as medium, verbal style is a moral matter, and the experience of God's eloquence wars with the need to communicate, that the oral poet exists, and whose feeling for chants and formulas he exploits as Piero exploited Italy's for sacks and barrels. "I memorized the Quran," one such poet said, trying hard, to explain his art. "Then I forgot the verses and remembered the words."

He forgot the verses during a three-day meditation at the tomb of a saint renowned for inspiring poets, but he remembers the words in the context of performance. Poetry here is not first composed and then recited; it is composed in the recitation, put together in the act of singing it in a public place.

Usually this is a lamp-lit space before the house of some wedding giver or circumcision celebrant. The poet stands, erect as a tree, in the center of the space, assistants slapping tambourines to either side of him. The male part of the audience squats directly in front of him, individual men rising from time to time to stuff currency into his turban, while the female part

[27]Ibid., vol. 2, p. 438.

either peeks discreetly out from the houses around or looks down in the darkness from their roofs. Behind him are two lines of sidewise dancing men, their hands on one another's shoulders and their heads swiveling as they shuffle a couple half-steps right, a couple left. He sings his poem, verse by verse, paced by the tambourines, in a wailed, metallic falsetto, the assistants joining him for the refrain, which tends to be fixed and only generally related to the text, while the dancing men ornament matters with sudden strange rhythmic howls.

Of course, like Albert Lord's famous Jugoslavs, he does not create his text out of sheer fancy, but builds it up, molecularly, a piece at a time, like some artistic Markov process, out of a limited number of established formulae. Some are thematic: the inevitability of death ("even if you live on a prayer rug"); the unreliability of women ("God help you, O lover, who is carried away by the eyes"); the hopelessness of passion ("so many people gone to the grave because of the burning"); the vanity of religious learning ("where is the schoolman who can whitewash the air?"). Some are figurative: girls as gardens, wealth as cloth, worldliness as markets, wisdom as travel, love as jewelry, poets as horses. And some are formal—strict, mechanical schemes of rhyme, meter, line, and stanza. The singing, the tambourines, the dancing men, the genre demands, and the audience sending up you-yous of approval or whistles of censure, as these things either come effectively together or do not, make up an integral whole from which the poem can no more be abstracted than can the Quran from the reciting of it. It, too, is an event, an act; constantly new, constantly renewable.

And, as with the Quran, individuals, or at least many of them, punctuate their ordinary speech with lines, verses, tropes, allusions taken from oral poetry, sometimes from a particular poem, sometimes one associated with a particular poet whose work they know, sometimes from the general corpus, which though large, is, as I say, contained within quite definite formulaic limits. In that sense, taken as a whole, poetry, the performance of which is widespread and regular, most especially in the countryside and among the common classes in the towns, forms a kind of "recitation" of its own, another collection, less exalted but not necessarily less valuable, of memorizable truths: lust is an incurable disease, women an illusory cure; contention is the foundation of society, assertiveness the master virtue; pride is the spring of action, unworldliness moral hypocrisy; pleasure is the flower of life, death the end of pleasure. Indeed, the word for poetry, $\check{s}^c ir$, means "knowledge," and though no Muslim would explicitly put it that way, it stands as a kind of secular counterpoise, a worldly footnote, to the Revelation itself. What man hears about God and the duties owed Him in the Quran, fix-worded facts, he hears about human beings and the consequences of being one in poetry.

The performance frame of poetry, its character as a collective speech act, only reinforces this betwixt and between quality of it—half ritual song, half plain talk—because if its formal, quasi-liturgical dimensions cause it to resemble Quranic chanting, its rhetorical, quasi-social ones cause it to resemble everyday speech. As I have said, it is not possible to describe here the general tone of interpersonal relations in Morocco with any concreteness; one can only claim, and hope to be believed, that it is before anything else combative, a constant testing of wills as individuals struggle to seize what they covet, defend what they have, and recover what they have lost. So far as speech is concerned, this gives to all but the most idle conversation the quality of a catch-as-catch-can in words, a head-on collision of curses, promises, lies, excuses, pleading, commands, proverbs, arguments, analogies, quotations, threats, evasion, flatteries, which not only puts an enormous premium on verbal fluency but gives to rhetoric a directly coercive force; ʿandu klām, "he has words, speech, maxims, eloquence," means also, and not just metaphorically, "he has power, influence, weight, authority."

In the poetic context this agonistic spirit appears throughout. Not only is the content of what the poet says argumentational in this way—attacking the shallowness of townsmen, the knavery of merchants, the perfidy of women, the miserliness of the rich, the treachery of politicians, and the hypocrisy of moralists—but it is directed at particular targets, usually ones present and listening. A local Quran teacher, who has criticized wedding feasts (and the poetry sung at them) as sinful, is excorciated to his face and forced from the village:[28]

> See how many shameful things the teacher did;
> He only worked to fill his pockets.
> He is greedy, venal.
> By God, with all this confusion.
> Just give him his money and tell him "go away";
> "Go eat cat meat and follow it with dog meat."
>
>   . . .
>
> They found out that the teacher had memorized only

[28]I am grateful to Hildred Geertz, who collected most of these poems, for permission to use them.

> four Quran chapters [this a reference to his
> claim to have memorized the whole].

If he knew the Quran by heart and could call himself a scholar,
He wouldn't hurry through the prayers so fast.
He has evil thoughts in his heart.
Why, even in the midst of prayer, his mind is on girls;
> he would chase one if he could find any.

A stingy host fares no better:

> As for him who is stingy and weak, he just sits there
> and doesn't dare say anything.
>
> . . .
>
> They who came for dinner were as in a prison [the food
> was so bad],
> The people were hungry all night and never satisfied.
>
> . . .
>
> The host's wife spent the evening doing as she pleased,
> By God, she didn't even want to get up and get the coffee
> ready.

And a curer, a former friend, with whom the poet has fallen out, gets thirty lines of the following sort of thing:

> Oh, the curer is no longer a reasonable man.
> He followed the road to become powerful,
> And changed into a mad betrayer.
> He followed a trade of the devil; he said he was
> successful, but I don't believe it.

And so on. Nor is it merely individuals the poet criticizes (or can be paid to criticize; for most of these verbal assassinations are contract jobs): the inhabitants of a rival village, or faction, or family; a political party (poetic confrontation between members of such parties, each led by their own poet, have had to be broken up by the police when words began to lead to blows); even whole classes of people, bakers or civil servants, may be targets. And he can shift his immediate audience in the very midst of performance. When he laments the inconstancy of women, he speaks up into the shadows of the roofs; when he attacks the lechery of men, his gaze drops to the crowd at his feet. Indeed, the whole poetic performance has an agonistic tone as the audience cries out in approval (and presses money on the poet) or whistles and hoots in disapproval, sometimes to the point of causing his retirement from the scene.

But perhaps the purest expressions of this tone are the direct combats between poets trying to outdo each other with their verses. Some subject—it may be just an object like a glass or a tree—is chosen to get things going, and then the poets sing alternately, sometimes the whole night long, as the crowd shouts its judgment, until one retires, bested by the other. From a three-hour struggle I give some brief excerpts, in which just about everything is lost in translation except the spirit of the thing:

Well into the middle of the battle, Poet A, challenging, "stands up and says:"

> That which God bestowed on him [the rival poet] he
>   wasted to buy nylon clothes for a girl; he will
>   find what he is looking for,
> And he will buy what he wants [that is, sex] and
>   go visiting around all sorts of [bad] places.

Poet B, responding:

> That which God bestowed on him [that is, himself,
>   Poet B] he used for prayer, tithe, and charity,
> And he didn't follow evil temptations, nor stylish
>   girls, nor tatooed girls; he remembers to run
>   away from Hell-fire.

Then, an hour or so later on, Poet A, still challenging, and still being effectively responded to, shifts to metaphysical riddling:

> From one sky to the other sky it would take 500,000 years,
> And after that, what was going to happen?

Poet B, taken off guard, does not respond directly, but, sparring for time, erupts in threats:

> Take him [Poet A] away from me,
> Or I'll call for bombs,
> I'll call for airplanes,
> And soldiers of fearful appearance.
>   .   .   .
> I will make, oh gentlemen, war now,
> Even if it is just a little one.
> See, I have the greater power.

Still later, the aroused Poet B recovers and replies to the riddle about the skies, not by answering it but by satirizing it with a string of unanswer-

able counterriddles, designed to expose its angels-on-the-head-of-a-pin sort
of foolishness:

> I was going to respond to that one who said, "Climb
>   up to the sky and see how far it is from sky
>   to sky, by the road."
> I was going to tell him, "Count for me all the things
>   that are in the earth."
> I will answer the poet, though he is crazy.
> Tell me, how much oppression have we had, which will
>   be punished in the hereafter?
> Tell me how much grain is there in the world, that
>   we can feast ourselves on?
> Tell me, how much wood is there in the forest, that
>   you can burn up?
> Tell me, how many electricity bulbs are there, from west to east?
> Tell me, how many teapots are filled with tea?

At which point, Poet A, insulted, hooted, angry, and defeated, says,

> Give me the teapot.
> I am going to bathe for prayer.
> I have had enough of this party.

and retires.

In short, in speech terms, or more exactly speech-act terms, poetry lies
in between the divine imperatives of the Quran and the rhetorical thrust
and counterthrust of everyday life, and it is that which gives it its uncertain
status and strange force. On the one hand, it forms a kind of para-Quran,
sung truths more than transitory and less than eternal in a language style
more studied than the colloquial and less arcane than the classical. On the
other, it projects the spirit of everyday life into the realm of, if not the holy,
at least the inspired. Poetry is morally ambiguous because it is not sacred
enough to justify the power it actually has and not secular enough for that
power to be equated to ordinary eloquence. The Moroccan oral poet inhab-
its a region between speech types which is at the same time a region between
worlds, between the discourse of God and the wrangle of men. And unless
that is understood neither he nor his poetry can be understood, no matter
how much ferreting out of latent structures or parsing of verse forms one
engages in. Poetry, or anyway this poetry, constructs a voice out of the
voices that surround it. If it can be said to have a "function," that is it.

"Art," says my dictionary, a usefully mediocre one, is "the conscious production or arrangement of colors, forms, movements, sounds or other elements in a manner that affects the sense of beauty," a way of putting the matter which seems to suggest that men are born with the power to appreciate, as they are born with the power to see jokes, and have only to be provided with the occasions to exercise it. As what I have said here ought to indicate, I do not think that this is true (I do not think that it is true for humor either); but, rather, that "the sense of beauty," or whatever the ability to respond intelligently to face scars, painted ovals, domed pavillions, or rhymed insults should be called, is no less a cultural artifact than the objects and devices concocted to "affect" it. The artist works with his audience's capacities—capacities to see, or hear, or touch, sometimes even to taste and smell, with understanding. And though elements of these capacities are indeed innate—it usually helps not to be color-blind—they are brought into actual existence by the experience of living in the midst of certain sorts of things to look at, listen to, handle, think about, cope with, and react to; particular varieties of cabbages, particular sorts of kings. Art and the equipment to grasp it are made in the same shop.

For an approach to aesthetics which can be called semiotic—that is, one concerned with how signs signify—what this means is that it cannot be a formal science like logic or mathematics but must be a social one like history or anthropology. Harmony and prosody are hardly to be dispensed with, any more than composition and syntax; but exposing the structure of a work of art and accounting for its impact are not the same thing. What Nelson Goodman has called "the absurd and awkward myth of the insularity of aesthetic experience," the notion that the mechanics of art generate its meaning, cannot produce a science of signs or of anything else; only an empty virtuosity of verbal analysis.[29]

If we are to have a semiotics of art (or for that matter, of any sign system not axiomatically self-contained), we are going to have to engage in a kind of natural history of signs and symbols, an ethnography of the vehicles of meaning. Such signs and symbols, such vehicles of meaning, play a role in the life of a society, or some part of a society, and it is that which in fact gives them their life. Here, too, meaning is use, or more carefully, arises from use, and it is by tracing out such uses as exhaustively as we are accustomed to for irrigation techniques or marriage customs that we are going to be able to find out anything general about them. This is not a plea for

[29]N. Goodman, *Languages of Art* (Indianapolis, 1968), p. 260.

inductivism—we certainly have no need for a catalogue of instances—but for turning the analytic powers of semiotic theory, whether Peirce's, Saussure's, Lévi-Strauss's, or Goodman's, away from an investigation of signs in abstraction toward an investigation of them in their natural habitat—the common world in which men look, name, listen, and make.

It is not a plea, either, for the neglect of form, but for seeking the roots of form not in some updated version of faculty psychology but in what I have called in chapter 2 "the social history of the imagination"—that is, in the construction and deconstruction of symbolic systems as individuals and groups of individuals try to make some sense of the profusion of things that happen to them. When a Bamileke chief took office, Jacques Maquet informs us, he had his statue carved; "after his death, the statue was respected, but it was slowly eroded by the weather as his memory was eroded in the minds of the people."[30] Where is the form here? In the shape of the statue or the shape of its career? It is, of course, in both. But no analysis of the statue that does not hold its fate in view, a fate as intended as is the arrangement of its volume or the gloss of its surface, is going to understand its meaning or catch its force.

It is, after all, not just statues (or paintings, or poems) that we have to do with but the factors that cause these things to seem important—that is, affected with import—to those who make or possess them, and these are as various as life itself. If there is any commonality among all the arts in all the places that one finds them (in Bali they make statues out of coins, in Australia drawings out of dirt) that justifies including them under a single, Western-made rubric, it is not that they appeal to some universal sense of beauty. That may or may not exist, but if it does it does not seem, in my experience, to enable people to respond to exotic arts with more than an ethnocentric sentimentalism in the absence of a knowledge of what those arts are about or an understanding of the culture out of which they come. (The Western use of "primitive" motifs, its undoubted value in its own terms aside, has only accentuated this; most people, I am convinced, see African sculpture as bush Picasso and hear Javanese music as noisy Debussy.) If there is a commonality it lies in the fact that certain activities everywhere seem specifically designed to demonstrate that ideas are visible, audible, and—one needs to make a word up here—tactible, that they can be cast in forms where the senses, and through the senses the emotions, can

[30]J. Maquet, "Introduction to Aesthetic Anthropology," in *A Macaleb Module in Anthropology* (Reading, Mass., 1971), p. 14.

reflectively address them. The variety of artistic expression stems from the variety of conceptions men have about the way things are, and is indeed the same variety.

To be of effective use in the study of art, semiotics must move beyond the consideration of signs as means of communication, code to be deciphered, to a consideration of them as modes of thought, idiom to be interpreted. It is not a new cryptography that we need, especially when it consists of replacing one cipher by another less intelligible, but a new diagnostics, a science that can determine the meaning of things for the life that surrounds them. It will have, of course, to be trained on signification, not pathology, and treat with ideas, not with symptoms. But by connecting incised statues, pigmented sago palms, frescoed walls, and chanted verse to jungle clearing, totem rites, commercial inference, or street argument, it can perhaps begin at last to locate in the tenor of their setting the sources of their spell.

Chapter 6 / Centers, Kings, and Charisma: Reflections on the Symbolics of Power

Introduction

Like so many of the key ideas in Weber's sociology—*verstehen,* legitimacy, inner-worldly asceticism, rationalization—the concept of charisma suffers from an uncertainty of referent: does it denote a cultural phenomenon or a psychological one? At once "a certain quality" that marks an individual as standing in a privileged relationship to the sources of being and a hypnotic power "certain personalities" have to engage passions and dominate minds, it is not clear whether charisma is the status, the excitement, or some ambiguous fusion of the two. The attempt to write a sociology of culture and a social psychology in a single set of sentences is what gives Weber's work its orchestral complexity and harmonic depth. But it is also what gives it, especially to ears less attuned to polyphony, its chronic elusiveness.

In Weber, a classic instance of his own category, the complexity was managed and the elusiveness offset by his extraordinary ability to hold together warring ideas. In more recent and less heroic times, however, the tendency has been to ease the weight of his thought by collapsing it into one of its dimensions, most commonly the psychological, and nowhere has this been more true than in connection with charisma.[1] Everyone from John Lindsay to Mick Jagger has been called charismatic, mainly on the grounds that he has contrived to interest a certain number of people in the glitter of his personality; and the main interpretation of the rather more genuine upsurge of charismatic leadership in the New States has been that it is a product of psychopathology encouraged by social disorder.[2] In the general psychologism of the age, so well remarked by Phillip Rieff, the study of personal authority narrows to an investigation of self-presentment and collective neurosis; the numinous aspect fades from view.[3]

A few scholars, among them prominently Edward Shils, have, however, sought to avoid this reduction of difficult richness to neo-Freudian cliché by facing up to the fact that there are multiple themes in Weber's concept of charisma, that almost all of them are more stated than developed, and that the preservation of the force of the concept depends upon developing them and uncovering thereby the exact dynamics of their interplay. Between the blur produced by trying to say too much at once and the banality produced by dismissing mysteries there remains the possibility of articulating just what it is that causes some men to see transcendency in others, and what it is they see.

In Shils's case, the lost dimensions of charisma have been restored by stressing the connection between the symbolic value individuals possess and their relation to the active centers of the social order.[4] Such centers, which have "nothing to do with geometry and little with geography," are essentially concentrated loci of serious acts; they consist in the point or points in a society where its leading ideas come together with its leading institutions to create an arena in which the events that most vitally affect its mem-

[1]For an excellent general review of the issue, see S. N. Eisenstadt's introduction to his collection of Weber's charisma papers, *Max Weber on Charisma and Institution Building* (Chicago, 1968), pp. ix–lvi. For the psychologization of "legitimacy," see H. Pitkin, *Wittgenstein and Justice* (Berkeley and Los Angeles, 1972); for "inner-worldly asceticism," D. McClelland, *The Achieving Society* (Princeton, 1961); for "rationalization," A. Mitzman, *The Iron Cage* (New York, 1970). All this ambiguity and even confusion of interpretation are, it should be said, not without warrant in Weber's own equivocalness.
[2]For some examples, see "Philosophers and Kings: Studies in Leadership," *Daedalus,* Summer 1968.
[3]P. Rieff, *The Triumph of the Therapeutic* (New York, 1966).
[4]E. Shils, "Charisma, Order, and Status," *American Sociological Review,* April 1965; idem, "The Dispersion and Concentration of Charisma," in *Independent Black Africa,* ed. W. J. Hanna (New York, 1964); idem, "Centre and Periphery," in *The Logic of Personal Knowledge: Essays Presented to Michael Polanyi* (London, 1961).

bers' lives take place. It is involvement, even oppositional involvement, with such arenas and with the momentous events that occur in them that confers charisma. It is a sign, not of popular appeal or inventive craziness, but of being near the heart of things.

There are a number of implications of such a glowing-center view of the matter. Charismatic figures can arise in any realm of life that is sufficiently focused to seem vital—in science or art as readily as in religion or politics. Charisma does not appear only in extravagant forms and fleeting moments but is an abiding, if combustible, aspect of social life that occasionally bursts into open flame. There is no more a single charismatic emotion than there is a single moral, aesthetic, or scientific one; though passions, often enough distorted ones, are undeniably involved, they can be radically different from case to case. But my concern here is not to pursue these issues, as important as they are to a general theory of social authority. It is to probe into another matter Shils's approach causes to appear in a novel light: the inherent sacredness of sovereign power.

The mere fact that rulers and gods share certain properties has, of course, been recognized for some time. "The will of a king is very numinous," a seventeenth-century political divine wrote; "it has a kind of vast universality in it"—and he was not the first to say so. Nor has it gone unstudied: Ernst Kantorowicz's extraordinary *The King's Two Bodies*—that magisterial discussion of, as he put it, "medieval political theology"—traced the vicissitudes of royal charisma in the West over two hundred years and a half-dozen countries, and more recently there has been a small explosion of books sensitive to what now tends to be called, a bit vaguely, the symbolic aspects of power.[5] But the contact between this essentially historical and ethnographic work and the analytical concerns of modern sociology has

[5] E. Kantorowicz, *The King's Two Bodies: A Study in Medieval Political Theology* (Princeton, 1957); R. E. Giesey, *The Royal Funeral Ceremony in Renaissance France* (Geneva, 1960); R. Strong, *Splendor at Court: Renaissance Spectacle and the Theater of Power* (Boston, 1973); M. Walzer, *The Revolution of the Saints* (Cambridge, Mass., 1965); M. Walzer, *Regicide and Revolution* (Cambridge, England, 1974); S. Anglo, *Spectacle, Pageantry, and Early Tudor Policy* (Oxford, 1969); D. M. Bergeron, *English Civic Pageantry, 1558–1642* (London, 1971); F. A. Yates, *The Valois Tapestries* (London, 1959); E. Straub, *Repraesentatio Maiestatis oder Churbayerische Freudenfeste* (Munich, 1969); G. R. Kernodle, *From Art to Theatre* (Chicago, 1944). For a recent popular book on the American presidency in this vein, see M. Novak, *Choosing Our King* (New York, 1974). Anthropological studies, especially those done in Africa, have of course been sensitive to such issues for a long time (for an example: E. E. Evans-Pritchard, *The Divine Kingship of the Shilluk of the Nilotic Sudan* [Cambridge, England, 1948]), and both E. Cassirer's *Myth of the State* (New Haven, 1946) and M. Bloch's *Les rois thaumaturges* (Paris, 1961) have to be mentioned, along with Kantorowicz, as seminal. The internal quotation is from N. Ward, as given in the OED under "Numinous."

been weak at best, a situation the art historian Panofsky once analogized, in a different context, to that of two neighbors who share the right to shoot over the same district, but one of them owns the gun and the other all the ammunition.

Though still very much in process, and cast sometimes on too apodictic a level, Shils's reformulations promise to be of enormous value in overcoming this unuseful estrangement because they encourage us to look for the vast universality of the will of kings (or of presidents, generals, führers, and party secretaries) in the same place as we look for that of gods: in the rites and images through which it is exerted. More exactly, if charisma is a sign of involvement with the animating centers of society, and if such centers are cultural phenomena and thus historically constructed, investigations into the symbolics of power and into its nature are very similar endeavors. The easy distinction between the trappings of rule and its substance becomes less sharp, even less real; what counts is the manner in which, a bit like mass and energy, they are transformed into each other.

At the political center of any complexly organized society (to narrow our focus now to that) there is both a governing elite and a set of symbolic forms expressing the fact that it is in truth governing. No matter how democratically the members of the elite are chosen (usually not very) or how deeply divided among themselves they may be (usually much more than outsiders imagine), they justify their existence and order their actions in terms of a collection of stories, ceremonies, insignia, formalities, and appurtenances that they have either inherited or, in more revolutionary situations, invented. It is these—crowns and coronations, limousines and conferences—that mark the center as center and give what goes on there its aura of being not merely important but in some odd fashion connected with the way the world is built. The gravity of high politics and the solemnity of high worship spring from liker impulses than might first appear.

This is, of course, more readily apparent (though, as I shall eventually argue, not any more true) in traditional monarchies than in political regimes, where the ingenerate tendency of men to anthropomorphize power is better disguised. The intense focus on the figure of the king and the frank construction of a cult, at times a whole religion, around him make the symbolic character of domination too palpable for even Hobbesians and Utilitarians to ignore. The very thing that the elaborate mystique of court ceremonial is supposed to conceal—that majesty is made, not born—is demonstrated by it. "A woman is not a duchess a hundred yards from a carriage," and chiefs are changed to rajahs by the aesthetic of their rule.

This comes out as clearly as anywhere else in the ceremonial forms by which kings take symbolic possession of their realm. In particular, royal progresses (of which, where it exists, coronation is but the first) locate the society's center and affirm its connection with transcendent things by stamping a territory with ritual signs of dominance. When kings journey around the countryside, making appearances, attending fêtes, conferring honors, exchanging gifts, or defying rivals, they mark it, like some wolf or tiger spreading his scent through his territory, as almost physically part of them. This can be done, as we shall see, within frameworks of expression and belief as various as sixteenth-century English Protestantism, fourteenth-century Javanese Hinduism, and nineteenth-century Moroccan Islam; but however it is done, it is done, and the royal occupation gets portrayed as being a good deal more than merely hedged with divinity.

Elizabeth's England: Virtue and Allegory

On 14 January 1559, the day before her coronation, Elizabeth Tudor—"a daughter, whose birth disappointed her father's hopes for succession, and thus, indirectly, caused her mother's early demise; an illegitimized Princess whose claim to the throne was, nevertheless, almost as valid as those of her half-brother and half-sister; a focus of disaffection during Mary's reign; and a survivor of constant agitation by Imperial and Spanish emissaries to have her eliminated"—rode in a great progress (there were a thousand horses, and she sat, awash in jewels and gold cloth, in an open litter) through the historical districts of the City of London. As she moved, a vast didactic pageant unfolded, stage by stage, before her, settling her into the moral landscape of the resilient capital that five years earlier had done as much, or tried to, for Philip of Spain.[6]

[6]There are a number of descriptions of Elizabeth's London progress (or "entry"), of which the fullest is Bergeron, *English Civic Pageantry*, pp. 11–23. See also R. Withington, *English Pageantry: An Historical Outline*, vol. 1 (Cambridge, Mass., 1918), pp. 199–202; and Anglo, *Spectacle, Pageantry*, pp. 344–59. The text quotation is from Anglo, *Spectacle, Pageantry*, p. 345. The city was resplendent too: "The houses on the way were all decorated; there being on both sides of the street, from Blackfriars to St. Paul's, wooden barricades on which mer-

Starting at the Tower (where she aptly compared her seeing the day to God's delivery of Daniel from the lions), she proceeded to Fenchurch Street, where a small child offered her, for the town's sake, two gifts—blessing tongues to praise her and true hearts to serve her. At Gracechurch Street she encountered a *tableau vivant* called "The Uniting of the Houses of Lancaster and York." It took the form of an arch spanning the street, covered with red and white roses and divided into three levels. On the lowest, two children, representing Henry VII, enclosed in a rose of red roses, and his wife Elizabeth, enclosed in one of white, sat holding hands. On the middle level there were two more children, representing Henry VIII and Ann Boleyn, the bank of red roses rising from the Lancaster side and the bank of white ones from the York converging upon them. And at the top, amid mingled red and white, perched a single child, representing the honored (and legitimate) Elizabeth herself. At Cornhill, there was another arch with a child on it representing the new queen, but this one was seated on a throne held up by four townsmen dressed to represent the four virtues—Pure Religion, Love of Subjects, Wisdom, and Justice. They, in turn, trod their contrary vices—Superstition and Ignorance, Rebellion and Insolence, Folly and Vainglory, Adulation and Bribery (also impersonated by costumed citizens)—roughly under foot. And lest the iconography be too oblique, the child addressed an admonitory verse to the sovereign she mirrored, spelling out its message:

> While that religion true, shall ignorance suppresse
> And with her weightie foote, break superstitions heade
> While love of subjectes, shall rebellion distresse
> And with zeale to the prince, insolencie down treade
>
> While justice, can flattering tonges and briberie deface
> While follie and vaine glory to wisedome yelde their handes
> So long shall government, not swarve from her right race
> But wrong decayeth still, and rightwisenes up standes.[7]

chants and artisans of every trade leant in long black gowns lined with hoods of red and black cloth . . . with all their ensigns, banners, and standards" (quotation from the Venetian ambassador to London, in Bergeron, *English Civic Pageantry,* p. 14). For Mary and Philip's 1554 entry, see Anglo, *Spectacle, Pageantry,* pp. 324–43, and Withington, *English Pageantry,* p. 189.
[7]Quoted in Bergeron, *English Civic Pageantry,* p. 17. The queen is supposed to have replied: "I have taken notice of your good meaning toward mee, and will endeavour to Answere your severall expectations" (ibid., p. 18).

Thus instructed, the queen moved on to Sopers-Lane, where there were no less than eight children, arranged in three levels. These, as tablets hung above their heads announced, represented the eight beatitudes of Saint Matthew, which a poem recited there described as grained into the character of the queen by the hurts and perils she had surmounted en route to the throne ("Thou has been viii times blest, O quene of worthy fame / by meekness of thy spirite, when care did thee besette").[8] From there she passed on to Cheapside, confronting at the Standard painted likenesses of all the kings and queens arranged in chronological order down to herself; receiving at the Upper End two thousand marks in gold from the City dignitaries ("Perswade you selues," she replied in thanks, "that for the safetie and quietness of you all, I will not spare, if nede be to spend my blood");[9] and arriving, in the Little Conduit, at the most curious image of all—two artificial mountains, one "cragged, barren and stony," representing "a decayed commonweal"; one "fair, fresh, green, and beautiful," representing "a flourishing commonweal." On the barren mountain there was a dead tree, an ill-dressed man slumped disconsolately beneath it; on the green one a flowering tree, a well-appointed man standing happily beside it. From the branches of each hung tablets listing the moral causes of the two states of political health: in the one, want of the fear of God, flattering of princes, unmercifulness in rulers, unthankfulness in subjects; in the other, a wise prince, learned rulers, obedient subjects, fear of God. Between the hills was a small cave, out of which a man representing Father Time, complete with scythe, emerged, accompanied by his daughter, Truth, to present to the queen an English Bible ("O worthy Queene . . . words do flye, but writing doth remain"), which Elizabeth took, kissed, and, raising it first above her head, pressed dramatically to her breast.[10]

After a Latin oration by a schoolboy in Saint Paul's churchyard, the queen proceeded to Fleet Street, where she found, of all people, Deborah, "the judge and restorer of the house of Israel," enthroned upon a tower shaded by a palm tree and surrounded by six persons, two each representing the nobility, the clergy, and the commonalty. The legend inscribed on a tablet before them read, "Deborah with her estates consulting for the good gouerment of Israel." All this, its designer writes, was to encourage the

[8]Anglo, *Spectacle, Pageantry,* p. 349.
[9]Bergeron, *English Civic Pageantry,* p. 15.
[10]The quotation is given in Anglo, *Spectacle, Pageantry,* p. 350.

queen not to fear, "though she were a woman; for women by the spirite
and power of Almyghtye God have ruled both honorably and pollitiquely,
and that a great tyme, as did Deborah."[11] At Saint Dunstan's Church, another child, this one from Christ's Hospital, made another oration. Finally,
at Temple Bar, two giants—Gogmagog, the Albion, and Corineus, the
Briton—bore a tablet on which were written verses summarizing all the
pageants that had been displayed, and the progress ended.

This progress. In 1565 she goes to Coventry; in 1566 to Oxford; in 1572
she makes a long journey through the provinces, stopping for "masques and
pageants" at a whole host of noble houses. She also enters Warwyck in that
year, and the next she is in Sandwich, greeted with gilt dragons and lions, a
cup of gold, and a Greek Testament. In 1574 it is Bristol's turn (there is a
mock battle in which a small fort called "Feeble Policy" is captured by a
large one called "Perfect Beauty"). In 1575 she visits the earl of Kenilworth's
castle near Coventry, where there are Triton on a mermaid, Arion on a dol-
phin, the Lady of the Lake, and a nymph called Zabeta who turns lovers into
trees; and later she enters Worcester. In 1578 the red and white roses and
Deborah reappear in Norwich, accompanied by Chastity and Philosophy
putting Cupid to rout. And they go on, "these endless peregrinations, which
were so often the despair of her ministers"—in 1591 to Sussex and Hamp-
shire, in 1592 to Sudeley, and, once again, Oxford.[12] In 1602, the year before
she dies, there is the last one, at Harefield Place. Time emerges, as he had that
first day in Cheapside, but with clipped wings and a stopped hourglass.[13] The
royal progress, Strong remarks of Elizabeth—"the most legendary and successful of all [its] exponents"—was "the means by which the cult of the imperial virgin was systematically promoted."[14] The charisma that the center had
(rather deliberately, as a matter of fact) fashioned for her out of the popular
symbolisms of virtue, faith, and authority she carried, with a surer sense of

[11]Grafton, quoted in ibid., p. 352. He was not unprescient: Deborah ruled for forty years, Elizabeth for forty-five.
[12]The quotation is from Strong, *Splendor at Court,* p. 84.
[13]For Elizabeth's progresses outside London, see Bergeron, *English Civic Pageantry,* pp. 25 ff.;
Withington, *English Pageantry,* pp. 204 ff.
[14]Strong, *Splendor at Court,* p. 84. The progress was, of course, an all-European phenomenon.
Emperor Charles V, for example, made ten to the Low Countries, nine to Germany, seven to
Italy, six to Spain, four to France, two to England, and two to Africa, as he reminded his audience at his abdication (ibid., p. 83). Nor was it confined to the sixteenth century: for fifteenth-century Tudor ones, see Anglo, *Spectacle, Pageantry,* pp. 21 ff.; for seventeenth-century
Stuart ones, see Bergeron, *English Civic Pageantry,* pp. 65 ff., and Strong, *Splendor at Court,* pp.
213 ff.

statecraft than those pragmatical ministers who objected, to the countryside, making London as much the capital of Britain's political imagination as it was of its government.

That imagination was allegorical, Protestant, didactic, and pictorial; it lived on moral abstractions cast into emblems. Elizabeth was Chastity, Wisdom, Peace, Perfect Beauty, and Pure Religion as well as queen (at an estate in Hertford she was even Safety at Sea); and being queen she was these things. Her whole public life—or, more exactly, the part of her life the public saw—was transformed into a kind of philosophical masque in which everything stood for some vast idea and nothing took place unburdened with parable. Even her meeting with Anjou, possibly the man she came closest to marrying, was turned into a morality; he entered her presence seated on a rock, which was drawn toward her by Love and Destiny pulling golden chains.[15] Whether you want to call this romanticism or neo-Platonism matters little; what matters is that Elizabeth ruled a realm in which beliefs were visible, and she but the most conspicuous.

The center of the center, Elizabeth not only accepted its transformation of her into a moral idea, she actively cooperated in it. It was out of this—her willingness to stand proxy, not for God, but for the virtues he ordained, and especially for the Protestant version of them—that her charisma grew. It was allegory that lent her magic, and allegory repeated that sustained it. "How striking and meaningful it must have been to the spectators," Bergeron writes of that gift of an English Bible from the daughter of Time, "to see Truth in visible union with their new sovereign. . . . Morally Truth has chosen between good—the flourishing hill, the future, Elizabeth—and evil—the sterile mount, the past, false religion and a false queen. Such is the path to salvation."[16]

Hayam Wuruk's Java: Splendor and Hierarchy

There are other ways of connecting the character of a sovereign to that of his realm, however, than enveloping him in pictured homilies; as moral

[15]Yates, *The Valois Tapestries*, p. 92.
[16]Bergeron, *English Civic Pageantry*, p. 21.

imaginations differ, so do political, and not every progress is that of a Pilgrim. In the Indic cultures of classical Indonesia the world was a less improvable place, and royal pageantry was hierarchical and mystical in spirit, not pious and didactic.[17] Gods, kings, lords, and commoners formed an unbroken chain of religious status stretching from Siva-Buddha—"Ruler over rulers of the world . . . Spirit of the spiritual . . . Unconceivable of the unconceivable"—down to the ordinary peasant, barely able to look toward the light, the higher levels standing to the lower as greater realities to lesser.[18] If Elizabeth's England was a swirl of idealized passions, Hayam Wuruk's Java was a continuum of spiritualized pride. "The peasants honor the chiefs," a fourteenth-century clerical text reads, "the chiefs honor the lords, the lords honor the ministers, the ministers honor the king, the kings honor the priests, the priests honor the gods, the gods honor the sacred powers, the sacred powers honor the Supreme Nothingness."[19]

Yet even in this unpopulist a setting, the royal progress was a major institution, as can be seen from Indic Java's greatest political text, the fourteenth-century narrative poem *Negarakertagama,* which is not only centered around a royal progress but is in fact part of it.[20] The basic principle of Indonesian statecraft—that the court should be a copy of the cosmos and the realm a copy of the court, with the king, liminally suspended between gods and men, the mediating image in both directions—is laid out in almost diagrammatic form. At the center and apex, the king; around him and at his feet, the palace; around the palace, the capital, "reliable, submissive"; around the capital, the realm, "helpless, bowed, stooping, humble"; around the realm, "getting ready to show obedience," the outside

[17]Java was Hindu from about the fourth century to about the fifteenth, when it became at least nominally Islamized. Bali remains Hindu until today. Much of what follows here is based on my own work; see C. Geertz *Negara: The Theatre State in Nineteenth-Century Bali* (Princeton, 1980). For Hindu Java generally, see N. J. Krom, *Hindoe-Javaansche Geschiedenis,* 2d ed. (The Hague, 1931).

[18]T. Pigeaud, *Java in the 14th Century: A Study in Cultural History,* 5 vols. (The Hague, 1963), 1:3 (Javanese); 3:3 (English). The chain actually continues downward through animals and demons.

[19]Ibid., 1:90 (Javanese); 3:135 (English). I have made alterations in the translation for clarity. Even then, "sacred powers" and "The Supreme Nothingness" (that is, Siva-Buddha) remain weak renderings of difficult religious conceptions, a matter not pursuable here. For an even more differentiated hierarchy, see the *Nawantaya* text, ibid., 3:119–28.

[20]Ibid. (despite its title, the work is essentially a text, translation, and commentary of the *Negarakertagama*). Of the poem's 1,330 lines, no less than 570 are specifically devoted to descriptions of royal progresses, and the bulk of the rest are ancillary to those. Literally, "Negarakertagama" means "manual for the cosmic ordering of the state," which is what it is really about rather than, as has so often been assumed, the history of Majapahit. It was written in 1365 by a Buddhist cleric, resident in the court of King Hayam Wuruk (r. 1350–89).

world—all disposed in compass-point order, a configuration of nested circles that depicts not just the structure of society but, a political mandala, that of the universe as a whole:

> The royal capital in Majapahit is Sun and Moon,
>   peerless;
> The numerous manors with their encircling groves
>   are halos around the sun and moon;
> The numerous other towns of the realm . . . are stars
>   and planets;
> And the numerous other islands of the archipelago
>   are ring-kingdoms, dependent states
>   drawn toward the royal Presence.[21]

It is this structure, the deep geometry of the cosmos, which the poem celebrates and into which, half as rite and half as policy, it fits the royal progress.

It opens with a glorification of the king. He is at once Siva in material form—"The Daymaker's Equal," upon whose birth volcanoes erupted and the earth shook—and a triumphant overlord who has vanquished all the darkness there is in the world ("Exterminated are the enemies . . . Rewarded, the good . . . Reformed, the bad").[22] Next, his palace is described: North, the reception areas; East, the religious shrines; South, the family chambers; West, the servants quarters; in the center, "The Interior of the Interior," his personal pavilion. Then, with the palace as center, the complex around it: East, the Sivaite clergy; South, the Buddhist clergy; West, the royal kinsmen; North, the public square. Then, with the complex as center, the capital in general: North, the chief ministers; East, the junior king; South, the Sivaite and Buddhist bishops; West, though not in fact mentioned, probably the ranking commoners.[23] Then, with the capital as center, the regions of

---

[21]*Negarakertagama,* canto 12, stanza 6. I have again reconstructed Pigeaud's English, this time more seriously, to convey better what I take to be the sense of the passage. On the mandala concept in Indonesia, where it means at once "sacred circle," "holy region," and "religious community," as well as being a symbol of the universe as such, see J. Gonda, *Sanskrit in Indonesia* (Nagpur, 1952), pp. 5, 131, 218, 227; Pigeaud, *Java,* 4:485–86. On this sort of imagery in traditional Asian states generally, see P. Wheatley, *The Pivot of the Four Quarters* (Chicago, 1971).

[22]Cantos 1–7. The royal family is also praised, as the first circle outward from the king. "Daymaker" is, of course, a metonym for the sun, identified with Siva-Buddha, "The Supreme Non-Entity" in Indic Indonesia.

[23]Cantos 8–12. There is much controversy here over details (cf. W. F. Stutterheim, *De Kraton van Majapahit* [The Hague, 1948]; H. Kern, *Het Oud-Javaansche Lofdicht Negarakertagama van Prapanca* [The Hague, 1919]), and not all of them are clear. The pattern has in any case

the realm, ninety-eight of them, stretching from Malaya and Borneo on the North and East to Timor and New Guinea on the South and West; and, finally, the outermost ring, Siam, Cambodia, Campa, Annam—"Other countries protected by the Illustrious Prince."[24] Virtually the whole of the known world (later parts of China and India are mentioned as well) is represented as turned toward Java, all of Java as turned toward Majapahit, and all of Majapahit as turned toward Hayam Wuruk—"Sun and Moon, shining over the earth-circle."[25]

In cold fact, hardly more than the eastern part of Java was so oriented, and most of that in an attitude not properly described as either helpless or humble.[26] It was to this region, where the kingdom, however invertebrate, at least was more than a poetic conceit, that the royal progresses were directed: west to Pajang, near present-day Surakarta, in 1353; north to Lasem on the Java Sea in 1354; south to Lodaya and the Indian Ocean in 1357; east to Lumajang, nearly to Bali, in 1359.[27]

Only the last of these, which was probably the greatest, is described in detail, however—more than four hundred lines being devoted to it. The king left the capital at the beginning of the dry season, visiting no less than 210 localities scattered over about ten thousand to fifteen thousand square miles in about two and a half months, returning just before the west monsoon brought the rains. There were about four hundred ox-drawn, solid-wheel carts; there were, more for effect than anything else, elephants, horses, donkeys, and even camels (imported from India); there were swarms of people on foot, some carrying burdens, some displaying regalia, some no doubt dancing and singing—the whole lurching along like some archaic traffic jam a mile or two an hour over the narrow and rutted roads lined with crowds of astonished peasants. The core section of the proces-

---

been simplified here (it really is a 16-8-4-point system about a center, and of course it is cosmological, not exactly geographical). "Ranking commoners" is an interpolation of mine on the basis of knowledge of later examples. "Junior king" does not indicate a dauphin but refers to the second-ranking line in the realm. This "double-king" system is general in Indonesian Indic states but is too complex to go into here. See my *Negara* for a full discussion.
[24]Cantos 13–16.
[25]Canto 92.
[26]On the exaggeration of the size of Majapahit, see, with caution, C. C. Berg, "De Sadèng oorlog en de mythe van Groot Majapahit," *Indonesie* 5 (1951): 385–422. See also my "Politics Past, Politics Present: Some Notes on the Uses of Anthropology in Understanding the New States," in C. Geertz, *The Interpretation of Cultures* (New York, 1973), pp. 327–41.
[27]Canto 17. Other minor progresses, for special purposes, are also mentioned for the 1360s; see cantos 61 and 70.

sion, which seems to have come in the middle, was led by the cart of the
chief minister, the famous Gajah Mada. Behind him came the four ranking
princesses of the realm—the sister, mother's sister's daughter, mother's sister, and mother of the king—together with their consorts. And behind
them, seated on a palanquin and surrounded by dozens of wives, body-
guards, and servants, came the king, "ornamented with gold and jewels,
shining." Since each of the princesses represented one of the compass points
(marked on her cart by traditional symbols and on her person by her title,
which associated her with the quarter of the country in the appropriate direction from the capital), and the king represented the center in which they
all were summed, the very order of the march conveyed the structure of
the cosmos—mirrored in the organization of the court—to the countryside.[28] All that was left to complete this bringing of Heaven's symmetry
to earth's confusion was for the countryside, struck with the example, to
shape itself, in turn, to the same design.

The stops this lumbering caravan made—at forest hermitages, sacred
ponds, mountain sanctuaries, priestly settlements, ancestral shrines, state
temples, along the strand (where the king, "waving to the sea," composed
some verses to placate the demons in it)—but reinforce the image of a metaphysical road show.[29] Everywhere Hayam Wuruk went, he was showered
with luxuries—textiles, spices, animals, flowers, drums, fire drills, vir-
gins—most of which, the last excepted, he redistributed again, if only because he could not carry them all. There were ceremonies everywhere,
crowded with offerings: in Buddhist domains Buddhist, in Sivaite ones Sivaite, in many places both. Anchorites, scholars, priests, abbots, shamans,
sages, entered into his Presence, seeking contact with sacred energies; and
in virtually every town, sometimes at mere encampments, he held public
audiences, also largely ceremonial, for local authorities, merchants, and
leading commoners. When there were places he could not reach—Bali,
Madura, Blambangan—their chieftains journeyed to meet him, bearing
gifts, "trying to outvie each other" in the forms of deference. The whole

---

[28]Cantos 13–18. The directional system was integrated with a color symbolism, the four primary colors—red, white, black, and yellow—being disposed about a variegated center. The
five days of the week, five periods of the day, and five life-cycle stages, as well as plants, gods,
and a number of other natural and social symbolic forms, were fused into the same pattern,
which was thus extremely elaborate, a picture of the whole cosmos.

[29]Cantos 13–38, 55–60. Four or five stops are described in detail; but there must have been
ten or fifteen times that many.

was a vast ritual seeking to order the social world by confronting it with magnificence reaching down from above and a king so exactly imitative of the gods that he appeared as one to those beneath him.

In short, instead of Christian moralism, Indic aestheticism. In sixteenth-century England, the political center of society was the point at which the tension between the passions that power excited and the ideals it was supposed to serve was screwed to its highest pitch; and the symbolism of the progress was, consequently, admonitory and covenantal: the subjects warned, and the queen promised. In fourteenth-century Java, the center was the point at which such tension disappeared in a blaze of cosmic symmetry; and the symbolism was, consequently, exemplary and mimetic: the king displayed, and the subjects copied. Like the Elizabethan, the Majapahit progress set forth the regnant themes of political thought—the court mirrors the world the world should imitate; society flourishes to the degree that it assimilates this fact; and it is the office of the king, wielder of the mirror, to assure that it does. It is analogy, not allegory, that lends the magic here:

> The whole of Java is to be as the capital of the King's
>   realm;
> The thousands of peasant huts are to be as the courtiers'
>   manors surrounding the palace;
> The other islands are to be as the cultivated lands,
>   happy, quiet;
> The forests and mountains are to be as the parks, all
>   set foot on by Him, at peace
>   in His mind.[30]

Hasan's Morocco: Movement and Energy

It is not necessary, of course, that power be dressed up in virtue or set round with cosmology to be perceived as more than force in the service of interest: its numinousness can be symbolized directly. In traditional Morocco, "the Morocco that was," as Walter Harris called it, personal power, the ability

[30]Canto 17, stanza 3. Again I have altered the translation; in particular I have rendered *negara* as "capital" rather than "town." For the multiple meanings of this word, see my *Negara*.

to make things happen the way one wants them to happen—to prevail—was itself the surest sign of grace.[31] In a world of wills dominating
wills, and that of Allah dominating them all, strength did not have to be
represented as other than what it was in order to suffuse it with transcendent meaning. Like God, kings desired and demanded, judged and decreed,
harmed and rewarded. *C'est son métier:* one did not need an excuse to rule.

One, of course, did need the capacity, and that was not so easily come
by in a vast and shifting field of literally hundreds of political entrepreneurs,
each concerned to build a smaller or larger configuration of personal support about himself. Morocco did not have either the hierarchism of medieval Hinduism or the salvationism of Reformation Christianity to canonize
its sovereign; it had only an acute sense of the power of God and the belief
that his power appeared in the world in the exploits of forceful men, the
most considerable of whom were kings. Political life is a clash of personalities everywhere, and in even the most focused of states lesser figures resist
the center; but in Morocco such struggle was looked upon not as something
in conflict with the order of things, disruptive of form or subversive of virtue, but as its purest expression. Society was agonistic—a tournament of
wills; so then was kingship and the symbolism exalting it. Progresses here
were not always easy to tell from raids.

Politically, eighteenth- and nineteenth-century Morocco consisted of a
warrior monarchy centered in the Atlantic Plain, a cloud of at least sporadically submissive "tribes" settled in the fertile regions within its immediate
reach, and a thinner cloud of only very occasionally submissive ones scattered through the mountains, steppes, and oases that rim the country.[32] Re-
ligiously, it consisted of a sharifian dynasty (that is, one claiming descent
from Muhammad), a number of Koranic scholars, jurists, teachers, and
scribes *(ulema),* and a host of holy men, living and dead, possessed of miraculous powers, the famous marabouts.[33] In theory, Islamic theory, the

[31]W. B. Harris, *Morocco That Was* (Boston, 1921). The following discussion is confined to
the period of the Alawite dynasty, that is, from the seventeenth to twentieth centuries (it still
continues), with most of the material coming from the eighteenth and nineteenth centuries.
Again, I have depended heavily on my own research (see C. Geertz, *Islam Observed: Religious
Development in Morocco and Indonesia* [New Haven, 1968]); C. Geertz, H. Geertz, and L.
Rosen, *Meaning and Order in Moroccan Society* (Cambridge, England, and New York, 1979).
[32]The best study of the traditional Moroccan state is E. Aubin, *Morocco of Today* (London,
1906). The term "tribe" is difficult of application in Morocco, where social groups lack stability
and definition, See J. Berque, "Qu'est-ce qu'une 'tribu' nord-africaine?" in *Eventail de l'histoire
vivante: Hommage à Lucien Febvre* (Paris, 1953).
[33]See A. Bel, *La Religion Musulmane en Berbérie,* (Paris, 1938), vol. 1; E. Gellner, *Saints of
the Atlas* (Chicago, 1969); C. Geertz, *Islam Observed.* Many of the ulemas and marabouts

political and religious realms were one, the king was caliph and head of both, and the state was thus a theocracy; but it was not a theory that anyone, even the king, could regard as more than a lost ideal in the face of a situation where charismatic adventurers were constantly arising on all sides. If Moroccan society has any chief guiding principle, it is probably that one genuinely possesses only what one has the ability to defend, whether it be land, water, women, trade partners, or personal authority: whatever magic a king had he had strenuously to protect.

The magic was perceived in terms of another famous North African idea: *baraka*. [34] *Baraka* has been analogized to a number of things in an attempt to clarify it—mana, charisma, "spiritual electricity"—because it is a gift of power more than natural which men, having received it, can use in as natural and pragmatical a way, for as self-interested and mundane purposes, as they wish. But what most defines *baraka*, and sets it off somewhat from these similar concepts, is that it is radically individualistic, a property of persons in the way strength, courage, energy, or ferocity are and, like them, arbitrarily distributed. Indeed, it is in one sense a summary term for these qualities, the active virtues that, again, enable some men to prevail over others. To so prevail, whether at court or in a mountain camp, was to demonstrate that one had baraka, that God had gifted one with the capacity to dominate, a talent it could quite literally be death to hide. It was not a condition, like chastity, or a trait, like pride, that shines by itself but a movement, like will, that exists in its impact. Like everything the king did, progresses were designed to make that impact felt, most particularly by those who might imagine their own to be comparable.

Rather than occasional or periodic—and therefore a schedule of set pieces—the Moroccan progress was very nearly continuous. "The king's throne is his saddle," one saying went, "the sky his canopy." "The royal tents are never stored," went another. The great late-seventeenth-to-early-eighteenth-century consolidator of the dynasty, the man who made its *baraka* real, Mulay Ismail, seems to have spent most of his reign "under canvas" (during the first half of it, a chronicler notes, he did not pass a single uninterrupted year in his palace); and even Mulay Hasan (d. 1894), the last of the old-regime kings of Morocco, normally spent six

---

were also sharifs. On Moroccan sharifs in general, see E. Lévi-Provençal, *Les Historiens des Chorfa* (Paris, 1922).

[34] On *baraka*, see E. Westermarck, *Ritual and Belief in Morocco*, 2 vols. (London, 1926); C. Geertz, *Islam Observed.*

months of the year on the move, demonstrating sovereignty to skeptics.[35] The kings did not even keep a single capital but instead shifted the court restlessly among the so-called Imperial Cities—Fez, Marrakech, Meknes, and Rabat—in none of which they were really at home. Motion was the rule, not the exception; and though a king could not, like God, quite be everywhere at once, he could try, at least, to give the impression that he was: "No one could be sure that the Sultan would not arrive at the head of his troops on the morrow. During such times the most adamant peoples were ready to negotiate with [his] officials and reach terms which suited the sovereign."[36] Like its rivals, the center wandered: "Roam and you will confound adversaries," another Moroccan proverb runs, "sit and they will confound you."

The court-in-motion was referred to either as a *mehalla,* literally, "way station," "camp," "stopover," or as a *harka,* literally, "movement," "stirring," "action," depending upon whether one wanted to emphasize the governmental or military aspects of it. Normally the king would remain camped in an area for anywhere from several days to several months and would then move, by gradual stages, to another, where he would remain for a similar period, receiving local chieftains and other notables, holding feasts, sending out punitive expeditions when need be, and generally making his presence known. This last was hardly difficult, for a royal camp was an impressive sight, a great sea of tents, soldiers, slaves, animals, prisoners, armaments, and camp followers. Harris estimated that there were nearly 40,000 people in Mulay Hasan's encampment (a "strange mixture of boundless confusion and perfect order that succeeded each other in . . . quick succession") in the Tafilalt in 1893, and fifty or sixty tents within the royal compound alone. Even as late as 1898, when all this was

---

[35]On Mulay Ismail's truly astounding mobility, see O. V. Houdas, *Le Maroc de 1631–1812 par Ezziani* (Amsterdam, 1969), pp. 24–55; text reference at p. 46. On Mulay Hasan, see S. Bonsal, *Morocco As It Is* (New York and London, 1893), pp. 47 ff.; cf. Harris, *Morocco That Was,* pp. 1 ff.

[36]S. Schaar, *Conflict and Change in Nineteenth-Century Morocco* (Ph.D. diss., Princeton University, 1964), p. 72. The constant mobility also shaped, and similarly, the nature of the court: "The very life that the greater part of the members of the [court] must lead, uproots them and cuts them off from any contact with their tribe or their native town, and attaches them, to the exclusion of all other ties, to the institution on which they are dependent. The bulk of the [court] . . . centres around the Sultan, and becomes nomadic like him. Their life is passed under canvas, or else, at unequal intervals, in one of the imperial cities—constant change, in fact, and no ties anywhere. The horizon narrows, everything outside disappears, and the members of the [court] have no eye for anything but this powerful mechanism, mistress of their lives and their fortune" (Aubin, *Morocco of Today,* p. 183).

more or less drawing to a close, Weisgerber speaks of "thousands of men and beasts" in Mulay Abdul Aziz's encampment in the Chaouia, which he also describes, less romantically, as a vast lake of infected mud.[37]

The mobility of the king was thus a central element in his power; the realm was unified—to the very partial degree that it was unified and was a realm—by a restless searching-out of contact, mostly agonistic, with literally hundreds of lesser centers of power within it. The struggle with local big men was not necessarily violent or even usually so (Schaar quotes the popular maxim that the king employed ninety-nine ruses, of which firearms were but the hundredth), but it was unending, especially for an ambitious king, one who wished to make a state—one scuffle, one intrigue, one negotiation succeeded by another.[38] It was an exhausting occupation, one only the tireless could pursue. What chastity was to Elizabeth, and magnificence to Hayam Wuruk, energy was to Mulay Ismail or Mulay Hasan: as long as he could keep moving, chastening an opponent here, advancing an ally there, the king could make believable his claim to a sovereignty conferred by God. But only that long. The traditional shout of the crowds to the passing king, *Allāh ybarak f-camer Sīdī*—"God give you *baraka* forever, my Master"—was more equivocal than it sounds: "forever" ended when mastery did.

There is no more poignant example of the degree to which this fact dominated the consciousness of Morocco's rulers, and no bitterer witness to its truth, than the terrible last progress of Mulay Hasan. Frustrated by the failure of his administrative, military, and economic reforms to bear fruit, threatened on all sides by intruding European powers, and worn out by twenty years of holding the country together by the main force of his per-

---

[37]W. B. Harris, *Tafilet* (London, 1895), pp. 240–43; F. Weisgerber, *Au Seuil du Maroc modern* (Rabat, 1947), pp. 46–60 (where one can also find a plan of the camp). On the move it was no less impressive; for a vivid description, complete with snake charmers, acrobats, lepers, and men opening their heads with hatchets, see Harris, *Morocco That Was*, pp. 54–60. The harkas were multitribal enterprises, the core of which was composed of the so-called military —*jaysh*—tribes, who served the court as soldiers in return for land and other privileges. One can't resist one more proverb here: *f-l-harka, baraka:* "There is blessing in movement."

[38]Schaar, *Conflict and Change in Morocco,* p. 73. The violence mostly consisted of burning settlements and cutting off the heads of particularly recalcitrant opponents (which, salted by the Jews, were then displayed over the entrance to the king's tent or palace). Meditation, which was more common, was conducted by royal officials or, often, various sorts of religious figures, specialized for the task. Schaar (ibid., p. 75) remarks that kings, or anyway wise ones, took care not to be overly harsh: "The ideal was to hit the enemy lightly, collect tribute payments, establish a firm administration in their midst, and move on to the next target."

sonality, he decided, in 1893, to lead a massive expedition to the shrine of his dynasty's founder in the Tafilalt, a desert-edge oasis three hundred miles south of Fez. A long, arduous, dangerous, expensive journey, undertaken in the face of what seems to have been nearly universal advice to the contrary, it was quite possibly the greatest mahalla ever made in Morocco—a dramatic, desperate, and, as it turned out, disastrous effort at self-renewal.

The expedition, of thirty thousand men drawn from the loyal tribes of the Atlantic Plain, mounted mostly on mules, left Fez in April, crossed the middle and high Atlases in the summer and early autumn, and arrived in the Tafilalt in November.[39] Since only one European, a French doctor, was permitted to go along, and he was an indifferent observer (there do not seem to be any native accounts), we do not know much about the trip except that it was grueling. Aside from the simply physical obstacles (the highest passes reached nearly eight thousand feet, and the road was hardly more than a trail scratched across the rocks), the burden of baggage, tents, and armaments (even cannons were dragged along), and the logistical problems involved in feeding so many people and animals, the whole area was dotted with contentious Berber tribes, who had to be prevented, half with threats and half with bribes, occasionally with force, from "eating the caravan." But though there were some difficult moments and the expedition was seriously delayed, nothing particularly untoward seems to have happened. The sheikhs came, accompanied by dozens of tribesmen; royal hospitality was extended; and, amid flamboyant riding and shooting displays, gifts were exchanged, tea drunk, bulls sacrificed, taxes gathered, and loyalty promised. It was only after the shrine had been reached and the prayers accomplished that the trouble began.

It is likely that the king, his timetable disrupted by the slowness of the Atlas passage and his army fevered and malnourished, would have preferred to remain in the oasis through the winter, but a combination of fac-

[39]Material on the Tafilalt mehalla can be found in Harris, *Tafilet,* pp. 213 ff.; R. Lebel, *Les Voyageurs français du Maroc* (Paris, 1936), pp. 215–20; R. Cruchet, *La Conquête pacifique du Maroc et du Tafilalet,* 2d ed. (Paris, 1934), pp. 223–41; G. Maxwell, *Lords of the Atlas* (New York, 1966), pp. 31–50; F. Linarès, "Voyage au Tafilalet," *Bulletin de l'Institut de la Hygiène du Maroc,* nos. 3–4 (1932). Cf. R. E. Dunn, *Resistance in the Desert* (Madison, Wisconsin, 1977), who stresses the king's desire to stabilize the Tafilalt against French incursion as a motive for the trip. Ten women of the royal harem also accompanied the king, and Cruchet estimates about 10,000 hangers-on, merchants, "et autres parasites qui sont la rançon d'une troupe, n'est pas une sinécure," as well (*La Conquête pacifique,* p. 223).

tors caused him to stay less than a month. The Berber tribes were still a
worry, particularly as the southern ones were even more belligerent; there
was a fear of assassination by French agents directed from southern Alge-
ria; and there were reports of severe fighting between Moroccans and
Spaniards at the other, Mediterranean, end of the country. But perhaps
the most important factor in the decision to try to make it back to the
plains at so unsuitable a time was Mulay Hasan's own failing powers.
Harris, who saw him at Tafilalt, found him terribly aged from only two
years earlier (he was apparently in his mid-forties)—tired, sallow, prema-
turely gray; and the same sense of lost momentum that propelled him
south apparently turned him north again when his journey to his origins
failed to restore it.

In any case, the expedition, now but about ten thousand strong, left in
December for Marrakech—three weeks' march over the High Atlas to the
east, through a region even more forbidding, geographically and politically,
than that through which it had already passed. In addition, it was winter
now, and the whole affair soon turned into a retreat from Moscow:

By the time his army had reached the foothills the winter snows had begun; as they
climbed higher into the main massif more and more of the camels, mules and horses,
weak with starvation, stumbled into deep snowdrifts and died. Little but their car-
casses stood between the remnants of the *harka* and starvation, and the surviving
beasts staggered on and upwards laden with what little meat could be salvaged from
the corpses of their companions. The army was attended by clouds of ravens, kites
and vultures. Hundreds of men died daily, they were left unburied in the snow,
stripped of whatever rags they had still possessed.[40]

By the time Marrakech was reached, more than a third of the already reduced army had been lost; and the himself rather mobile Harris (he was
the London *Times* correspondent), who was on hand for the arrival, found
the king no longer merely aging but dying:

What was noticeable at Tafilet was doubly apparent now. The Sultan had become
an old man. Travel-stained and weary, he rode his great white horse with its mockery of green-and-gold trapping, while over a head that was the picture of suffering
waved the imperial umbrella of crimson velvet. Following him straggled into the
city a horde of half-starved men and animals, trying to be happy that at last their
terrible journey was at an end, but too ill and too hungry to succeed.[41]

[40]Maxwell, *Lords of the Atlas,* pp. 39–40.
[41]Harris, *Tafilet,* p. 333.

The king remained in Marrakech until spring, attempting to regather his powers; but then, renewed anxiety about the deteriorating situation in the North, and the need for his presence there, set him in motion again. He had got as far as Tadla, about a hundred miles from Marrakech, when he collapsed and died. The death was, however, concealed by his ministers. They were concerned that, with the king gone, the caravan would dissolve and the tribes fall upon it and that conspirators supporting other candidates would contrive to prevent the accession of Mulay Hasan's chosen successor, his twelve-year-old son, Mulay Abdul Aziz. So he was represented as being merely indisposed and resting privately, his corpse was laid in a curtained palanquin, and the expedition was launched into a forced march, brutal in the summer heat, toward Rabat. Food was brought to the king's tent and then taken away again as though consumed. The few knowledgeable ministers hurried in and out of his presence as though conducting business. A few local sheikhs, cautioned that he was sleeping, were even permitted to look in upon him. By the time that the progress neared Rabat, two days later, the king's corpse had so begun to stink that his death announced itself; but by then the dangerous tribes had been left behind, and Abdul Aziz, his backers informed of events by a runner, had been proclaimed king in the city. In two more days the company, largely reduced to the old king's ministers and personal bodyguard—the others having drifted away or straggled behind—limped into Rabat, engulfed in the stench of royal death:

It must have been a gruesome procession from the description his son Mulai Abdul Aziz gave me [Walter Harris wrote]: the hurried arrival of the swaying palanquin bearing its terrible burden, five days dead in the great heat of summer; the escort, who had bound scarves over their faces—but even this precaution could not keep them from constant sickness—and even the mules that bore the palanquin seemed affected by the horrible atmosphere, and tried from time to time to break loose.[42]

And so, its motion spent, the progress that had begun more than a year before ended, and with it two decades of rushing about from one corner of the country to another, defending the idea of religious monarchy. Indeed, this was more or less the end of the whole pattern; for the next two kings—one of whom reigned for fourteen years, the other for four—attempted only a few rather desultory *harka*s in a rapidly disintegrating situation, and the French, who took over after them, made palace prisoners of the two kings who fol-

[42]Harris, *Morocco That Was,* pp. 13–14; for a fuller description, see Harris, *Tafilet,* pp. 345–51.

lowed. Immobilized, Moroccan kings were as dead as Hasan, their *baraka* impotent and theoretical. It was neither as embodiments of redemptive virtue nor as reflections of cosmic order but as explosions of divine energy that Moroccan kings recommended themselves to their subjects, and even the smallest explosion needs room in which to happen.

Conclusion

Now, the easy reaction to all this talk of monarchs, their trappings, and their peregrinations is that it has to do with a closed past, a time, in Huizinga's famous phrase, when the world was half-a-thousand years younger and everything was clearer. All the golden grasshoppers and bees are gone; monarchy, in the true sense of the word, was ritually destroyed on one scaffold in Whitehall in 1649 and on another in the Place de la Révolution in 1793; the few fragments left in the Third World are just that—fragments, relic kings whose likelihood of having successors diminishes by the hour.[43] England has a second Elizabeth, who may be as chaste—more so, probably—as the first, and who gets properly lauded on public occasions, but the resemblance rather ends there; Morocco has a second Hasan, but he is more a French colonel than an Arab prince; and the last of the great line of Javanese Indic kings, Hamengku Buwono IX, his royal office legally abolished, is (1977) the self-effacing, rather ineffectual, vaguely socialist vice-president of the Indonesian Republic, around whom not even the smallest planets revolve.

Yet, though all this is true enough, it is superficial. The relevance of historical fact for sociological analysis does not rest on the proposition that there is nothing in the present but the past, which is not true, or on easy

[43]For the argument concerning the ritual destruction of the monarchy, see Walzer, *Regicide and Revolution*. With Walzer's argument that the trials and executions of Charles and Louis were symbolic acts designed to kill not just kings but kingship, I am in agreement; concerning his further argument that they altered the whole landscape of English and French political life permanently and utterly—that is, that these rituals were availing—I am less convinced. The other wing of this sort of argument is, of course, that democracy makes the anthropomorphization of power impossible: "Die Repräsentation [that is, of "majesty"] verlangt eine Hierarchie, die der Gleichheit des demokratischen Staates widerspricht, in der jeder Bürger Soverain ist und Majestas hat. So aber alle Könige sind, da kann keiner mehr als König auftreten, und die Repräsentation wird unmöglich" (Straub, *Repraesentatio Maiestatis*, p. 10). But along with a number of other people, from Tocqueville to Talmon, I am not persuaded of this either.

analogies between extinct institutions and the way we live now. It rests on the perception that though both the structure and the expressions of social life change, the inner necessities that animate it do not. Thrones may be out of fashion, and pageantry too; but political authority still requires a cultural frame in which to define itself and advance its claims, and so does opposition to it. A world wholly demystified is a world wholly depoliticized; and though Weber promised us both of these—specialists without spirit in a bureaucratic iron cage—the course of events since, with its Sukarnos, Churchills, Nkrumahs, Hitlers, Maos, Roosevelts, Stalins, Nassers, and de Gaulles, suggests that what died in 1793 (to the degree that it did) was a certain view of the affinity between the sort of power that moves men and the sort that moves mountains, not the sense that there is one.

The "political theology" (to revert to Kantorowicz's term) of the twentieth century has not been written, though there have been glancing efforts here and there. But it exists—or, more exactly, various forms of it exist—and until it is understood at least as well as that of the Tudors, the Majapahits, or the Alawites, a great deal of the public life of our times is going to remain obscure. The extraordinary has not gone out of modern politics, however much the banal may have entered; power not only still intoxicates, it still exalts.

It is for this reason that, no matter how peripheral, ephemeral, or free-floating the charismatic figure we may be concerned with—the wildest prophet, the most deviant revolutionary—we must begin with the center and with the symbols and conceptions that prevail there if we are to understand him and what he means. It is no accident that Stuarts get Cromwells and Medicis Savonarolas—or, for that matter, that Hindenburgs get Hitlers. Every serious charismatic threat that ever arose in Alawite Morocco took the form of some local power figure's laying claim to enormous *baraka* by engaging in actions—*siba,* literally, "insolence"—designed to expose the weakness of the king by showing him up as unable to stop them; and Java has been continuously beset by local mystics emerging from meditative trances to present themselves to the world as its "Exemplary Ruler" *(Ratu Adil),* corrective images of a lost order and an obscured form.[44] This is the paradox of charisma: that though it is rooted in the sense of being near to the heart of things, of being caught up in the realm of the serious, a senti-

[44]For a description of some of the *siba* activities at the end of the Protectorate, see E. Burke, *Prelude to Protectorate in Morocco* (Chicago, 1976). On *ratu adil,* see Sartono Kartodirdjo, *Protest Movements in Rural Java* (Singapore, 1973).

ment that is felt most characteristically and continuously by those who in fact dominate social affairs, who ride in the progresses and grant the audiences, its most flamboyant expressions tend to appear among people at some distance from the center, indeed often enough at a rather enormous distance, who want very much to be closer. Heresy is as much of a child of orthodoxy in politics as it is in religion.

And both orthodoxy and heresy, however adept the secret police, are universal, as we learn when workers explode in East Germany, Tolstoyan romantics reappear in Russia, or, strangest of all, soldier-populists surface in Portugal. The enfoldment of political life in general conceptions of how reality is put together did not disappear with dynastic continuity and divine right. Who gets What, When, Where, and How is as culturally distinctive a view of what politics is, and in its own way as transcendental, as the defense of "wisdom and rightwiseness," the celebration of "The Daymaker's Equal," or the capricious flow of *baraka*. Nor is it any less capable of yielding spectacle, center-praising or center-challenging:

I accompany the Humphrey press to one of Hubert's stops, a school for handicapped children, for the deaf and the retarded. He shakes hands with every single Sister. Every one. And every child he can reach. Schedule allows for twenty minutes. Thirteen used for shaking hands. The talk goes on for twenty minutes, *on* for twenty-five, *on* for thirty. The hands of the poor priest who is trying to translate into sign language are wearing out . . . thirty-five minutes—another man takes over as translator . . . "And some of the greatest men in history had handicaps"—he tries to think of one, his eyes flash, cheeks acquire that familiar beaming, knowing look.—"Thomas Edison. We *all* have handicaps . . ." "What's the most important word in the English language?" "Service!" "And the other most important word is 'love!' " "And what are the last four letters in the word American? I CAN. Look at them. Spell it. I can. You *can.* You're great. You're wonderful. God bless you." The tears are in the corners of his eyes, the tears that cause him such grief on television. His head chucks up and down happily as he wades back through the crowd of distracted, uncertain, uncomprehending kids.

In Madison Square Garden, then, on July 14, a celebration of moral purity is held. "Together with McGovern at the Garden," it is called. Its purpose is to raise funds. Mike Nichols and Elaine May come back together just for the event; so do Peter, Paul, and Mary; and Simon and Garfunkel. The contrast between such a rally and a Wallace rally—or, say, a gathering of Bob Hope and Billy Graham for Richard Nixon—explodes the circuits of the mind. Comparative liturgies! June 14 is Flag Day. But there are no flags on stage. No flags surround the Garden. The evening celebrates the resurrection of the youth culture. The liturgy of a new class is performed. Peter, Paul, and Mary, Dionne Warwick, Simon and Garfunkel in every song celebrate the mobile, lonely, vulnerable, middle-class life. Dionne Warwick warbles in blue-flowered, cottony, innocent, white gown: "Imagine!—No heaven—no hell—no countries—no religions! When the world will live as one." Simon and Garfunkel offer "Jesus loves you, Mrs. Robinson!" and the most revealing line: "I'd rather be a hammer than a nail." No Lawrence Welk. No Johnny Cash. No Benny Goodman. The music is singlemindedly sectarian. At 11:05, the entire cast gathers on stage, flashing peace signs. Then a great chant goes up: WE WANT MC-GOVERN!" "It's a wonderful night of coming together," McGovern says. He tells them how he "loves this country enough to hold it to a higher standard, away from the killing, death, and destruction now going on in Southeast Asia." "I love this land and cherish its future. I want to set about making this country a great, decent, and good land . . . to be a bridge from war to peace . . . a bridge across the generation gap . . . a bridge across the gaps in justice in this country. . . . As the prophet wrote: 'Therefore, choose life . . . be on the side of blessing, not cursing' . . . on the side of hope, health, life. And peace for ourselves and peoples all around the globe."

At Racine, the rally is on again, this time in Memorial Hall, well after working hours and publicized through radio spots. The crowd assembles early; some are turned away at the door. 1200 sit inside, 330 in the balcony, standing room for 250. Excitement crackles. The loudspeakers are tuned just right, then turned up louder. "I've laid around and played around this ole town too long." Billy Grammer is singing, his blue eyes flashing. And: "Horseshoe diamond ring." Mr. Karl Prussian, twelve years a counterspy, is introduced by George Magnum, in the latter's high nasal best: "If you've been followin' the Conservative movement in the U.S., you'll know the man ah'm about to intr'duce to you." "George Wallace," Karl Prussian says, "is a man of God." "God bless you!" George Magnum says. We're in Protestant territory now and the symbols are colliding, and sparks are shooting. It's meetin' time, and everyone's at ease. George Wallace, Jr., his hair as long as John Lennon's, swings out gently. He flourishes his dark electric guitar, tenderly, with restraint. No wild vulgar rock, no Mick Jagger here, but son of a man misunderstood, a young, patient, and determined Alabaman. "Gentle on my mind . . ." is his first number, and his second is: "I shot a man in Reno just to watch him die." Then the Governor, half-reluctant, half-jubilant, explodes across the stage. Pandemonium. He likes the crowd. His eyes begin to shine. Nervousness falls away and his movements become fluid, confident. Each gesture draws a response. "I tell you we're gonna give St. Vitus dance to the leadership of the Democratic party." "Ah'm sick of permissiveness in this society. Ah'm tired of false liberals!" "Ah'm sick'n' tired of giving up 50 percent of my income to the United States, to waste half of it overseas on nations that spit on us and half of it on welfare." "An' now they tell us Vietnam was a mistake. A mistake that cost the average citizen 50,000 lives, 300,000 wounded, 120 billion dollars down the drain. Ah don' call that a mistake. It's a tragedy." Like David Halberstam, he puts the blame upon the best and brightest—"them." *This is how *they* run our lives.*[45]

---

[45]Novak, *Choosing Our King,* pp. 211, 224–28, and 205–8. I have omitted, without indication, so as not to clutter the page with ellipses, large segments of these passages, and have repunc-

So the progresses continue. If the material were from Germany or France, India or Tanzania (to say nothing of Russia or China), the idiom would be different, as would the ideological assumptions upon which it rested. But there would be an idiom, and it would reflect the fact that the charisma of the dominant figures of society and that of those who hurl themselves against that dominance stem from a common source: the inherent sacredness of central authority. Sovereignty may rest now in states or even in the populations of states, as Humphrey, McGovern, and Wallace alike· assume; but the "vast universality" that inheres in it remains, whatever has become of the will of kings. Neither nationalism nor populism has changed that. It is not, after all, standing outside the social order in some excited state of self-regard that makes a political leader numinous but a deep, intimate involvement—affirming or abhorring, defensive or destructive—in the master fictions by which that order lives.

---

tuated, reparagraphed, and even run some sentences together, both in the interests of brevity and to eliminate as many as possible of Novak's personal comments, some of which are extremely shrewd, others mere alternative clichés. Thus, though all the words are his (or those he is quoting), and nothing has been done to alter the meaning, these excerpts are better regarded as précis than as true quotations. For a similarly vivid view of 1972 presidential campaign theatrics from another part of the forest, see H. Thompson, *Fear and Loathing on the Campaign Trail, '72* (San Francisco, 1973).

Chapter 7 / The Way We Think Now: Toward an Ethnography of Modern Thought

I

"Thought," says my dictionary (suitably enough, given the nature of the occasion,* the *American Heritage*), has two primary meanings: (1) "The act or process of thinking; cogitation," and (2) "The product of thinking; idea; notion." In clarification of the first, "process" meaning, a number of, as we would put it, internal psychological phenomena are listed: "attention," "expectation," "intent," even "hope," with the implication that the set may be expanded to include everything from memory and dream to imagination and calculation in some way a "mental act." In clarification of the second, "product" meaning, we get, grand and undifferentiated, vir-

*This chapter originally given as a bicentennial address to the American Academy of Arts and Sciences.

tually the whole of culture: "The intellectual activity or production of a particular time or social class." Thought is what goes on in our heads. Thought is what, especially when we put them together, comes out of them.

Discrepant meanings for the same term are not, of course, in themselves surprising, at least in ordinary language; polysemy, as the linguists call it, is the natural condition of words. I bring this example of it forward because it takes us into the heart of the unity and diversity theme as it has appeared in the social sciences since, say, the twenties and thirties. The overall movement of those sciences during that period has been one in which the steady progress of a radically unific view of human thought, considered in our first, "psychological" sense as internal happening, has been matched by the no less steady progress of a radically pluralistic view of it in our second, "cultural" sense as social fact. And this has raised issues that have now so deepened as to threaten coherence. We are forced at last, whether we work in laboratories, clinics, slums, computer centers, or African villages, to consider what it is we really think about thought.

In my own particular corner of the social sciences, anthropology, this issue has been with us late and soon in a peculiarly unnerving form. Malinowski, Boas, and Lévi-Bruhl in the formative phases of the discipline, Whorf, Mauss, and Evans-Pritchard after them, Horton, Douglas, and Lévi-Strauss now, have all been unable to leave off worrying it. Formulated first as the "primitive mind" problem, later as the "cognitive relativism" problem, and most recently as the "conceptual incommensurability" problem—as always, what advances most in such matters is the majesty of the jargon—the disaccordance between a lowest common denominator view of the human mind ("even Papuans exclude middles, distinguish objects, and lay effects to causes") and an "other beasts, other notions" one ("Amazonians think they are parakeets, fuse the cosmos with village structure, and believe pregnancy disables males") has grown steadily more difficult to avoid noticing.

The primitive form of the "primitive thought" formulation—that is, that while we, the civilized, sort matters out analytically, relate them logically, and test them systematically, as can be seen by our mathematics, physics, medicine, or law, they, the savage, wander about in a hodgepodge of concrete images, mystical participations, and immediate passions, as can be seen by their myth, ritual, magic, or art—has, of course, been progressively undermined as more about how the other half thinks has become known (and more, too, about just how unvirginal reason is); though it persists in certain sorts of developmental psychology, certain styles of comparative history, and certain circles of the diplomatic service. The error, as in rather different ways both Boas and Malinowski gave much of their careers to demonstrating, lay in attempting to interpret cultural materials as though they were individual expressions rather than social institutions. Whatever the connection between thought as process and thought as product might be, the Rodin model—the solitary thinker mulling facts or spinning fantasies—is inadequate to clarify it. Myths are not dreams, and the rational beauties of mathematical proof are guarantees of no mathematician's sanity.

The second, "cognitive relativism" formulation of the issue consisted, then, in a series of attempts, more or less desperate, to avoid this culture-is-the-mind-writ-large fallacy and the we-logical, you-confused provincialism that went with it. Particular cultural products (American Indian grammatical forms, seasonal variations in Arctic settlement patterns, African divination techniques) were related to particular mental processes (physical perception, temporal sense, causal attribution). The truth value of the specific hypotheses proposed—that the Hopi see the natural world as composed of events rather than objects; that the Eskimo experience time as cyclic rather than serial; that the Azande conceive causal chains in mechanical terms but explain their intersection in moral ones—may be problematic. But such studies did at least open up the distinction between the vehicles in terms of which persons must think, given who they are and where they are, and the perceiving, imagining, remembering, or whatever that they engage in when they get down in fact actually to doing so.

Where they were less successful was in, once they had opened it, avoiding the "every people gets the psychology it deserves" particularism that tends to go with it. If verb forms, camp layouts, or chicken-poisoning rituals yield somehow specific modes of mental functioning, it becomes profoundly unclear how individuals enclosed in one culture are able to penetrate the thought of individuals enclosed in another. As the work of the cognitive relativists itself rested on a claim to such penetration, and of a rather deep-going sort at that, this was, and remains, an uncomfortable situation. Hopi tensors (words denoting intensity, tendency, duration, or strength as autonomous phenomena) drive reasonings so abstract, Whorf said, as to be almost beyond our power to follow. "We feel," Evans-Pritchard sighed, confronted on the upper Nile by cow poems and cucumber sacrifices, "like spectators at a shadow show watching insubstantial shadows on the screen . . . what the eye sees and the ear hears is not the same as what the mind perceives."

The situation was made even more difficult because, as I mentioned, at the same time as this radical pluralization of the "product" side of thought was taking place, not only in anthropology but in certain regions of history, philosophy, literature, and sociology as well, a number of powerfully unitive approaches to the "process" side were gathering force, most especially in psychology, linguistics, and such latter day originalities as game theory and computer science. These approaches have themselves been disparate. The only thing that links Freud, Piaget, von Neumann, and Chomsky (to say nothing of Jung and B. F. Skinner) is the conviction that the mechanics of human thinking is invariable across time, space, culture, and circumstance, and that they know what it is. But the general movement toward universalistic conceptions of, to use the most neutral word I can think of, ideation has naturally come to have its effects upon the pluralizers too. The fundamental identity of mental functioning in *homo sapiens,* the so-called "psychic unity of mankind," had remained a background article of faith among even the most thoroughgoing of them, anxious as they were to do away with any notion of primitive minds or cultural racism. But the content of that identity was confined to the most generalized of general capacities, hardly more than the ability to learn, feel, abstract, and analogize. With the appearance of more circumstantial pictures of such matters, however incompatible with one another or difficult to swallow whole, this sort of evasiveness—everything is general in general but particular in particular—seemed increasingly strained.

The reaction from those (ethnographers, sociologists of knowledge, historians of science, devotees of ordinary language) whose *en plein air* working conditions make it hard for them to ignore the fact that, however computers may work, grammar arise, or eros unfold, thinking as we find it lying about "in nature" is nothing if not various, has been to move the issue out of the cobweb world of mentality and restate it in terms of the supposedly more tensile one of meaning. For structuralists, Lévi-Strauss *cum suis,* the product side of thought becomes so many arbitrary cultural codes, diverse indeed, with their jaguars, tattoos, and rotting meat, but which, when properly deciphered, yield as their plain text the psychological invariants of the process side. Brazilian myth or Bach fugue, it is all a matter of perceptual contrasts, logical oppositions, and relation-saving transformations. For neo-Durkheimians, such as Mary Douglas, though the persuasion is widespread to the point of orthodoxy in social anthropology, social history, and social psychology, the product side and the process side are reconnected through a new and improved brand of sociological determinism in which meaning systems become a middle term between social structures, which vary, and psychological mechanisms, which do not. Hebrew dietary laws, endlessly sorting out foods, represent the boundary-obsessed consciousness of an hermetic community threatened on all sides with social absorption. For symbolic action theorists (a smaller band, but hardy, to whom, with some reservations, I would give my own allegiance), thinking is a matter of the intentional manipulation of cultural forms, and outdoor activities like ploughing or peddling are as good examples of it as closet experiences like wishing or regretting. But whatever the approach (and there are others), what formerly was seen as a question of the comparability of psychological processes from one people to the next is now seen, given how much more one would have to deny these days in denying that, as a question of the commensurability of conceptual structures from one discourse community to the next, a change of formulation that has led some inquirers into what I suppose we might call practical epistemology, Victor Turner, Edmund Leach, Mircea Eliade, or Melford Spiro, for example, out of relativism and others, Thomas Kuhn, Michel Foucault, Nelson Goodman, or myself, for example, more complexly into it.

That thought is spectacularly multiple as product and wondrously singular as process has thus not only come to be a more and more powerful animating paradox within the social sciences, driving theory in all sorts of directions, some of them reasonable, but the nature of that paradox has more and more come to be regarded as having to do with puzzles of translation, with how meaning in one system of expression is expressed in another—cultural hermeneutics, not conceptive mechanics. In such a form it may not be any more tractable than it was before; but it does at least bring the war back home, because the problem of how a Copernican understands a Ptolemaian, a fifth republic Frenchman an *ancien régime* one, or a poet a painter is seen to be on all fours with the problem of how a Christian understands a Muslim, a European an Asian, an anthropologist an aborigine, or vice versa. We are all natives now, and everybody else not immediately one of us is an exotic. What looked once to be a matter of finding out whether savages could distinguish fact from fancy now looks to be a matter of finding out how others, across the sea or down the corridor, organize their significative world.

II

It is that, then—how the presented diversity of modern thought is to be itself understood—that I want now for a bit to pursue. Not that I aim actually to produce such an understanding. That is not only far beyond my competence, it is far beyond anybody's. It is a task, like poetics or paleontology, for a continuing body of scholars working with what Kuhn, who keeps coining terms for speed-readers to abuse, calls "a disciplinary matrix." Indeed, it is toward the formation of such a matrix, by outlining what I think some of its characteristics should be, that my remarks are directed. To call, as I am about to do, for an ethnography of thought is to take a stand on what thought is by taking a stand on how it is to be thought about.

To name the study of thinking as it goes on in the fora and agorae of modern life "ethnography" may seem to claim it for my own indisciplinary matrix, anthropology. But such is in no way my intention. Just about everybody knows more about the matter than we do, still bemused as we are by cockfights and pangolins. My intention is to stress a certain bent of its character: namely, that it is (or, anyway, ought to be) an historical, sociological, comparative, interpretive, and somewhat catch-as-catch-can enterprise, one whose aim is to render obscure matters intelligible by providing them with an informing context. What connects Victor Turner, shuffling through the color symbolism of passage rites, Philippe Ariès, parading funeral images of death or schoolhouse ones of childhood, and Gerald Holton, ferreting out themata from oil drops, is the belief that ideation, subtle or otherwise, is a cultural artifact. Like class or power, it is something to be characterized by construing its expressions in terms of the activities that sustain them.

There are a number of practical implications that flow fairly directly from this notion that thinking (any thinking: Lord Russell's or Baron Corvo's; Einstein's or some stalking Eskimo's) is to be understood "ethnographically," that is, by describing the world in which it makes whatever sense it makes. But there are also a number of fears, powerful, engulfing, and so far anyway extraordinarily difficult to calm, that it stimulates more diffusely. What to some, heritors of the social fact tradition and its pluralizing impulses, looks like the introduction of more profitable ways of thinking about thinking looks to others, heritors of the internal happening tradition and its unifying drives, like a blowing up of the foundations of reason.

The most obvious of the directer implications is that, as thinking in this view is a matter of trafficking in the symbolic forms available in one or another community (language, art, myth, theory, ritual, technology, law, and that conglomerate of maxims, recipes, prejudices, and plausible stories the smug call common sense), the analysis of such forms and such communities is ingredient to interpreting it, not ancillary. The sociology of knowledge, to use the rubric, rather too Kantian for my taste, most often invoked here, is not a matter of matching varieties of consciousness to types of social organization and then running causal arrows from somewhere in the recesses of the second in the general direction of the first—rationalists wearing square hats sitting in square rooms thinking square thoughts, they should try sombreros, as Stevens says. It is a matter of conceiving of cognition, emotion, motivation, perception, imagination, memory . . . whatever, as themselves, and directly, social affairs.

How precisely to accomplish this, how to analyze symbol use as social action and write thereby an outdoor psychology is, of course, an exceedingly difficult business at which everyone from Kenneth Burke, J. L. Austin, and Roland Barthes to Gregory Bateson, Jurgen Habermas, and Erving Goffman has had some sort of pass. But what is clear, if anything is, is that to do so is to attempt to navigate the plural/unific, product/process paradox by regarding the community as the shop in which thoughts are constructed and deconstructed, history the terrain they seize and surrender, and to attend therefore to such muscular matters as the representation of authority, the marking of boundaries, the rhetoric of persuasion, the expression of commitment, and the registering of dissent.

It is here, where the imagery gets political, or worse, that the uneasiness of those for whom the mind (or the id) is a thing apart, Ryle's secret grotto, Rorty's glassy essence, grows serious—an uneasiness expressed in a number of not altogether concordant ways: as a fear of particularism, a fear of subjectivism, a fear of idealism, and, of course, summing them all into a sort of intellectualist *Grande Peur,* the fear of relativism. If thought is so much out in the world as this, what is to guarantee its generality, its objectivity, its efficacy, or its truth?

This fear of particularism, which (I suppose it is clear by now) I regard as a bit of academic neurosis, is especially prominent in my own field, anthropology, where those of us who attend with care to specific cases, usually peculiar, are constantly being told that we are undermining thereby the possibility of general knowledge and should take up instead something properly scientific like comparative sexology or cultural energetics; but it appears with some force as well in relation to history, of which one of its practitioners once wrote the terror is that simply in knowing everything in particular one will end by knowing nothing in particular. The subjectivism charge, which certain sorts of sociologists and historians of science attract perhaps a bit more than the rest of us, is that if one interprets ideologies or theories wholly in terms of the conceptual horizons of those who hold them one is left without a means of judging either their cogency or the degree to which one represents an advance over another. And by idealism, what usually seems to be meant is not adherence to some identifiable philosophical doctrine, *esse est percipi* or whatever, but merely that if one pays much attention to surface manifestations, symbols and so on, the deeper realities, neurons and so on, will be obscured by forceless appearances. It is all these sins, plus global accusations of moral laxity and logical confusion (Hitler is usually brought in at this point), that relativism evokes. The view that thought is where you find it, that you find it in all sorts of cultural shapes and social sizes, and that those shapes and sizes are what you have to work with is somehow taken to be a claim that there is nothing to say about it except, when in Rome, to each his own, across the Pyrenees, and not in the South.

But there is a great deal more to say. A great deal more about, as I mentioned, translation, how meaning gets moved, or does not, reasonably intact from one sort of discourse to the next; about intersubjectivity, how separate individuals come to conceive, or do not, reasonably similarly similar things; about how thought frames change (revolutions and all that), how thought provinces are demarcated ("today we have naming of fields"), how thought norms are maintained, thought models acquired, thought labor divided. The ethnography of thinking, like any other sort of ethnography—of worship, or marriage, or government, or exchange—is an attempt not to exalt diversity but to take it seriously as itself an object of analytic description and interpretive reflection. And as such it poses a threat neither to the integrity of our moral fiber nor to whatever linguists, psychologists, neurologists, primatologists, or artificers of artificial intelligence might contrive to find out about the constancies of perception, affect, learning, or information processing. What it forms a threat to is the prejudice that the pristine powers (to borrow a term from Theodore Schwartz) that we all have in common are more revelatory of how we think than the versions and visions (to borrow one from Nelson Goodman) that, in this time or that place, we socially construct.

III

The bearing of what one of these sorts of inquirer uncovers upon what the other sort does itself presents, of course, no small translation problem; one which, to the degree it can in fact be negotiated and the communities conceptually connected, will doubtless bring something of a sea change in the thinking of both. But rather than pursue that, which would involve too much technical detail and might anyway be premature, I want to render the ethnographic approach a bit more visible by tracing out what it comes to when one trains it on the general subject of our discussions here; the prismal and singular life of the mind. My argument that the diversity side of the issue, the one that appeals to fieldwork foxes, has as much to tell us as the unity side, the one that appeals to hypothesis hedgehogs, clearly demands, if not demonstration, at least something more in the way of spelling out in terms of methodological assumptions and research procedures.

The first of such assumptions, and the most important, is that the various disciplines (or disciplinary matrices), humanistic, natural scientific, social scientific alike, that make up the scattered discourse of modern scholarship are more than just intellectual coigns of vantage but are ways of being in the world, to invoke a Heideggerian formula, forms of life, to use a Wittgensteinian, or varieties of noetic experience, to adapt a Jamesian. In the same way that Papuans or Amazonians inhabit the world they imagine, so do high energy physicists or historians of the Mediterranean in the age of Phillip II—or so, at least, an anthropologist imagines. It is when we begin to see this, to see that to set out to deconstruct Yeats's imagery, absorb oneself in black holes, or measure the effect of schooling on economic achievement is not just to take up a technical task but to take on a cultural frame that defines a great part of one's life, that an ethnography of modern thought begins to seem an imperative project. Those roles we think to occupy turn out to be minds we find ourselves to have.

The development of methods of research designed to explicate such métier-made mentalities and render them intelligible to those to whom they seem foreign or worse (as well as, indeed, to those who have them, to whom they seem merely inevitable) is, of course, hardly without precedents to guide it. The reduction of puzzlement in the face of unfamiliar ways of looking at things has been something of a speciality of at least one strand of my own discipline; that concerned to make Tewas, Turks, or Trukese less riddles wrapped inside enigmas. But others have addressed it as well: historians, especially those concerned with more than how we got to be so much cleverer than we used to be; literary critics, especially those who have read something beside Twain and Melville in the original; and lately even philosophers, to whom it has occurred that if grammar glosses the world for English (or, facing page, German) speakers it should do so as well, and otherwise, for Chinese. Yet so far, whatever has been learned about how to get at the curve of someone else's experience and convey at least something of it to those whose own bends quite differently has not led to much in the way of bringing into intersubjective connection historians and sociologists, psychiatrists and lawyers, or, to rub a wound, entomologists and ethnographers.

In any case, sticking only to my own field, there are a number of methodological themes I might discuss as relevant to an ethnographic understanding of modern thought. But I will contain myself and refer, and that briefly, to only three: the use of convergent data; the explication of linguistic classifications; and the examination of the life cycle.

By convergent data I mean descriptions, measures, observations, what you will, which are at once diverse, even rather miscellaneous, both as to type and degree of precision and generality, unstandardized facts, opportunistically collected and variously portrayed, which yet turn out to shed light on one another for the simple reason that the individuals they are descriptions, measures, or observations of are directly involved in one another's lives; people, who in a marvelous phrase of Alfred Schutz's, "grow old together." As such they differ from the sort of data one gets from polls, or surveys, or censuses, which yield facts about classes of individuals not otherwise related: all women who took degrees in economics in the 1960s; the number of papers published on Henry James by two-year periods since World War II. The focus in anthropology on natural communities, groups of people engaged with one another in multiple ways, makes it possible to turn what looks like a mere collection of heterogeneous material into a mutually reinforcing network of social understandings. And as modern scholars are no more solitaires than are Bushmen the same should be possible for them.

Indeed, when we get down to the substance of things, unbemused by covering terms like "literature," "sociology" or "physics," most effective academic communities are not that much larger than most peasant villages and just about as ingrown. Even some entire disciplines fit this pattern: it is still true, apparently, that just about every creative mathematician (those men a quattrocento aesthetician once finely dismissed as people who quiet their intellect with proofs) knows about every other one, and the interaction, indeed the Durkheimian solidarity, among them would make a Zulu proud. To some extent the same thing seems to be true of plasma physicists, psycholinguists, Renaissance scholars, and a number of other of what have come to be called, adapting Boyle's older phrase, "invisible colleges." From such units, intellectual villages if you will, convergent data can be gathered, for the relations among the inhabitants are typically not merely intellectual, but political, moral, and broadly personal (these days, increasingly, marital) as well. Laboratories and research institutes, scholarly societies, axial university departments, literary and artistic cliques, intellectual factions, all fit the same pattern: communities of multiply connected individuals in which something you find out about A tells you something about B as well, because, having known each other too long and too well, they are characters in one another's biographies.

The second methodological theme that seems transferable from ethnography generally to the ethnography of thought, the concern with linguistic categories, is, of course, not something peculiar to anthropology; everyone is, as they say, "into" language these days. But the anthropological concern, which dates from its founding and long discussions about "mana," "tabu," "potlatch," "lobola" and so on, does have a somewhat special twist. It tends to focus on key terms that seem, when their meaning is unpacked, to light up a whole way of going at the world.

Since I am pretuned to be interested in such matters, the vocabularies in which the various disciplines talk about themselves to themselves naturally fascinates me as a way of gaining access to the sorts of mentalities at work in them. Whether it be mathematicians, discoursing, like so many wine-tasters, on the differences, apparently extremely real to them and invisible to everybody else, between "deep," "elegant," "beautiful," "powerful," and "subtle" proofs; physicists invoking such peculiar words of praise and blame as "tact" or "skimming"; or literary critics invoking the relative presence of a mysterious property, to outsiders anyway, called "realization," the terms through which the devotees of a scholarly pursuit represent their aims, judgments, justifications, and so on seems to me to take one a long way, when properly understood, toward grasping what that pursuit is all about.

Even the larger, grand classifications, containing as they do strong "persuasive definition" type elements, including the hallowed "Science" versus "Humanities" divide itself, are ripe for this sort of examination. In our intermediary sort of grand subarea, the "Third Culture" Snow forgot, whether one likes to call the whole enterprise the Social, the Behavioral, the Life, or the Human Sciences (or indeed deny the "Science" accolade altogether) tells a great deal about what one thinks the whole enterprise is, or at least ought to be, or at least ought strenuously to be prevented from becoming. And the "hard/soft," "pure/applied," "mature/immature" distinctions in the sciences, or the "creative arts"/"critical studies" one in the humanities, bear similar ideological overtones worth more reflection than, an occasional outburst against think-tank technocrats or New Haven mandarins aside, they usually get.

My third theme, the concern with the life cycle, is not precisely biological in nature, though it stems from a sensitivity to the biological foundations of human existence. Nor is it precisely biographical, though it sets social, cultural, and psychological phenomena in the context of careers. Passage rites, age and sex role definitions, intergenerational bonds (parent/child, master/apprentice) have been important in ethnographic analysis because, marking states and relationships almost everyone experiences, they have seemed to provide at least reasonably fixed points in the swirl of our material.

There are a number of ways in which this way of looking at things could prove of use in thinking about thought. I mention just two.

The first is the extremely peculiar career pattern that marks the academic disciplines: namely, that one starts at the center of things and then moves toward the edges. Induction into the community takes place at or near the top or center. But most people are not settled at or near the top or center but at some region lower down, further out—whatever the image should be. Put concretely, the overwhelming proportion of doctorates in my profession, for example, are still awarded by seven or eight universities; but only a very small proportion of those who receive them work in those universities. There are some doctorates awarded elsewhere, of course, and perhaps (but the most recent figures do not support the idea very much) there has been some diffusion in recent years. But it is, for all that, still true that the majority of people follow a career pattern in which they are for several years at the perceived heart of things and then, in differing degrees and with different speeds, are, in the jargon, "downwardly mobile"—or, again, at least perceive themselves to be. And in some other disciplines the phenomenon is even more marked. The physics departments of the whole country are dotted with people who were "around MIT (or Cal Tech) for awhile"; and to study English history at Princeton and teach it at Louisiana State can lend a particular tone to your life.

To see how odd this pattern is (I don't want to go into its justice), consider the police, where everyone is inducted at the bottom and moves, grade by grade, toward the top; or the two-caste, officer and enlisted man career path of the army; or the Catholic Church, where there is almost nothing between parish priest and bishop so that the great majority of people stay at the same general level of the hierarchy for thirty or forty years. So far as I know, no one has investigated the consequences for thought of this peculiar pattern of incorporating people into academia. But I am convinced that someone should, and that what one might call the "exile from Eden syndrome" is rather more important in shaping our general cast of mind (and accounts for some good part of the nature of our ritual life—professional meetings, for example) than we have allowed ourselves to realize.

The second, and rather closely related, matter I want to mention in this connection is the different, or anyway supposed so, maturation cycles in the various scholarly fields. Mathematics is, of course, one extreme of this, at least in popular imagery: people seem to blossom at eighteen and be washed up at twenty-five. History, where fifty-year-old men are sometimes thought to be still not mature enough to tackle a major work, is, of course, the other. A visitor to the Institute for Advanced Study, where one can see virtually the whole range of cycles in marvelously cacophonic operation at once, is supposed to have asked a mathematician and an historian at tea one afternoon how things were around the place these days. "Oh, you can see," said the historian, waving his hand at the beardless youths about, "it's still a nursery for mathematicians." "And a nursing home for historians," said the mathematician.

Clearly, the facts of the matter are more complex than this and demand subtler concepts than these to determine what they are. I have no substantive propositions to defend in this matter, nor in the others I have so cursorily raised. My point is that "the natives' " notions about maturation (and postmaturation) in the various fields, together with the anxieties and expectations those notions induce, shape much of what any given one is like, "mentally," from inside. They give a distinctive, life-cycle, age-structure tone to it, a structure of hope, fear, desire, and disappointment that permeates the whole of it and that ought to be, as it has for Pueblo Indians and Andaman Pygmies but not for chemists or philosophers, looked into.

As I say, one could go on this way, advising thinkers how to go about understanding what it is they are up to. But as we are here concerned with an issue both more pointedly specific and more grandly general, unity and diversity in the life of the mind, some implications of thinking about thought as a social activity, diversely animated, organized, and aimed, need to be drawn out.

In particular, the hard dying hope that there can again be (assuming there ever was) an integrated high culture, anchored in the educated classes and setting a general intellectual norm for the society as a whole, has to be abandoned in favor of the much more modest sort of ambition that scholars, artists, scientists, professionals, and (dare we hope?) administrators who are radically different, not just in their opinions, or even in their passions, but in the very foundations of their experience, can begin to find something circumstantial to say to one another again. The famous answer that Harold Nicholson is supposed to have given to a lady on a London street in 1915 as to why he was not, young man, off defending civilization—"Madam, I *am* civilization"—is no longer possible at even the highest of High Tables. All we can hope for, which if it were to happen would be that rarest of phenomena, a *useful* miracle, is that we can devise ways to gain access to one another's vocational lives.

IV

The question of where the "general" went in "general education" and how one might contrive to get it back so as to avoid raising up a race of highly trained barbarians, Weber's "specialists without spirit, sensualists without heart," is one that haunts anyone who thinks seriously about the intellectual life these days. But most of the discussions that arise around it seem to me condemned to a certain sterility, an endless oscillation of equally defensible but rather academical positions, because they take as their starting point the notion that what should be restored (or should not be restored) is some kind of diffuse humanism, one "revised," as Max Black has put it somewhere, so as to be "relevant to our own pressing problems, rather than those of Athenian gentlemen or Renaissance courtiers." However attractive such a program may be (and I, myself, don't wholly find it so) it is a simple impossibility.

The hallmark of modern consciousness, as I have been insisting to the point of obsession, is its enormous multiplicity. For our time and forward, the image of a general orientation, perspective, *Weltanschauung*, growing out of humanistic studies (or, for that matter, out of scientific ones) and shaping the direction of culture is a chimera. Not only is the class basis for such a unitary "humanism" completely absent, gone with a lot of other things like adequate bathtubs and comfortable taxis, but, even more important, the agreement on the foundations of scholarly authority, old books and older manners, has disappeared. If the sort of ethnography of thought work I have here projected is in fact carried out, it will, I am sure, but strengthen this conclusion. It will deepen even further our sense of the radical variousness of the way we think now, because it will extend our perception of that variousness beyond the merely professional realms of subject matter, method, technique, scholarly tradition, and the like, to the larger framework of our moral existence. The conception of a "new humanism," of forging some general "the best that is being thought and said" ideology and working it into the curriculum, will then seem not merely implausible but utopian altogether. Possibly, indeed, a bit worrisome.

But if a more accurate perception of how deeply into our lives the specificities of our vocations penetrate, how little those vocations are simply a trade we ply and how much a world we inhabit, dissolves the hope that some new form of *culture générale de l'esprit* can turn their force, it need not leave us resigned to anarchy, grantsmanship, and the higher solipsism. The problem of the integration of cultural life becomes one of making it possible for people inhabiting different worlds to have a genuine, and reciprocal, impact upon one another. If it is true that insofar as there is a general consciousness it consists of the interplay of a disorderly crowd of not wholly commensurable visions, then the vitality of that consciousness depends upon creating the conditions under which such interplay will occur. And for that, the first step is surely to accept the depth of the differences; the second to understand what these differences are; and the third to construct some sort of vocabulary in which they can be publicly formulated—one in which econometricians, epigraphers, cytochemists, and iconologists can give a credible account of themselves to one another.

To show that this problem, the deep dissimilarity of métier-formed minds, is not just in my head, the contrivance of an anthropologist drumming his trade, let me quote, in way of conclusion, two *Op. Ed.* items from the *New York Times* of a couple years back. The first is a letter, written by a young, and apparently quite brilliant, associate professor of mathematics at Rutgers, in response to a *Times* editorial concerning some of his work which the paper, in its usual style of sedate apocalypse, had entitled "Crisis in Mathematics." The "crisis," as the *Times* had it, was that two independent teams of researchers, one American, one Japanese, had produced two mutually contradictory proofs that were so long and complicated that reconciliation could not be effected. This was not quite correct, the letter writer, who, as a member of the American team, ought to know, said. As he felt it, at least, the crisis cut a great deal nearer the bone than mere methodology:

The issue [of the proofs] remained open for somewhat more than a year [he wrote]—which is not at all unusual when economists, biologists, or even physicists argue; the conflict drew attention precisely because such things are almost unheard of in mathematics. In any case [the Japanese team] found an error in their proof in July, 1974.

The problem, you see, is not that the proofs were too long and complicated—ours, for instance, took just thirteen pages. Rather because homotopy theory is an abstract field of no interest outside mathematics, only one worker bothered to verify the proofs independently. Partly for this reason, I have come to my own "Crisis in Mathematics." Precisely because there is no "maybe" in mathematics, and because pure mathematics has become so relentlessly detached from reality, I have decided that I cannot afford any more such victories. This fall I will enroll in medical school.

The other quotation is from a brief article that appeared, quite unrelated, a week or so later, entitled "What Physicists Do: Neaten Up the Cosmos," by a professor at the Fermi Institute at the University of Chicago. *He* is exercised by the fact that students, and beyond them the rest of us, consider physics to be "sharp, clear-cut and dried." Physics isn't like that, he says, with a certain asperity, and life isn't like that. He goes on to give some examples of the fact so far as physics is concerned—the standard ant on the standard expanding balloon, and so on—concluding:

Physics is like life; there's no perfection. It's never all sewed up. It's all a question of better, better yet, and how much time and interest do you really have in it. Is the universe really curved? It's not that cut and dried. Theories come and go. A theory isn't right and wrong. A theory has a sort of sociological position that changes as new information comes in.

"Is Einstein's theory correct?" You can take a poll and have a look. Einstein is rather "in" right now. But who knows if it is "true?" I think there is a view that physics has a sort of pristineness, rightness, trueness that I don't see in physics at all. To me, physics is the activity you do between breakfast and supper. Nobody said anything about Truth. Perhaps Truth is "out." One thinks, "Well, this idea looks bad for or looks good for general relativity."

Physics is confusing; like life it would be so easy were it otherwise. It's a human activity and you have to make human judgments and accept human limitations.

This way of thinking implies a greater mental flexibility and a greater tolerance for uncertainty than we tend toward naturally, perhaps.

The point is not that there is metaphysical malaise in mathematics and homey cheerfulness in physics. One could produce the inverse impression by quoting the more familiar expressions by mathematicians of the tremendous aesthetic rewards of their work—with fishermen and musicians, they are perhaps the last true poets—and the more familiar ones by physicists of the dispiriting disorder of the charmed, colored, and quarked particle world, from which neatness, cosmic or otherwise, seems to have fled altogether. The point is that to practice an art in which there is no "maybe" or, contrariwise, one that lives by the creed of "perhaps" has an effect on one's general approach to things. It is not just a proposition in homotopy theory that is likely to seem the more aloof the more perfect, the more perfect the more aloof, or adherence to the doctrine of general relativity that is likely to look like a sociological position that changes as new information comes in. The reaction to these compelling facts of scholarly experience is, as I say, of course not uniform. Some individuals embrace a clean, well-lighted place, some are repelled by it; some are drawn toward the confusion of everyday, some long for escape from it. Nor would comparable quotations from Milton specialists or ethnomusicologists, if they could be induced to write honest letters to newspapers, fail to show similar intensities.

But of all this, we know very little. We know very little about what it is like, these days, to live a life centered around, or realized through, a particular sort of scholarly, or pedagogical, or creative activity. And until we know a great deal more, any attempt even to pose, much less to answer, large questions about the role of this or that sort of study in contemporary society—and contemporary education—is bound to break down into passionate generalities inherited from a past just about as unexamined in this regard as the present. It is that, not psychological experiment, neurological investigation, or computer modeling, against which an ethnographic approach to thought sets its face.

PART III

Chapter 8 / Local Knowledge:

Fact and Law in

Comparative Perspective

I

Like sailing, gardening, politics, and poetry, law and ethnography are crafts of place: they work by the light of local knowledge. The instant case, Palsgraff or the Charles River Bridge, provides for law not only the ground from which reflection departs but also the object toward which it tends; and for ethnography, the settled practice, potlatch or couvade, does the same. Whatever else anthropology and jurisprudence may have in common—vagrant erudition and a fantastical air—they are alike absorbed with the artisan task of seeing broad principles in parochial facts. "Wisdom," as an African proverb has it, "comes out of an ant heap."

Given this similarity in cast of mind, a to-know-a-city-is-to-know-its-streets approach to things, one would imagine lawyers and anthropologists were made for each other and that the movement of ideas and arguments between them would proceed with exceptional ease. But a feel for immediacies divides as much as it connects, and though the yachtsman and the wine-grower may admire one another's sense of life it is not so clear what they have to say to one another. The lawyer and the anthropologist, the both of them connoisseurs of cases in point, cognoscenti of matters at hand, are in the same position. It is their elective affinity that keeps them apart.

A number of the curiosities that mark what lawyers tend to call legal anthropology and anthropologists the anthropology of law stem from this so near and yet so far relationship between those whose job, to quote Holmes, is to equip us with "what we want in order to appear before judges or . . . to keep . . . out of court" and those occupied, to quote Hoebel quoting Kluckhohn, with constructing a great mirror in which we can "look at [ourselves] in [our] infinite variety."[1] And of these curiosities, surely the most curious is the endless discussion as to whether law consists in institutions or in rules, in procedures or in concepts, in decisions or in codes, in processes or in forms, and whether it is therefore a category like work, which exists just about anywhere one finds human society, or one like counterpoint, which does not.

Long after this issue—the problematic relationship between rubrics emerging from one culture and practices met in another—has been recognized as neither avoidable nor fatal in connection with "religion," "family," "government," "art," or even "science," it remains oddly obstructive in the case of "law." Not only has a wedge been driven between the logical aspects of law and the practical, thus defeating the purposes of the whole enterprise (one more quotation of "the life of the law . . . has been experience" will do it in altogether), but the forensic approach to juridical analysis and the ethnographic have been unusefully set against one another, so that the stream of books and articles with such titles as law without lawyers, law without sanctions, law without courts, or law without precedent would seem to be appropriately concluded only by one called law without law.

The interaction of two practice-minded professions so closely bound to special worlds and so heavily dependent on special skills has yielded, thus, rather less in the way of accommodation and synthesis than of ambivalence and hesitation. And instead of the penetration of a juridical sensibility into anthropology or of an ethnographic one into law, we have had a fixed set of becalmed debates as to whether Western jurisprudential ideas have useful

[1]O. W. Holmes, Jr., "The Path of Law," reprinted in *Landmarks of Law,* ed. R. D. Henson (Boston, 1960), pp. 40–41. E. A. Hoebel, *The Law of Primitive Man: A Study in Comparative Legal Dynamics* (Cambridge, Mass., 1954), p. 10.

application in non-Western contexts, whether the comparative study of law has to do with how justice is conceived among Africans or Eskimos or with how disputes get dealt with in Turkey or Mexico, or whether jural rules constrain behavior or merely serve as masking rationalizations for what some judge, lawyer, litigant, or other machinator wants anyway to do.

I make these rather querulous comments not to dismiss what has been done in the name of legal anthropology—*Crime and Custom, The Cheyenne Way, The Judicial Process Among the Barotse,* and *Justice and Judgment Among the Tiv* remain the classic analyses of social control in tribal societies that they are—nor to draw a bead on what is now being done, some intriguing exceptions apart (Sally Falk Moore on strict liability, Lawrence Rosen on judicial discretion), about the same sort of thing in the same sort of terms, but to take my distance from it.[2] In my view, by conceiving of the product of the encounter of ethnography and law to be the development of a specialized, semi-autonomous subdiscipline within their own field, like social psychology, exobiology, or the history of science, anthropologists (to confine myself for the moment to them; I will have at the lawyers later) have attempted to solve the local knowledge problem in precisely the wrong way. The evolution of new branches of established fields may make sense when the problem is the emergence of genuinely interstitial phenomena neither the one thing nor the other, as with biochemistry, or where it is a question of deploying standard notions in unstandard domains, as with astrophysics. But with law and anthropology, where each side merely wonders, now wistfully, now skeptically, whether the other might have something somewhere that could be of some use to it in coping with some of its own classic problems, the situation is not like that. What these would-be colloquists need is not a centaur discipline—nautical wine-growing or *vigneron* sailing—but a heightened, more exact awareness of what the other is all about.

This, in turn, seems to me to imply a somewhat more disaggregative approach to things than has been common; not an attempt to join Law, *simpliciter,* to Anthropology, *sans phrase,* but a searching out of specific analyti-

[2]B. Malinowski, *Crime and Custom in Savage Society* (London, 1926); K. Llewellyn and E. A. Hoebel, *The Cheyenne Way* (Norman, Oklahoma, 1941); M. Gluckman, *The Judicial Process Among the Barotse of Northern Rhodesia* (Manchester, 1955, rev. ed. 1967); P. Bohannan, *Justice and Judgment Among the Tiv of Nigeria* (London, 1957).

S. F. Moore, "Legal Liability and Evolutionary Interpretation," in *Law as Process* (London, 1978), pp. 83–134; L. Rosen, "Equity and Discretion in a Modern Islamic Legal System," *Law and Society Review* 15 (1980–81): 217–45.

cal issues that, in however different a guise and however differently addressed, lie in the path of both disciplines. It also implies, I think, a less
internalist, we raid you, you raid us, and let gain lie where it falls, approach;
not an effort to infuse legal meanings into social customs or to correct juridical reasonings with anthropological findings, but an hermeneutic tacking
between two fields, looking first one way, then the other, in order to formulate moral, political, and intellectual issues that inform them both.

The issue I want to address in this way is, stated in its most general
terms—so general, indeed, as to lack much outline—the relationship between fact and law. As the is/ought, *sein/sollen* problem, this issue and
all the little issues it breeds has, of course, been a staple of Western philosophy since Hume and Kant at least; and in jurisprudence any debate about
natural law, policy science, or positive legitimation tends to make of it the
crux of cruxes. But it appears as well in the form of quite specific concerns
quite concretely expressed in the practical discourse of both law and anthropology: in the first case, in connection with the relation between the evidentiary dimensions of adjudication and the nomistic, what happened and was
it lawful; in the second, in connection with the relation between actual patterns of observed behavior and the social conventions that supposedly govern them, what happened and was it grammatical. Between the skeletonization of fact so as to narrow moral issues to the point where determinate
rules can be employed to decide them (to my mind, the defining feature
of legal process) and the schematization of social action so that its meaning
can be construed in cultural terms (the defining feature, also to my mind,
of ethnographic analysis) there is a more than passing family resemblance.[3]
At the anthill level, our two sorts of workaday cleverness may find something substantial to converse about.

The place of fact in a world of judgment, to tack now for awhile in the jural
direction (as well as to abuse a famous title), has been something of a vexed

---

[3]On the skeletonization of fact, see J. T. Noonan, Jr., *Persons and Masks of the Law: Cardozo,
Holmes, Jefferson, and Whythe as Makers of the Masks* (New York, 1976). On narrowing
moral issues for adjudication, see L. A. Fallers, *Law Without Precedent* (Chicago, 1969); cf.
H. L. A. Hart, *The Concept of Law* (Oxford, 1961). On the "interpretive" view of ethnographic
analysis, see C. Geertz, "Thick Description: Toward an Interpretive Theory of Culture," in
The Interpretation of Cultures (New York, 1973), pp. 3–30.

question since the Greeks raised it with their grand opposure of nature and convention; but in modern times, when *physis* and *nomos* no longer seem such unmixed realities and there seems somehow so much more to know, it has become a chronic focus of legal anxiety. Explosion of fact, fear of fact, and, in response to these, sterilization of fact confound increasingly both the practice of law and reflection upon it.

The explosion of fact can be seen on all sides. There are the discovery procedures that produce paper warriors dispatching documents to each other in wheelbarrows and taking depositions from anyone capable of talking into a tape recorder. There is the enormous intricacy of commercial cases through which not even the treasurer of IBM much less a poor judge or juror could find his way. There is the vast increase in the use of expert witnesses; not just the icy pathologist and bubbling psychiatrist of long acquaintance but people who are supposed to know all about Indian burial grounds, Bayesian probability, the literary quality of erotic novels, the settlement history of Cape Cod, Filipino speech styles, or the conceptual mysteries—"What is a chicken? Anything that is not a duck, a turkey, or a goose"—of the poultry trade. There is the growth of public law litigation—class action, institutional advocacy, *amicus* pleading, special masters, and so on—which has gotten judges involved in knowing more about mental hospitals in Alabama, real estate in Chicago, police in Philadelphia, or anthropology departments in Providence than they might care to know. There is the technological restlessness, a sort of rage to invent, of contemporary life which brings such uncertain sciences as electronic bugging, voice printing, public opinion polling, intelligence testing, lie detecting and, in a famous instance, doll play under juridical scrutiny alongside the more settled ones of ballistics and fingerprinting. But most of all there is the general revolution of rising expectations as to the possibilities of fact determination and its power to settle intractable issues that the general culture of scientism has induced in us all; the sort of thing that perhaps led Mr. Justice Blackmun into the labyrinths of embryology (and now following him with less dispassionate intent, various congressmen) in search of an answer to the question of abortion.

The fear of fact that all this has stimulated in the law and its guardians is no less apparent. As a general wariness about how information is assessed in court, this fear is, of course, a long-standing judicial emotion, particularly in common law systems where such assessment has tended to be given to amateurs to accomplish. It is a handbook commonplace that the rules of evidence, and the Manichaean dispersion of Being into Questions of Law and Questions of Fact they represent, are motivated less by a concern for relevancy than by a distrust of juries as "rational triers of fact," whatever that may mean. The judge's job in admissibility questions is to decide, as one such recent handbook finely puts it, when "the trial [will be] better off without the evidence."[4] The general decline of jury trials in civil cases, the growth of empirical studies of jury operation, the stream of proposals for jury reform, for the importation of inquisitorial procedures from civilian systems, or for *de novo* review, as well as the spread of moral misgivings of the A. P. Herbert sort as to whether "shutting . . . ten good men and true and two women in a cold room with nothing to eat" is really a sensible way of deciding "questions that baffle the wisest brains of Bench and Bar," all bespeak the same anxiety: the world of occurrence and circumstance is getting out of juridical hand.[5]

Nor is depreciation of the jury (an institution Judge Frank once compared to the useless man-size fish-hooks coveted by prestige-mad Pacific islanders) the only expression of a growing desire to keep fact at bay in legal proceedings.[6] The increasing popularity of strict liability conceptions in tort law, which reduce the "what happened?" side of things to levels a mere behaviorist can deal with, or of no-fault ones, which reduce it to virtually nothing at all; the expansion of plea-bargaining in criminal cases, which avoids undue exertion in organizing evidence for all concerned and brings the factual side of things to court largely stipulated; and the rise of "economic" theories of jurisprudence, which displace empirical interest from the ragged history of issues to the calculable consequences of their resolution, from sorting material claims to assigning social costs, all point in the same direction. Uncluttered justice has never seemed more attractive.

Of course, the trial cannot go on wholly without the evidence or the simulacrum of such, and some intelligence, real or purported, from the world in which promises are made, injuries suffered, and villanies committed must seep through, however attenuated, even to appeal courts. The skeletonization of fact, the reduction of it to the genre capacities of the law note, is in itself, as I have already said, an unavoidable and necessary process. But

[4]P. Rothstein, *Evidence in a Nutshell* (St. Paul, 1970), p. 5.
[5]A. P. Herbert, *Uncommon Law* (London, 1970), p. 350; I have reordered the quote.
[6]J. Frank, *Courts on Trial* (Princeton, 1949).

it grows increasingly tenuous as empirical complexity (or, a critical distinction, the sense of empirical complexity) and the fear of such complexity grows, a phenomenon that has rather seriously disquieted a number of prominent legal thinkers from, again, Judge Frank to Lon Fuller and John Noonan, as well as, and I daresay even more seriously, a far larger number of plaintiffs and defendants made suddenly aware that whatever it is that the law is after it is not the whole story.[7] The realization that legal facts are made not born, are socially constructed, as an anthropologist would put it, by everything from evidence rules, courtroom etiquette, and law reporting traditions, to advocacy techniques, the rhetoric of judges, and the scholasticisms of law school education raises serious questions for a theory of administration of justice that views it as consisting, to quote a representative example, "of a series of matchings of fact-configurations and norms" in which either a "fact-situation can be matched with one of several norms" or "a particular norm can be . . . invoked by a choice of competing versions of what happened."[8] If the "fact-configurations" are not merely things found lying about in the world and carried bodily into court, show-and-tell style, but close-edited diagrams of reality the matching process itself produces, the whole thing looks a bit like sleight-of-hand.

It is, of course, not sleight-of-hand, or anyway not usually, but a rather more fundamental phenomenon, the one in fact upon which all culture rests: namely, that of representation. The rendering of fact so that lawyers can plead it, judges can hear it, and juries can settle it is just that, a rendering: as any other trade, science, cult, or art, law, which is a bit of all of these, propounds the world in which its descriptions make sense. I will come back to the paradoxes this way of putting things seems to generate; the point here is that the "law" side of things is not a bounded set of norms, rules, principles, values, or whatever from which jural responses to distilled events can be drawn, but part of a distinctive manner of imagining the real. At base, it is not what happened, but what happens, that law sees; and if law differs, from this place to that, this time to that, this people to that, what it sees does as well.

Rather than conceiving of a legal system, our own or any other, as di-

[7]J. Frank, *Law and the Modern Mind* (New York, 1930); L. Fuller, "American Legal Realism," *University of Pennsylvania Law Review* 82 (1933–34):429–62; Noonan, *Persons and Masks of the Law.*
[8]M. Barkun, *Law Without Sanctions* (New Haven, 1968), p. 143.

vided between trouble over what is right and trouble over what is so (to use Llewellyn's piquant formulation, if only because it has been so influential among anthropologists) and of "juristic technique," our own or any other, as a matter of squaring ethical decisions responding to the what is right sort with empirical determinations responding to the what is so sort, it would seem better—more "realistic," if I may say so—to see such systems as describing the world and what goes on in it in explicitly judgmatical terms and such "technique" as an organized effort to make the description correct.[9] The legal representation of fact is normative from the start; and the problem it raises for anyone, lawyer or anthropologist, concerned to examine it in reflective tranquillity is not one of correlating two realms of being, two faculties of mind, two kinds of justice, or even two sorts of procedure. The problem it raises is how that representation is itself to be represented.

The answer to this question is far from clear and awaits, perhaps, developments in the theory of culture that jurisprudence itself is unlikely to produce. But surely better than the matching image of fitting an established norm to a found fact, jural mimesis as it were, is a discourse-centered formulation that, to borrow from a young Swiss anthropologist, Franz von Benda-Beckmann, sees adjudication as the back and forth movement between the "if-then" idiom of general precept, however expressed, and the "as-therefore" one of the concrete case, however argued.[10] This remains a rather too Western way of putting things to make an ethnographer, whose subjects are not always given to explicitly conditional reasoning and even less to contrasting general thought to particular, altogether happy, nor doubtless is it without methodological problems of its own. Yet it does, at least, focus attention on the right place: on how the institutions of law translate between a language of imagination and one of decision and form thereby a determinate sense of justice.

Put this way, the question of law and fact changes its form from one having to do with how to get them together to one having to do with how to tell them apart, and the Western view of the matter, that there are rules that sort right from wrong, a phenomenon called judgment, and there are methods that sort real from unreal, a phenomenon called proof, appears

---

[9]K. Llwellyn and E. A. Hoebel, *The Cheyenne Way,* p. 304. *Cf.* on "justice of fact" vs. "justice of law" L. Pospisil, *Anthropology of Law: A Comparative Perspective,* pp. 234 ff.; M. Gluckman, *The Judicial Process* p. 336.

[10]F. von Benda-Beckmann, *Property in Social Continuity,* Verhandelingen van het Instituut voor Taal-, Land- en Volkenkunde, 86, (The Hague, 1979), pp. 28 ff.

as only one mode of accomplishing this. If adjudication, in New Haven or New Hebrides, involves representing concrete situations in a language of specific consequence that is at the same time a language of general coherence, then making a case comes to rather more than marshaling evidence to support a point. It comes to describing a particular course of events and an overall conception of life in such a way that the credibility of each reinforces the credibility of the other. Any legal system that hopes to be viable must contrive to connect the if-then structure of existence, as locally imagined, and the as-therefore course of experience, as locally perceived, so that they seem but depth and surface versions of the same thing. Law may not be a brooding omnipresence in the sky, as Holmes insisted rather too vehemently, but it is not, as the down-home rhetoric of legal realism would have it, a collection of ingenious devices to avoid disputes, advance interests, and adjust trouble-cases either. An *Anschauung* in the marketplace would be more like it.

And: other marketplaces, other *Anschauungen.* That determinate sense of justice I spoke of—what I will be calling, as I leave familiar landscapes for more exotic locales, a legal sensibility—is, thus, the first object of notice for anyone concerned to speak comparatively about the cultural foundations of law. Such sensibilities differ not only in the degree to which they are determinate; in the power they exercise, vis-à-vis other modes of thought and feeling, over the processes of social life (when faced with pollution controls, the story goes, Toyota hired a thousand engineers, Ford a thousand lawyers); or in their particular style and content. They differ, and markedly, in the means they use—the symbols they deploy, the stories they tell, the distinctions they draw, the visions they project—to represent events in judiciable form. Facts and law we have perhaps everywhere; their polarization we perhaps have not.

So much for dictum, the hallmark figure of legal rhetoric. To change the voice to a more anthropological register for a while, let me, mimicking the famous wind-in-the-palm-trees style of Malinowski, invite you to come with me now to a peasant village perched amid shining terraces on the green-clad volcanic slopes of a small sun-drenched South Pacific island where the operations of something that looks very much like law have driven a native mad. The island is Bali, the village we can leave nameless, and the native (who, as all this happened in 1958, may well be dead) we may call Regreg.

Regreg's problem began when either his wife ran off with a man from another village, a man from another village ran off with her, or they ran off together: the marriage by mock-capture pattern of Bali makes these events more or less indistinguishable, or anyway not worth distinguishing, to local eyes. Properly incensed, Regreg demanded that the village council, a body of some hundred and thirty or so men which assembles once every thirty-five days to make decisions concerning village matters, take action to bring about her return. Though virtually everyone in the council sympathized with his predicament, they pointed out to him that, as of course he already very well knew, marriage, adultery, divorce, and that sort of thing were not a village concern. They were matters for kin-groups, which in Bali tend to be well defined and jealous of their prerogatives, to deal with. The issue was outside their jurisdiction, and he was pleading in the wrong forum. (Balinese villages have explicit rules, inscribed and reinscribed, generation after generation, onto palm leaves, defining in essentially religious, but nonetheless quite specific, terms the rights and obligations of the various bodies—councils, kin-groups, irrigation societies, temple congregations, voluntary associations—which, in a rather federative way, make them up.)[11] The council members would sincerely have liked to have done something for him, for they agreed that he had been badly used, but constitutionally, if I may put it that way, they could not. And as Regreg's kin-group, even more sympathetic, for his wife, being his patri-cousin, belonged to it too, was a small, weak, and rather low-status one, there was not much it could do either except try to comfort him with banalities of the that's life, by-gones-are-bygones, and there are other pebbles, other cousins even, on the beach variety.

Regreg would not, however, thus be comforted. When, seven or eight months later, his turn to take office as one of the, in this village, five council chiefs happened to come up, he balked and his troubles really began. One becomes chief, again in this village at least (no two do things exactly alike; if they find that they do, one of them changes something), in automatic rotation, the term being three years; and when your time comes round (quite rarely as a matter of fact; Regreg was not blessed with much luck in all

[11]C. Geertz, "Form and Variation in Balinese Village Structure," *American Anthropologist* 61 (1949): 991–1012; idem "Tihingan: A Balinese Village," *Bijdragen tot Taal-, Land- en Volkenkunde* 120 (1964): 1–33.

this), you simply must serve. This *is* a council matter, inscribed again on those palm leaves together with the god-produced disasters, exact and elaborate, attending its neglect; and refusal (so far as anyone could remember, this was the first example) is tantamount to resigning not just from the village but from the human race. You lose your house-land, for that is village-owned here, and become a vagrant. You lose your right to enter the village temples, and thus are cut off from contact with the gods. You lose, of course, your political rights—seat on the council, participation in public events, claims to public assistance, use of public property, all matters of great substance here; you lose your rank, your inherited place in the caste-like order of regard, a matter of even greater substance. And beyond that, you lose the whole social world, for no one in the village may speak to you on pain of fine. It is not precisely capital punishment. But for the Balinese, who have a proverb, "to leave the community of agreement [*adat,* a sovereign word whose ambiguities I shall be returning to at some length later on] is to lie down and die," it is the next best thing to it.

Why Regreg was so uncharacteristically resistant to public obligation for a Balinese, who obey their own rules to a degree an anthropologist, especially one who has come there from Java, not to speak of the United States, can greet only with personal astonishment and professional delight, is unclear. His co-citizens were, anyway, totally uninterested in the question of what his motivations might be and could hardly be brought to speculate on it. ("Who knows? He wants his wife back.") Rather, conscious of the disaster for which he was headed, they sought, in every way they could devise, to dissuade him from his course and induce him to take the damned office. The council assembled a half dozen times over the course of several months in special session simply to this end—to talk him into changing his mind. Friends sat up all night with him. His kin pleaded, cajoled, threatened. All to no avail. Finally, the council expelled him (unanimously; all its decisions are unanimous), and his kin-group, after one last desperate effort to bring him round, did so as well, for, given the precedence of the council's concerns over its own in *this* matter, if it had not done so, all of its members would have shared his fate. Even his immediate family—parents, siblings, children—had to abandon him in the end. Though, of course, their view, reasonably enough I suppose, was that it was he who had abandoned them.

He was, at any rate, abandoned. He wandered, homeless, about the streets and courtyards of the village like a ghost, or more exactly like a dog.

(Which the Balinese, though they have lots of them—mangy, emaciated, endlessly barking creatures, kicked about like offal in the road—despise with an almost pathological passion born of the notion that they represent the demonic end of a god-to-human-to-animal hierarchy.) For although people were forbidden to speak with him, they did now and then throw him scraps to eat, and he foraged in garbage heaps, when not driven off by stones, for the rest. After several months of this, growing more disheveled by the day, he became virtually incoherent, unable any longer to shout his case to deafened ears, perhaps unable any longer even to remember what it was.

At this point, however, a quite unexpected, and in its own way unprecedented, thing occurred. The highest ranking traditional king on Bali, who was also, under the arrangements in effect at the time, the regional head of the new Republican government, came to the village to plead Regreg's case for him. This man, who in the Indic state pattern of Southeast Asia as it was found in Bali (and to some, partly altered, partly reinforced extent, still is found), is situated along that gods-to-animals hierarchy I mentioned just at the point where its human ranges shade off into its divine; or, as the Balinese, who see rank progressing downward from the top, prefer to put it, the divine into the human.[12] He is, therefore, a half- or quasi-god (he is called *Dewa Agung*—"Great God"), the most sacred figure on the island, as well as, in 1958 anyway, the most elevated politically and socially. People still crawled in his presence, spoke to him in hyper-formal phrases, considered him shot through with cosmic power at once terrible and benign. In the old days, a local exile such as Regreg would most likely have ended up in his palace, or in that of one of his lords, as a powerless, protected, outcaste dependent—not precisely enslaved, but not precisely free either.

When this incarnation of Siva, Vishnu, and other empyrean persons came to the village—that is, to the council gathered in special session to receive him—he squatted on the floor of the council pavilion to symbolize that in *this* context he was but a visitor, however distinguished, and not a king, much less a god. The council members listened to him with enormous deference, a grand outpouring of traditional politesse, but what he had to say was far from traditional. This was, he told them, a new era. The country was independent. He understood how they felt, but they really ought not to exile people anymore, confiscate their house-land, refuse them political

[12]C. Geertz, *Negara: The Theatre State in Nineteenth-Century Bali* (Princeton, 1980).

and religious rights, and so on. It was not modern, up-to-date, democratic, the Sukarno-way. They should, in the spirit of the new Indonesia and to demonstrate to the world that the Balinese were not backward, take Regreg back and punish him, if they must, in some other way. When he finished (it was a long oration), they told him, slowly, obliquely, and even more deferentially, to go fly a kite. Village affairs, as he well knew, were their concern not his, and his powers, though unimaginably great and superbly exercised, lay elsewhere. Their action in the Regreg case was supported by the hamlet constitution, and if they were to ignore it, poxes would fall upon them, rats would devour their crops, the ground would tremble, the mountains explode. Everything he had said about the new era was right, true, noble, beautiful, and modern, and they were as committed to it as he was. (This was true: the village was an unusually "progressive" one; more than half the population were socialists.) But, well, no—Regreg could not be readmitted to human company. His traditional status reacknowledged, his modern duty done, or anyway attempted, the divine king-cum-civil servant said, may the village prosper, thanks for the tea, and left amid kowtows to his foot, and the issue never resurfaced. The last time I saw Regreg he had sunk into an engulfing psychosis, wandering now in a world largely hallucinatory, beyond pity, beyond remark.

There are clearly a great number of things to say about this terrible little episode, which may remind those who are fans of Storrs lectures of Grant Gilmore's description of Hell as a place where there is nothing but law and due process is meticulously observed; and I shall be referring back to it now and then as a sort of touchstone as I proceed to grander matters.[13] But what is of immediate relevance is that we have here events, rules, politics, customs, beliefs, sentiments, symbols, procedures, and metaphysics put together in so unfamiliar and ingenious a way as to make any mere contrast of "is" and "ought" seem—how shall I put it?—primitive. Nor can one, I think, deny the presence of a powerful legal sensibility here: one with form, personality, bite, and, even without the aid of law schools, jurisconsults, restatements, journals, or landmark decisions, a firm, developed, almost willful awareness of itself. Certainly Regreg (were he still capable of having a view) would not want to deny it.

Event and judgment flow along together here in, to adopt a phrase of Paul Hyams's about English ordeals, an effortless mix that encourages nei-

---

[13]G. Gilmore, *The Ages of American Law* (New Haven, 1977), p. 111.

ther extensive investigation into factual detail nor systematic analysis of legal principle.[14] Rather, what seems to run through the whole case, if it properly can be called a case, reaching as it does from cuckoldry and contumacy to kingship and madness, is a general view that the things of this world, and human beings among them, are arranged into categories, some hierarchic, some coordinate, but all clear-cut, in which matters out-of-category disturb the entire structure and must be either corrected or effaced. The question was not whether Regreg's wife had done this or that to him, or he had done this or that to her, or even whether in his present state of mind he was fit for the post of village chief. No one cared or made any effort to find out. Nor was it whether the rules under which he was judged were repellent. Everyone I talked to agreed that they were. The question was not even whether the council had acted admirably. Everyone I talked to thought, that, in his own terms, the king had a point, and they were indeed a rather backward lot. The question, to put it in a way no Balinese, of course, either would or could, was how do the constructional representations of if-then law and the directive ones of as-therefore translate one into the other. How, given what we believe, must we act; what, given how we act, must we believe.

Such an approach to things, one not of a legal anthropologist or an anthropologist of law, but of a cultural anthropologist turned away for a moment from myths and kin charts to look at some matters Western lawyers should find at least reminiscent of those they deal with, brings to the center of attention neither rules nor happenings, but what Nelson Goodman has called "world versions," and others "forms of life," *"epistemés,"* *"Sinnzusammenhange,"* or "noetic systems."[15] Our gaze fastens on meaning, on the ways in which the Balinese (or whoever) make sense of what they do—practically, morally, expressively . . . juridically—by setting it within larger frames of signification, and how they keep those larger frames in place, or try to, by organizing what they do in terms of them. The segregation of domains of authority—kin-group from council, council from king; the definition of fault as disruption not of political order (Regreg's obstinacy was not regarded as any threat to that) but of public etiquette; and the remedy employed, the radical effacement of social personality, all point to a powerful, particular, to our minds even peculiar,

[14]P. R. Hyams, "Trial by Ordeal, the Key to Proof in the Common Law," in press.
[15]N. Goodman, *Ways of Worldmaking* (Indianapolis and Cambridge, Mass., 1978).

conception of, to use another of Goodman's compendious tags, "the way the world is."[16]

The way the Balinese world is would take a monograph even to begin to describe: an extravagance of gods, groups, ranks, witches, dances, rites, kings, rice, kinship, ecstasis, and artisanry, set in a maze of politesse. The key to it, so far as it has one, is probably the politesse, for manners have a force here difficult for us even to credit, much less to appreciate. But however that may be, and I shall try later on to make all this seem a little less Martian, the cultural contextualization of incident is a critical aspect of legal analysis, there, here, or anywhere, as it is of political, aesthetic, historical, or sociological analysis. If there are any features general to it, it is in this that they must lie: in the ways in which such contextualization is accomplished when the aim is adjudication rather than, say, causal explanation, philosophical reflection, emotional expression, or moral judgment. The fact that we can—that is, that we think that we can—take so much of this context for granted in our own society obscures from us a large part of what legal process really is: seeing to it that our visions and our verdicts ratify one another, indeed that they are, to borrow an idiom less offhand, the pure and the practical faces of the same constitutive reason.

It is here, then, that anthropology, or at least the sort of anthropology I am interested in, a sort I am trying, with indifferent success, to get people to call "interpretive," enters the study of law, if it enters it at all. Confronting our own version of the council-man mind with other sorts of local knowledge should not only make that mind more aware of forms of legal sensibility other than its own but make it more aware also of the exact quality of its own. This is, of course, the sort of relativization for which anthropology is notorious: Africans marry the dead and in Australia they eat worms. But it is one that neither argues for nihilism, eclecticism, and anything goes, nor that contents itself with pointing out yet once again that across the Pyrenees truth is upside down. It is, rather, one that welds the processes of self-knowledge, self-perception, self-understanding to those of other-knowledge, other-perception, other-understanding; that identifies, or

[16]N. Goodman, "The Way the World Is," in *Problems and Projects* (Indianapolis and Cambridge, Mass., 1972), pp. 24–32.

very nearly, sorting out who we are and sorting out whom we are among. And as such, it can help both to free us from misleading representations of our own way of rendering matters judiciable (the radical dissociation of fact and law, for example) and to force into our reluctant consciousness disaccordant views of how this is to be done (those of the Balinese, for example) which, if no less dogmatical than ours, are no less logical either.

The turn of anthropology, in some quarters at least, toward a heightened concern with structures of meaning in terms of which individuals and groups of individuals live out their lives, and more particularly with the symbols and systems of symbols through whose agency such structures are formed, communicated, imposed, shared, altered, reproduced, offers as much promise for the comparative analysis of law as it does for myth, ritual, ideology, art, or classification systems, the more tested fields of its application.[17] "Man," as A. M. Hocart remarked, "was not created governed," and the realization that he has become so, severally and collectively, by enclosing himself in a set of meaningful forms, "webs of signification he himself has spun," to recycle a phrase of my own, leads us into an approach to adjudication that assimilates it not to a sort of social mechanics, a physics of judgment, but to a sort of cultural hermeneutics, a semantics of action.[18] What Frank O'Hara said of poetry, that it makes life's nebulous events tangible and restores their detail, may be true as well, and no less variously accomplished, of law.

As I suggested earlier, such a tack runs counter, or at least at some obtuse sort of angle, to what has been the mainstream of the analysis of law by anthropologists and their would-be fellow travelers in the other social sciences and in the legal profession. Michael Barkun's view, which he claims to draw from M. G. Smith, that what we comparativists of legal systems must do is "draw pure structure from its culture-specific accretions" seems to me a proposal for a perverse sort of alchemy to turn gold into lead.[19] P. H. Gulliver's self-styled "declaration of faith," formulated for him, he says, by my only anthropological predecessor to the Storrs platform, Max Gluckman, that he is concerned with "the social processes which largely determine the outcome of a dispute" not "the analysis of the processes of ratiocination by which negotiations proceed," seems to me, as befits such

[17]C. Geertz, *The Interpretation of Cultures;* P. Rabinow and W. M. Sulivan, eds., *Interpretive Social Science: A Reader* (Berkeley and Los Angeles, 1979).
[18]A. M. Hocart, *Kings and Councillors: An Essay in the Comparative Anatomy of Human Society* (Chicago, 1970), p. 128.
[19]Barkun, *Law Without Sanctions,* p. 33.

declarations, incoherent.[20] And Elizabeth Colson's notion, derived from god knows where, that those interested in symbolic systems are so interested because, shy of the dust and blood of social conflict and anxious to please the powerful, they retreat to realms assumed to be impersonal, above the battle, and to operate by their own logic, seems to me idle slander.[21] Again, I growl this way not to dismiss what others have done or are doing (though I am critical of a lot of it), nor to divide my profession into warring camps (that it does quite well by itself). I do it to lay a different course. I am going to revel in culture-specific accretions, pore over processes of ratiocination, and plunge headlong into symbolic systems. That does not make the world go away; it brings it into view.

Or rather, it brings worlds into view. I am going to try, in too brief a compass to be in any way persuasive and too extended a one wholly to avoid actually saying something, to outline three quite different varieties of legal sensibility—the Islamic, the Indic, and a so-called customary-law one found throughout the "Malayo" part of Malayo-Polynesia—and connect them to the general views of what reality really is embodied within them. And I am going to do this by unpacking three terms, that is, three concepts, central, so I think, to these views: *haqq,* which means "truth," and very great deal more, for the Islamic; *dharma,* which means "duty," and a very great deal more, for the Indic; and *adat,* which means "practice," and a very great deal more, for the Malaysian.

It is the "very great deal more" that will absorb me. The intent is to evoke outlooks, not to anatomize codes, to sketch, at least, something of the if/thens within which the as/therefores are set in each of these particular cases (which will be even more particular because I shall be relying on my Moroccan and Indonesian work to construct them) and gain a sense thereby of what the fact-law issue comes to in them as against what it comes to for us.

That little job done over the course of my next forty pages or so, there remains only the minor question of how such distinct legal visions are going to relate, indeed are relating and have for some good time been relating, to one another as we all become more and more involved in each other's business; how local knowledge and cosmopolitan intent may comport, or fail to, in the emerging world disorder. Undeterred by either modesty or

[20]P. H. Gulliver, "Dispute Settlement Without Courts: The Ndenduli of Southern Tanzania," in *Law in Culture and Society,* ed. L. Nader (Chicago, 1969), p. 59.
[21]E. Colson, *Tradition and Contract: The Problem of Order* (Chicago, 1974), p. 82.

common sense, I will turn then finally to that in the third part of this essay, arguing, I suppose, that it is anyone's guess, but that anthropological guesses are at least worth juristic attention.

II

I said in the first part of this essay that "law," here, there, or anywhere, is part of a distinctive manner of imagining the real. I would like now to present some evidence that this is so—evidence only, schematic, peremptory, and, as I speak not from a bench but a podium, hardly conclusive, hardly even systematically marshaled, yet for all that I trust instructive. I want less to prove something, whatever "proof" could mean for so groping an enterprise, than to evoke something: namely, other forms of juristical life. And for that, and to risk sounding merely outrageous, what we need, or anyway can best expect to get, is not exact propositions, exactly established. What we need, or can best expect to get, is what Nelson Goodman, whose attitudes in these matters again closely resemble my own, sees even that modern paragon of naked truth, the scientific law, as being: "the nearest amenable and illuminating lie."[22]

If one looks at law this way, as a view of the way things are, like, say, science or religion or ideology or art—together, in this case, with a set of practical attitudes toward the management of controversy such a view seems to entail to those wedded to it—then the whole fact/law problem appears in an altered light. The dialectic that seemed to be between brute fact and considered judgment, between what is so and what is right, turns out to be between, as I put it earlier, a language, however vague and unintegral, of general coherence and one, however opportunistic and unmethodical, of specific consequence. It is about such "languages" (that is to say,

[22]N. Goodman, *Ways of Worldmaking*, p. 121: "But, of course, truth is no more a necessary than a sufficient consideration for choice of statement. Not only may the choice often be of a statement that is the more nearly right in other respects over one that is the more nearly true, but where truth is too finicky, too uneven, and does not fit comfortably with other principles, we may choose the nearest amenable and illuminating lie. Most scientific laws are of this sort: not assiduous reports of detailed data but sweeping Procrustean simplifications."

symbol systems) and such a dialectic that I want now to try to say something at once empirical enough to be credible and analytical enough to be interesting.

I want to do that, as I also said earlier, by the somewhat unorthodox route of unpacking three resonant terms, each from a different moral world and connecting to a different legal sensibility: the Islamic, the Indic, and what, for want of a better designation, I will call the Malaysian, meaning by that not just the country of Malaysia but the Austronesian-speaking civilizations of Southeast Asia. As the invocation of these generalized culture-images indicates, the route is not only unorthodox, it is full of pitfalls of the sort into which a certain kind of anthropology—the kind that finds Frenchmen Cartesian and Englishmen Lockean—particularly likes to fall. Proposing, besides, to communicate something of the character of these mega-entities through the examination of single concepts, however rich, would seem merely to make disaster sure. Perhaps it does. But if certain precautions are taken and certain restraints observed, the absolute worst, mere stereotype, may yet be avoided.

The first precaution is to confess that the three terms I shall use—*haqq,* an Arabic word having something to do with what we, with hardly more precision, would call "reality," or perhaps "truth," or perhaps "validity"; *dharma,* a Sanskritic word, originally in any case, though one finds it now in everything from Urdu to Thai, which centers, in a linga-and-lotus sort of way, around notions of "duty," "obligation," "merit," and the like; and *adat,* also originally Arabic, but taken into Malaysian languages to mean something half-way between "social consensus" and "moral style"—are not only not the only three I might have used; they may not even be the best. *Šarīᶜa* ("path," "way") and *fiqh* ("knowledge," "comprehension") are cer-tainly more common starting points for reflections about the characteristic bent of Islamic law. *Āgama* ("precept," "doctrine") or *śāstra* ("treatise," "canon") might lead more directly into Indic conceptions of the legal. And either *patut* ("proper," "fitting") or *pantas,* ("suitable," "apposite") would have the advantage for Southeast Asia of at least being an indigenous word rather than an obliquely borrowed and worked-over one. What one really needs, in each case, is a cycle of terms defining not point concepts but a structure of ideas—multiple meanings, multiply implicated at multiple levels. But this is clearly not possible here. We must do with partials.

We must also do with a radical simplification of both the historical and regional dimensions of these matters. "Islam," "The Indic World," and *sensu lato* "Malaysia" are, as the bulk of my work in general has in fact been devoted to demonstrating, hardly homogeneous block entities, invariant over time, space, and populations.[23] Reifying them as such has been, indeed, the main device by means of which "The West," to add another nonentity to the collection, has been able to avoid understanding them or even seeing them very clearly. This may (or may not) have had its small uses in the past, when we were alternately self-absorbed and impassioned to shape others to our view of how life should be lived. It hardly has any now when, as I shall argue at some length in the concluding section of this essay, we are faced with defining ourselves neither by distancing others as counterpoles nor by drawing them close as facsimiles but by locating ourselves among them.

Yet, as my purpose is to put a comparative frame around certain of our ideas about what justice comes to, not to present "The East in a Nutshell," the necessity to gloss over internal variation and historical dynamics is perhaps less damaging than it might otherwise be; it may even serve to focus issues by blurring detail. And in any case, there is the further precaution one can take of remembering that, although I shall be drawing on material from all sorts of times and places, when I speak of "Islam," or "The Indic World," or "Malaysia," I usually have at the back of my mind one or another of the rather marginal cases quite recently observed on which I have happened as an anthropologist at an historical moment to work: Morocco, at the extreme western end of the Muslim world, far from the calls of Mecca; Bali, a small, detached, and extremely curious Hindu-Buddhist outlier in the eastern reaches of the Indonesian archipelago; and Java, a sort of anthology of the world's best imperialisms, where a "Malaysian" cultural base has been over-lain by just about every major civilization—South Asian, Middle Eastern, Sinitic, European—to thrust itself into the Asiatic trade over the past fifteen hundred years.

Finally, and then I shall be done with apologizing (it never does any good anyhow), I must stress that I am not engaged in a deductive enterprise in which a whole structure of thought and practice is seen to flow, according to some implicit logic or other, from a few general ideas, sometimes called postulates, but in an hermeneutic one—one in which such ideas are used

---

[23]For the disaggregation theme in my work, see especially my *Islam Observed* (New Haven, 1968), and *The Religion of Java* (Glencoe, Ill., 1960). Also, I should note that by "Islamic" I do *not* mean Middle Eastern; by "Indic" I do *not* mean Indian.

as a more or less handy way into understanding the social institutions and cultural formulations that surround them and give them meaning.[24] They are orienting notions, not foundational ones. Their usefulness does not rest on the presumption of a highly integrated system of behavior and belief. (There is none such, even on so tight a little island as Bali.) It rests on the fact that, ideas of some local depth, they can direct us toward some of the defining characteristics, however various and ill ordered, of what it is we want to grasp: a different sense of law.

Our three terms, to put all this in a somewhat different way, are more comparable to the Western notion of "right" *(Recht, droit)* than they are to that of "law" *(Gesetz, loi).* They center, that is, less around some sort of conception of "rule," "regulation," "injunction," or "decree" than around one, cloudier yet, of an inner connection, primal and unbreakable, between the "proper," "fitting," "appropriate," or "suitable" and the "real," "true," "genuine," or "veritable": between the "correct" of "correct behavior" and that of "correct understanding." And of none of them is this more true than it is of *ḥaqq.*

There is an Arabic word and term of Islamic jurisprudence at least generally correspondent to the "rules and regulations" idea, namely *ḥukm,* from a root having to do with delivering a verdict, passing a sentence, inflicting a penalty, imposing a restraint, or issuing an order, and it is from that root that the commonest words for judge, court, legality, and trial derive. But *ḥaqq* is something else again: a conception that anchors a theory of duty as a set of sheer assertions, so many statements of brute fact, in a vision of reality as being in its essence imperative, a structure not of objects but of wills. The moral and ontological change places, at least from our point of view. It is the moral, where we see the "ought," which is a thing of descriptions, the ontological, for us the home of the "is," which is one of demands.

It is this representation of the really real as a thing of imperatives to be responded to, a world of wills meeting wills, and that of Allah meeting them

---

[24]For the postulational approach, see E. A. Hoebel, *The Law of Primitive Man.* Again, I do not wish to dismiss this approach or deny its achievements, merely to distinguish mine from it.

all, rather than a thing of, say, forms to be contemplated, matter to be perceived, or noumena to be postulated, that I want to use *haqq* to light up; though, as this view is general to the legal sensibility we are after, any systematic consideration of juristical terms in the Islamic world would, I think, fairly promptly lead one to it.[25] The "real" here is a deeply moralized, active, demanding real, not a neutral, metaphysical "being," merely sitting there awaiting observation and reflection; a real of prophets not philosophers. Which brings us, as just about anything also eventually does in some devious way or other in this vehement part of the world, to religion.

Ḥaqq, as *al-Ḥaqq,* is in fact one of the names of God, as well as, along with such things as "speech," "power," "vitality," and "will," one of His eternal attributes. As such, it images, even for the unlearned Muslim, to whom these notions come wrapped in colloquial ethics, standard practices, quranic tags, mosque-school homilies, and proverbial wisdom, how things most generally are. As the Islamicist W. C. Smith has put it: "*Ḥaqq* refers to what is real in and of itself. It is a term par excellence of God. *Huwa al-Ḥaqq:* He is Reality as such. Yet every other thing that is genuine is also *haqq.* It means reality first, and God only for those [that is to say, Muslims] who [go on to] equate Him with reality. [It] is truth in the sense of the real, with or without the capital R."[26] Arabic script does not, as a matter of fact, employ majuscules. But the relation of the upper-case sense of R (or, more precisely, *ha'*) and the lower-case one is the heart of the matter: the connecting, again, of an overarching sense of how things are put together, the if/then necessities of *Anschauung* coherence, and particular judgments of concrete occasions, the as/therefore determinations of practical life.

This connection is made (semantically anyway—I am not arguing causes, which are as vast as mideastern history and society) by the word itself. For at the same time as it means "reality," "truth," "actuality," "fact," "God," and so on, it, or this being Arabic, morphophonemic permutations of it, also means a "right" or "duty" or "claim" or "obligation," as well as "fair," "valid," "just," or "proper." "The *haqq* is at you" (*ᶜandek*) means (again,

---

[25]Some passages here and elsewhere in this discussion are taken from previous works of mine, most especially, "*Sūq:* The Bazaar Economy in Morocco," in C. Geertz, H. Geertz, and L. Rosen, *Meaning and Order in Moroccan Society,* (Cambridge, England, and New York, 1979), pp. 123–313; C. Geertz, *Islam Observed.*

[26]W. C. Smith, "Orientalism and Truth" (T. Cuyler Young Lecture, Program in Near Eastern Studies, Princeton University, 1969); cf. W. C. Smith, "A Human View of Truth," *Studies in Religion* 1 (1971):6–24. I have, not to mar the page with dots, eliminated phrases and sentences without benefit of ellipses. On the question of attributes in Islamic theology, see H. A. Wolfson, *The Philosophy of the Kalam* (Cambridge, Mass., 1976), pp. 112–234.

I follow Moroccan usage) "you are right," "right is on your side." "The *ḥaqq* is in you" *(fīk)* means "you are wrong," "you are unfair, unjust," apparently in the sense that you know the truth but are not acknowledging it. "The *ḥaqq* is on you *(ᶜalīk)* means "it is your duty, your responsibility," "you must," "you are obligated to." "The *haqq* is with you" *(minek)* means "you are entitled to it," "it is your due." And in various forms and phrases it denotes a beneficiary; a participant in a business deal; a legitimate "property right" share in something, such as a profit, a bundle of goods, a piece of real estate, an inheritance, or an office. It is used for a contractual duty or, derivatively, even for a contract document as such; for a general responsibility in some matter; for a fine, for an indemnity. And its definite plural, *al-ḥuqūq,* means law or jurisprudence. A *ḥuqūqī,* the attributive form, and thus most literally I suppose, "(someone) affixed to the real, fastened to it," is a lawyer or a jurisprudent.

The conception of an identity between the right and the real is thus constant through every level of the term's application: on the religious (where it is used not only for God, but also for the Quran in which his Will is stated, for the Day of Judgment, for Paradise, for Hell, for the state that comes with the attainment of mystic gnosis); on the metaphysical (where it signifies not just factuality as such, but essence, true nature, "the intelligible nucleus of an existing thing"); on the moral, in the phrases heard every day in the Morocco I know, that I have just been quoting; and on the jural, where it becomes an enforceable claim, a valid title, a secured right, and justice and the law themselves.[27] And this identity of the right and the real informs the Islamic legal sensibility not just abstractly as tone and mood, but concretely as deliberation and procedure. Muslim adjudication is not a matter of joining an empirical situation to a jural principle; they come already joined. To determine the one is to determine the other. Facts are normative: it is no more possible for them to diverge from the good than for God to lie.

Men, of course, can lie, and, especially in the presence of judges, often do; and that is where the problems arise. The as/therefore level of things

[27]For a fuller discussion of the various levels of meaning for *ḥaqq,* see the entry under "Hakk" in *The Encyclopedia of Islam,* new ed. (Leiden and London, 1971), vol. 3, pp. 81–82, where it is argued, rather speculatively, that the legal meaning was the original (pre-Islamic) one, out of which the ethical and religious meanings developed. "To sum up, the meanings of the root [*ḥ-q-q*] started from that of carved [that is, in wood, stone, or metal] permanently valid laws, expanded to cover the ethical ideals of right and real, just and true, and developed further to include Divine, spiritual reality." For other dimensions of this extraordinarily productive root, see also the entries at "Hakika" (ibid, pp. 75–76) and "hukuk" (ibid, p. 551).

is as difficult of determination as the if/then level is (in theory, anyway) clear and inescapable. The Quran as the eternally existing words of God—the Inlibration of Divinity, as H. A. Wolfson has brilliantly called it in polemic contrast to the Incarnation conceptions of Christology—is considered crystalline and complete in its assertion of what it is that Allah would have those for whom he is in fact *al-Ḥaqq* do and not do.[28] There has been, of course, much commentary and dispute, formation of schools, secretarian dissent, and so on. But the notion of the certainty and comprehensiveness of the law as embooked (another of Wolfson's happy phrases) in the Quran powerfully reduces, if it does not wholly remove, any sense that questions of what is just and what unjust may be, in and of themselves, ambiguous, quixotic, or unanswerable. Jural analysis, though an intellectually complex and challenging activity, and often enough a politically risky one, is seen as a matter of stating public-square versions of divine-will truths—describing the Sacred House when it is out of sight, as Shafi'i, perhaps the greatest of the classical jurists, has it—not of balancing conflicting values. Where the value balancing comes in is in the recounting of incident and situation. And it is that which leads to what is to my mind the most striking characteristic of the Islamic administration of justice: the intense concern with what might be called "normative witnessing."

As is well known, at least by those whose business it is to know such things, all evidence that comes before a Muslim court—that is to say, one governed by the *šarīᶜa* and presided over by a *qāḍī*—is considered to be oral, even if it involves written documents or material exhibits. It is only spoken testimony—*šahāda*, "witnessing," from a root for "to see with one's own eyes"—that counts, and such written materials as come to be involved are regarded not as legal proof in themselves but merely as (normally rather suspect) inscriptions of what someone said to someone in the presence of morally reliable witnesses.[29] This denial of the legal validity of the written

[28]H. A. Wolfson, *Philosophy of the Kalam,* pp. 235–303.
[29]On documents and witnesses in classical Islamic law, see J. A. Wakin, *The Function of Documents in Islamic Law* (Albany, 1972). Cf. Rosen, "Equity and Discretion in a Modern Islamic Legal System"; A. Mez, *The Renaissance of Islam* (Beirut, 1973 [originally ca. 1917]), pp. 227–29; J. Schacht, *Islamic Law* (Oxford, 1964), pp. 192–94. The word for "martyr"—*šahīd*—developed from the same root, apparently in a "God's witness" sense. See the article, *"Shahīd,"* H. A. R. Gibb and J. H. Kramers, *Shorter Encyclopaedia of Islam* (Leiden and London, 1961), pp. 515–18. *Šahāda,* "testimony," "witnessing," is also, of course, the term for the famous Muslim "Profession of Faith:" "[I witness that] there is no God but God and [I witness that] Muḥammad is the Messenger of God." The strict witnessing requirements (for example, that "the party who bore [the burden of proof] . . . was obliged to produce two

act as such dates from the very earliest periods of Islam, and in the formative phases of Islamic law written evidence was often rejected altogether, as was what we would call circumstantial or material evidence. "The personal word of an upright Muslim," as Jeanette Wakin has written, "was deemed worthier than an abstract piece of paper or a piece of information subject to doubt and falsification."[30] Today, when written evidence is accepted, however reluctantly, it still remains the case that its worth is largely derivative of the moral character of the individual or individuals who, personally involved in its creation, lend to it their authenticity. It is not, to paraphrase Lawrence Rosen on contemporary Moroccan practice, the document that makes the man believable; it is the man (or, in certain contexts, the woman) who makes the document such.[31]

The development of the institutions of witnessing have thus been as elaborate as those of pleading have been rudimentary. The search has not been for knowledgeable individuals sufficiently detached to retail empirical particulars an umpire judge can weigh in legal scales but for perceptive individuals sufficiently principled to produce righteous judgments an exegete judge can cast into quranic rhetoric. And this search has taken a wide variety of directions and a wider variety of forms. The sort of attention our tradition gives to assuring and reassuring itself, with indifferent success, that its laws are fair, the Islamic, in no doubt on that score, gives to assuring and reassuring itself, not much more successfully, that its facts are reputable.

In classical times, this obsession (the word is not too strong) with the moral reliability of oral testimony gave rise to the institution of accredited witnesses, men (or again in special cases or with special limitations, women) considered to be "upright," "straightforward," "honorable," "decent," "moral" (ʿādil), as well as, of course, of local prominence and presumed acquaintance with the ins-and-outs of local affairs. Chosen by the qāḍī once and for all through a settled procedure of evaluation and formal certification, they thenceforth testified, over and over again, in cases appearing be-

male, adult, Muslim witnesses, whose moral integrity and religious probity were unimpeachable, to testify orally to their direct knowledge of the truth of his claim") has sometimes been asserted to be the chief reason for the progressive constriction of šarīʿa court jurisdiction in recent times (N. J. Coulson, "Islamic Law," in An Introduction to Legal Systems, ed. J. D. M. Derrett (New York and Washington, D.C., 1968), pp. 54–74, quotation at p. 70). There is truth in this but it neglects the degree to which such "strict" views of witnessing have influenced proceedure in the "secular" court successors of the šarīʿa courts.
[30]Wakin, Function of Documents in Islamic Law, p. 6.
[31]Rosen, "Equity and Discretion in a Modern Islamic Legal System."

fore the court as individuals "whose testimony," as Wakin puts it, ". . . could not be doubted"—at least not legally.[32]

Not only could the number of such official, permanent witnesses grow very large (they reach eighteen hundred in tenth-century Baghdad), but the choosing and validation of them, one of the main duties of the *qāḍī* (each of which appointed his own, dismissing his predecessor's), could be extremely elaborate, extending to the point of the even odder practice, to our eyes anyway, of creating a similar body of secondary witnesses—*šahāda ᶜalā šahāda*, "witnesses as to witnesses."[33] These secondary, meta-witnesses affirmed the probity of the primary witnesses, two of them for one of the primary, particularly where the latter had died or moved since giving their original testimony or for some other reason were unable to appear personally in court, but also where the *qāḍī* still had reservations as to their moral perfection. (Perhaps, as Joseph Schacht notes, one had been seen playing backgammon or entering a public bath without a loin cloth. At least one medieval *qāḍī* is reported to have gone about in disguise through the streets at night to check on his witnesses' characters.)[34] The *qāḍī*'s anxiety in this regard was understandable, as well as unallayable: if he accepted the word of a false witness, his judgment based on it was legally valid, judicially irreversible, and morally on his head.[35] Where the normative and the actual are ontologically conjoined—*Ḥaqq* with a capital *Ḥa'*—and oral testimony (or the record of oral testimony) is virtually the sole way in which what transpires in the world—*ḥaqq* with a small one—is represented juridically, perjury has a peculiar fatality. Indeed, it is not even a crime, punishable by human sanction, in Islamic law. Like violating the fast, not praying, or giving partners to God, it is a sacrilege, punishable by damnation.[36]

This specific institution of a community of official truth-tellers is rare to nonexistent now, even in *šarīᶜa* courts; and, of course much of legal life in the Islamic world has long since been administered by civil tribunals pre-

---

[32]Wakin, *Function of Documents in Islamic Law,* p. 7.
[33]On Baghdad, see Mez, *Renaissance of Islam,* p. 229. This was an unusually high figure. A few years later the number was cut to a more practical 303, which was still felt by the jurists to be a bit too high. On secondary witnesses, Wakin, *Function of Documents in Islamic Law,* pp. 66 ff. Schacht, *Islamic Law,* p. 194, notes two witnesses must testify to validate each primary witness. *Šahada ᶜalā šahada* is singular and refers technically in law to the act of "witnessing" rather than to "witnesses," and so should perhaps more properly be translated as "witnessing as to witnessing." See footnote 29.
[34]Schacht, *Islamic Law,* p. 193. On the incognito *qāḍī,* Mez, *Renaissance of Islam,* p. 228.
[35]Schacht, *Islamic Law,* pp. 122, 189.
[36]Ibid, p. 187. As with a number of other points in the text, the matter is not entirely consensual among legal commentators, but nearly so.

sided over by more or less secular magistrates applying more or less positive law according to more or less "modern" procedures, leaving hardly more than family and inheritance issues to the care of the *qāḍī*.[37] But in the same way that the whole mass of what, in our ignorance, we used to do and now, in our enlightenment, do only somewhat differently—the near-vanished distinction between equity and common law, the transmogrified one between presentment and trial, or the culturally sublimated institutions of ordeal, battle, compurgation, and form-of-action pleading—haunts our sense of due process, so the notion of a certified virtuous witness speaking moral truth to a rulebook jurist haunts the legal conscience of the Muslim, however desanctified that conscience may become. More exactly, the increasing sensitivity to the problematics of evidence that for us led to juries has, for Muslims, led to notaries.

Such notaries, again called *šuhūd ᶜudūl*, "just" or "upright" witnesses, but now appointed as full-time professional officers of the court at least somewhat trained in at least the practical forms of the law, have become in more recent times as central to the functioning of the *qāḍī* court as the *qāḍī* himself.[38] Indeed, as they mediate the process by which social disputes are given judiciable representation, are brought to the point where settled rules can, rather mechanically in most cases, decide them, they are perhaps even more central. In no mere metaphorical sense, notaries make evidence, or anyway legal evidence, and thus, in line with what I have been saying about the normative status of fact, and so of witnessing, they make the better part of judgment as well. Reality as a structure of divine imperatives—God's will *Ḥaqq*—may be in the *qāḍī*'s hands. But reality as a flow of moral occurrence—in-you, on-you, and at-you *ḥaqq*—is to a significant extent in theirs.

But not only theirs. Notaries proper, those attached to *qāḍī* courts, are but the type case of an approach to judicial inquiry now expanded like a vast intelligence net to virtually all realms of legal concern. Like the

[37]On the contemporary functioning of *sarīᶜa* courts, see Coulson, "Islamic Law."
[38]The terms usually gets shortened to *šuhūd* (sg. *sahīd;* see footnote 29) in the central Islamic regions, to *ᶜudūl* (sg. *ᶜadl*) in the Western and Eastern margins; Wakin, *Function of Documents in Islamic Law,* p. 7. As he functions not just to record what people say but to add to what people say the aura of his own character, *ᶜadl* should perhaps not be translated as "notary" (or even less, with its civil law overtones, *"notaire"*); but the rendering is standard and I have nothing better to offer, save the literal, but in its own way not quite right in English "reliable witness." On Islamic notaries (and the "reliable witness" usage) in general, see E. Tyan, *Le Notariat et le Preuve par Ecrit dans le Pratique du Droit Musulman* (Beirut, 1945). Again, I am indebted to Lawrence Rosen for much of what I know about the role of the *ᶜadl* in Morocco.

šarī͡a itself, the jurisdiction of notaries is now largely confined to matters of marriage and inheritance in most parts of the Islamic world, their power to turn complaints into evidence mainly exercised with respect to marital contracts, divorce agreements, succession claims, and deeds.[39] Beside them, there is now a host of similar official or quasi-official normative witnesses: people whose testimony, if not precisely incapable of being doubted—these are, after all, fallen times—carries, like that of the classical šahīd and unlike that of the ordinary litigant or defendant, the specific weight of their religious and moral stature.

Secular courts are quite literally surrounded by such certified truth-bringers—the general Arabic term for them usually being ͡arīf, from "to know," "be aware of," "recognize," "discover"; the usual English (and French) translation being "expert" *(expert)*. In Morocco, for example, there is the amīn (from the root for "faithful," "reliable," "trustworthy") in each craft or commercial trade, and in some professions as well, who is the fact-authority for disputes concerning it; there is the *jāri,* who is the same for irrigation matters; and there is the *muqqadem* for neighborhood quarrels. In each case, the disputants bring their problem to him first, and if they do not accept his mediation—the usual outcome—he serves as the main witness, most of the time the only one to whom the judge extends much credibility, in court. There is the *mezwār,* who acts in the same manner for particular religious status-groups; the *ṭāleb,* "student of religion," or the šurfa, "descendant of the Prophet," who may be called upon in a wide range of moral matters; and there is the rural holy man, *siyyid* or *murābit,* who serves in a similar capacity for country people. And, most important of all, there is a set of full-time investigator-reporters, called kebīr (from "to know by experience," "to be acquainted with"—the word for "news" in Arabic is kbar), some of them "expert" in agricultural matters, some in construction ones, some (women) in finding out who has made whom pregnant or who is sexually depriving or abusing whom, sent out in virtually every genuinely disputable case by the judges of the secular courts to visit the scene, interview those involved, and report back what the facts—never mind what the litigants say—"really are."

It is not possible to go into the operation of these institutions here, nor

---

[39]The šarī͡a, and with it presumably the notaries, has rather wider scope still in some of the more traditional Middle Eastern regimes, such as Saudi Arabia. Also, the recent so-called Islamic Revival seems to have led to at least a formal rewidening of its scope in Lybia, Iran, Pakistan, and so on.

into the problems this expansion of normative witnessing has brought with it—though, in my opinion, a just understanding of such matters is the key to a realistic comprehension of legal sensibilities in at least a great part of the contemporary Muslim world, where the "fact explosion" and the anxieties it induces that I spoke of earlier are hardly unknown. The essential point is that the energies that, in the Western tradition, have gone into distinguishing law from fact and into developing procedures to keep them from contaminating one another have, in the Islamic, gone into connecting them, and into developing procedures to deepen the connection. Normative witnessing is critical to the administration of justice in the Muslim world because it represents, so far as it can, the here-we-are-and-there-we-are of particular circumstance, *haqq* with a small *ha',* in the settled terms of general truth, *Haqq* with a big one.

When we turn to Indic law and to its animating idea, *dharma,* the problems inherent in trying to sum a sensibility in a lexeme grow yet more awkward.[40] For all its adaptation to local circumstance, its unevenness of impact, and its internal differentiation into schools and traditions, classical Islamic law has been, on balance, a homogenizing force, creating a legal *oikumenē* such that, in the fourteenth century for example, Ibn Battuta, himself a judge, could travel, *qāḍī* to *qāḍī,* from Morocco to Malaya and back without ever feeling himself in genuinely alien surroundings. Climate differed, and race, and with them custom; but the *šarīᶜa* was the *šarīᶜa,* in Samarkand as in Timbuktu, at least in the homes of legists.

But Indic law did not spread that way. It singularized what it encountered in the very act of universalizing it. Its realm was granular, segmented into a horde of hyper-particular, hyper-concrete manifestations of a hyper-general, hyper-abstract form; a world of avatars. Not only was it split at its origins by the great Hinduism-Buddhism divide; but, a vast, disheveled collection of obsessively specific rules, the eighteen this and the thir-

---

[40]I should reiterate that the use of the term "Indic" ("Indicised") rather than "Indian" (Indianized), "Hindu" (Hinduised"), and so on is an attempt to finesse the whole, highly vexed question of the degree, type, depth, or whatever of "Indian-ness," "Indian impact" in Southeast Asia. For more on this, see Geertz, *Negara,* p. 138. Cf. Derrett's "anything that is not a duck, a goose, or a turkey is a chicken" view of "Hinduism": "For the purposes of the application of the *codified* parts of personal law a Hindu [in India] is one who is not a Muslim, Parsi, Christian or Jew." J. D. M. Derrett, *Religion, Law and the State in India* (New York, 1968), p. 44 (italics original).

ty-four that, it was held together not by a single canonical scripture, copied
direct from the explicit speech of God, but by a set of maddeningly global
conceptions drawn from a Borgesian library of irregular texts of diverse
purpose, differing provenance, and unequal authority.[41] In every locality,
in almost every social group in every locality, it developed a distinct and
definite variant, joined to its cognates by only the most cousinish of family
resemblances. As with Divinity (or for that matter, Humanity, Beauty,
Power, or Love), in the Indic world Law was one but its expressions many.

As it diffused, fitfully and unevenly, first across India, then to Ceylon,
Burma, Siam, Cambodia, Sumatra, Java, and Bali, Indic high culture, and,
as an unseparated part of it, Indic law, absorbed into itself a vast plurality
of local practices, symbols, beliefs, and institutions. Hindu in some places,
Buddhist in others, Hindu-Buddhist in yet others, it conquered not by
anathema, ruling out, but by consecration, ruling in; by, as J. D. M. Derrett
has put it, subordinating "an infinitely vast and cumbersome medley of rules
. . . to a comprehensive pattern of life and thought."[42] On the deci-
sion-forming level of as/therefore, it was everywhere a scattered catalogue
of particulate formulae, derived indifferently from text, custom, legend, and
decree, adapted to place and changing with need. On the coherence-making
if/then level, it was everywhere grounded in a highly distinctive, extraordinarily stable grand idea, derived ultimately from immediate revelation,
Vedic or Bo-tree: a cosmic doctrine of duty in which each sort of being in
the universe, human, transhuman, infrahuman alike, has, by virtue of its
sort, an ethic to fulfill and a nature to express—the two being the same
thing. "Snakes bite, demons deceive, gods give, sages control their senses
. . . thieves steal . . . warriors kill . . . priests sacrifice . . . sons obey mothers,"
Wendy O'Flaherty has written. "It is their *dharma* to do so."[43]

[41]For discussions of classical Indian law texts (or, more exactly, texts from which juridical
ideas are drawn) see, for Hinduism, R. Lingat, *The Classical Law of India,* trans. J. D. M.
Derrett (Berkeley and Los Angeles, 1973), pp. 7–9, 18–122; for Buddhism, R. F. Gombrich,
Precept and Practice: Traditional Buddhism in the Rural Highlands of Ceylon (Oxford, 1971),
pp. 40–45; for the derivative works of Southeast Asia, M. C. Hoadley and M. B. Hooker, *An
Introduction to Javanese Law: A Translation of and Commentary on the Agama* (Tucson,
1981), pp. 12–31, and M. B. Hooker, "Law Texts of Southeast Asia," *The Journal of Asian
Studies* 37(1978):201–19.
[42]Derrett, *Religion, Law and the State,* p. 118.
[43]W. D. O'Flaherty, *The Origins of Evil in Hindu Mythology* (Berkeley and Los Angeles, 1976).
The quotation is portmanteau from pp. 94, 95, 96, 98, 109. This is, of course, a Hindu formulation; Buddhist ones differ in important ways (for a discussion, see W. Rahula, *What the Buddha Taught,* rev. ed. [London, 1978]). In the text discussion I have sought, as best I can, to
state matters in such a way as to at least generally apply at once to Hindu India, the Theravada
countries of northern Southeast Asia, and the more mixed situation of the Indonesian archipel-

Rendering *dharma* (and its converse *adharma*) into English is an even more difficult enterprise than is rendering *ḥaqq*. For the problem here is less a splintering of meaning, the partitioning of a semantic domain into a host of unexpected parts, than imprecision of meaning, the expansion of such a domain to near infinite dimensions. The Sanskritist J. Gonda calls *dharma* "untranslatable," remarking that it is glossed in bilingual dictionaries "by ten or twelve lines of English terms or phrases: 'law, usage, customary observance, duty, morality, religious merit, good works, etc.,' and many other equivalents must be added if we will do justice to all aspects of the concept and its unexhaustible wealth." From the Buddhist-Pali side, where the word is *dhamma,* Richard Gombrich says it "can be and has been translated in a thousand ways: 'righteousness,' 'truth,' 'the Way,' etc. It is best not translated at all." For Walpola Rahula, himself a Buddhist monk, "there is no term in Buddhist terminology wider than *dhamma* . . . there is nothing in the universe or outside, good or bad, conditioned or non-conditioned, relative or absolute, which is not included in this term." Robert Lingat begins his great treatise *The Classical Law of India,* at base an extended mediation on the term, with the comment that "Dharma is a concept difficult to define because it disowns—or transcends—distinctions that seem essential to us." And Soewojo Wojowasito's dictionary of Old Javanese defines it as "law, right, task, obligation, merit, service, pious deed, duty," and follows with a page and a half of distensive compounds from *dharmadeśanā* "[the] science of good conduct," and *dharmabuddhi,* "just, fair, impartial [of mind]," to *dhammayuddha,* "a . . . war [fought] according to [an established] code," and *dharmottama,* "[the] code of justice most appropriate to each class of society."[44]

So far as law is concerned, it is these last notions that are the most critical.

ago, though a more deep going analysis could no more avoid probing the differences in legal view of the two major Indic traditions than a deep going one of Western tradition could ignore probing those between Catholic and Protestant Christianity. But, like the Western (and, for all its sectarian splits, the Islamic, where I have equally ignored Sunni/Shi'i differences), Indic civilization does possess a distinctive form and tonality that its law projects. "If you ask a Buddhist his religious beliefs he will assume you are talking of Dharma. But these beliefs operate in the context of other beliefs, of more basic assumptions. This is true both logically and historically: The Buddha grew up in a Hindu society and accepted many Hindu assumptions" (Gombrich, *Precept and Practice,* p. 68).

[44] J. Gonda, *Sanskrit in Indonesia,* 2nd ed. (New Delhi, 1973), pp. 537, 157; Gombrich, *Precept and Practice,* p. 60; Rahula, *What the Buddha Taught,* p. 58; Lingat, *Classical Law of India,* p. 3; S. Wojowasito, *A Kawi Lexicon,* ed. R. F. Mills (Ann Arbor, 1979), pp. 287–88. For an excellent brief discussion of the meaning of *dharma* and its relation to law in the Hindu tradition, see L. Rocher, "Hindu Conceptions of Law," *The Hastings Law Journal* 29 (1978): 1280–1305.

For what most distinguishes the Indic legal sensibility from others is that right and obligation are seen as relative to position in the social order, and position in the social order is transcendentally defined. What is just for the absolute goose is not for the absolute gander; for the priest for the warrior, the monk the layman, the householder the hermit, the once-born the twice, the inhabitant of fallen times the inhabitant of golden ones. Social category, whether ritually characterized as in caste Hinduism or ethically so as in merit Buddhism, represents a sorting of groups and individuals into natural classes according to the rules they naturally live by. Status is substance. If *ḥaqq* negotiates "is" and "ought" by construing law as a species of fact, *dharma* does so by construing fact as a species of law, which is very much not the same thing.

The differencing of justice according to social location is, of course, hardly unique to the Indic world. Classical Chinese and tribal African law, for example, binding right to kinship relation, are at least as thoroughgoing in this regard, and something of it, whether in the form of juvenile courts or "mother knows best" presumptions in custody cases, remains in every legal system. It is the *dharma* idea—that the codes which govern the behavior of the various sorts of men and women (as well as gods, demons, spirits, animals, or, for that matter, things) define what they primordially are—that sets the Indic case apart. What Ronald Inden and Ralph Nicholas have said for Bengal is, suitably nuanced, true everywhere that Indian assumptions have penetrated, and to the degree that they have:

All beings are organized into [kinds]. Each [kind] is defined by its particular [nature] and [behavioral] code which are thought to be inseparable from one another. As a consequence of this cultural premise . . . no distinction is made, as [it is] in American culture, between an order of "nature" and an order of "law." Similarly, no distinction is made between a "material" or "secular" order and a "spiritual" or "sacred" order. Thus there is a single order of beings, an order that is in Western terms both natural and moral, both material and spiritual.[45]

And both legal and factual. Or as O'Flaherty puts it, summarizing the Indic conception of evil:

[45]R. B. Inden and R. W. Nicholas, *Kinship in Bengali Culture* (Chicago, 1977), p. xiv. I have omitted, without benefit of ellipses, Bengali vernacular terms and some passages that apply as such only to caste Hinduism. For similar formulations, see M. Davis, *Rank and Rivalry: The Politics of Inequality in Rural West Bengal* (Cambridge, England), and New York, forthcoming); M. Marriott and R. B. Inden, "Caste Systems," *Encyclopedia Brittanica,* 15th ed. 1974.

Dharma is the fact that there are rules that must be obeyed; it is the principle of order, regardless of what that order actually is. . . . [It] is both a normative and a descriptive term. . . . [Thus] the moral code *(dharma)* in India is nature, where in the West it usually consists of a conflict with nature. . . . The dharma of a [being] is both his characteristic as a type and his duty as an individual. . . . He may refuse his duty [and thus] deny his nature [the condition contemned as *adharma*], but Hindus regard this conflict as an unnatural one, one which must be resolved. . . .[46]

It must be resolved because, as the Code of Manu already says, somewhere just before or after the time of Christ, "destroyed *dharma* destroys, protected [it] protects."[47] The law is merely there, like the sun and cattle, both in its grand unbounded form as "what is firm and durable, what sustains and maintains, what hinders fainting and falling," and in its cabined, local form as particular duties embodied in particular rules incumbent on particular persons in particular situations according to their particular status.[48] What its guardians must do is guard it, so that it will guard them.

[46]O'Flaherty, *Origins of Evil,* pp. 94–95, again with emendations and interpollations to render the formulation more general. Both the Inden-Nicholas and O'Flaherty statements pertain, of course, to caste Hinduism, but once more, in this regard at least, the Buddhist view seems not all that different: "The [Buddhist] universe is full of living beings, in hierarchically ordered strata. Men are somewhere in the middle. . . . Above them are various classes of gods and spirits, below them are animals, ghosts, and demons. Above this world are heavens, below this world are hells. By and large, power, well-being and length of life increase as one goes up the scale. So do the power and inclination to do good. But at all levels there is death, the ineluctable reminder of the unsatisfactoriness of life. Death supplies the mobility between the different levels. Everywhere, constantly, are death and rebirth. One's station at birth is determined by *karma. Karma* is a Sanskrit word simply meaning "action," but it has acquired this technical sense. . . . All this is accepted by all kinds of Hindus and by Jains—by all the major Indian religious systems. However, Buddhism was the first system completely to ethicize the concept. For Buddhists *karma* consists solely of actions morally good or bad, not of other actions such as ritual." Gombrich, *Precept and Practice,* p. 68.
[47]*Manu,* VIII, 5, quoted in Lingat, *Classical Law of India,* p. 4, who dates the code ca. second century B.C. to second A.D. (ibid, p. 96).
[48]Ibid, p. 3, apparently from Manu. The unbounded sense of *dharma*—the word is etymologically related to Latin *firmus,* in the *terra firma* sense of "solid," "hard," "durable"—is as clearly expressed as it probably can be in the *Mahābhārata (Sāntip.* 109, 59; quoted in ibid, p. 3, n. 3): "Dharma is so called because it protects . . . everything; Dharma maintains everything that has been created. Dharma is thus that very principle which can maintain the universe." For the particular sense of the term *(svadharma),* see Davis, *Rank and Rivalry,* "Afterword": "*Dharma* refers to the natural and moral behavior appropriate to an individual or group of individuals and to society as a whole. [It] is defined in part by the . . . physical-cum-social community in which one lives, for each [such community] has a customary way of life that is in some ways different from all other[s]. . . . The *dharma* of [an individual] is also defined in part by the . . . time in which one lives, for every [community] has a history which is unique and dissimilar, and even in the same [community] what is deemed right and proper behavior has not been unvarying through time. And *dharma* [is also] defined in part by one's own qualities and . . . life stage, for the behavior appropriate to individuals differs

And chief among such guardians is, or anyway was until colonial rule half replaced him, not the jurist, who was a scholiast only, but the king. It is, to put the basic principle of Indic legality in an Indic nutshell, the *dharma* of the king to defend the *dharma.*

The critical place of the king, large, small, or medium sized (and some, it must be kept firmly in mind, could be very small indeed), in Indic adjudication is as characteristic of it as normative witnessing is of Islamic, and as fateful. For it was he, counseled by the appropriate savants, monks, or brahmins, who connected the coherence-making if/then paradigms of general *dharma* to the consequence-producing as/therefore determinations of concrete rule. A society without a king, *arājaka,* is a society without law, *adharma,* subject to "The Rule of the Fish." The ability of an individual to follow his natural code in a world teeming with natural codes and with temptations to evade them, depends on the protection of the king. As the *Mahābhārata* explicitly says, all dharmas rest on the royal *dharma*—"all have the *rāja-dharma* at their head."[49]

Despite its imperatorial accents, however—accents real enough not just in legal theory but, as we shall see, in the practical administration of decisionary justice—this is not an Austinian conception. For the law here is not a spelling out of the sovereign's commands; the sovereign's commands, when they are proper commands, are, like the acts of any other variety of person when they are proper acts, a spelling out of the law. The behavior of just kings is an illustration of law, as Lingat puts it; an embodiment of it, as David Wyatt does; a symbol of it as M. B. Hooker does; or an enactment of it, as David Engel does.[50] The problem, of course, is that kings may

according to their own nature and physical-cum-moral maturity. Place, time, qualities and life stage . . . are the four . . . constant[s] against which the *dharma* of any individual or group of individuals is defined. The specific behaviors which constitute [their] *dharma* are not similarly constant, for they differ across time and place, they differ among individuals living at the same time and in the same place, and they differ during the course of an individual's own life." For a perceptive discussion of the complex relations between general and personal *dharma,* see O'Flaherty, *Origins of Evil,* pp. 94 ff.

[49]Lingat, *Classical Law of India,* p. 208. Cf. Hoadley and Hooker, *Introduction to Javanese Law,* p. 14: "Particular *rules* of dharma obtain stability only through the proper exercise of the King's will and in this sense the *Rāja-dharma* has precedence over all other stated duties in the [classical law] world" (emphasis original). Cf. Rocher, "Hindu Conceptions of Law," p. 1294: "Those aspects of *dharma* in which Western civilization's category of law play a more prominent role are joined together around the central figure of the king." For *arājaka* and "The Rule of the Fish," Lingat, *Classical Law of India,* p. 207, and Derrett, *Religion, Law and the State,* p. 560.

[50]R. Lingat, "Evolution of the Conception of Law in Burma and Siam," *Journal of the Siam Society* 38(1980):9–31, quoted in R. A. O'Connor, "Law as Indigenous Social Theory," *American Ethnologist* 8(1980):223–37, D. K. Wyatt, *The Politics of Reform in Thailand* (New

not in fact be just, and perhaps but sporadically are. The issue that in the Islamic world is framed in terms of the reliability of witnesses—the conformance of as/therefore verdicts to if/then visions—is framed in the Indic in terms of the righteousness of kings. What lying, the denial of truth, symbolized in the one, self-interest, the unmindfulness of it, symbolizes in the other.

To keep the ruler mindful so that he will act to fulfill his own *dharma*, protect the dharmas of others, and thus maintain the whole within the cosmic balance that is *dharma* as such, is in turn the *dharma* of those who devote themselves not to the enforcement of law but to the knowing of it. The relation between the wielder of power, the punisher, and the master of learning, the purifier, is perhaps the most delicate and elusive in the whole of traditional Indic civilization—like that, as the Balinese put it, of a younger brother to an older, a student to a teacher, a ship to its helmsman, a dagger to its hilt, the instruments of an orchestra to the sound that it makes.[51] In the realm of practical adjudication it was, at every level from

Haven, 1969), p. 8, quoted in D. M. Engel, *Law and Kingship in Thailand During the Reign of King Chulalongkorn* (Ann Arbor, 1979), p. 3; M. B. Hooker, *A Concise Legal History of Southeast Asia* (Oxford, 1978), p. 31; Engel, *Law and Kingship*, p. 8.

The Wyatt passage indicates, again, the essential similarity in this regard of Buddhist and Hindu conceptions: "The Brahmanical concept of the *Devarāja*, the king as god, was modified to make the king the embodiment of the Law, while the reign of Buddhist moral principles ensured that he should be measured against the Law. The effect of this was to strengthen the checks which, in the Khmer [that is, Cambodian] empire, Brahmans had attempted to exercise against despotic excesses of absolute rule."

Remark should also be made of the other "differentiation" problem that arises here—that between India proper and the Indicised regions of Southeast Asia, between what the colonial Dutch, with useful ethnocentrism, referred to as *Voorindië* and *Achterindië*: The altered role of the king in Southeast Asia from what L. Dumont has called, for India, the "secularized type," (that is, one who "cannot be his own sacrificer [but] puts 'in front' of himself a priest . . . and *then* he loses the hierarchical preeminence in favor of the priests, retaining for himself power only" (*Homo Hierarchicus: An Essay on the Caste System,* trans. M. Swainsbury [Chicago, 1970], pp. 67–68; italics original), to the various sorts of "divine" or "semi-divine" or "exemplary" kingship types of Southeast Asia (see Engel, *Concise Legal History;* O'Connor, "Law as Indigenous Social Theory"; G. Coedés, *The Indianized States of Southeast Asia,* trans. S. B. Cowing, (Kuala Lumpur, 1958); and Geertz, *Negara,* pp. 121–36). In addition to the fact that this distinction may be a bit overdrawn in both directions, whatever its uses in inter-Indic comparisons, so far as comparisons between the Indic law world and others are concerned it fades to minor significance. The formulation of Coedés, "Indianization must be understood essentially as the expansion of an organized culture that was founded upon the Indian conception of royalty, was characterised by Hinduist or Buddhist cults, the mythology of the *Purānās,* and the observance of the *Dharmaśāstras,* and expressed itself in the Sanskrit language" (*Indianized States,* this note, pp. 15–16) seems overall the justest view of the matter, so long as the unevenness of the degree of "Indianization," thus defined, beyond India (and, indeed, within it as well) is kept firmly in mind.

[51]Geertz, *Negara,* pp. 37, 126, 240. There are similar images in classical Indian texts: the learned man is "he who conceives," the power-wielder "he who does"; the first is "intelli-

the state to the locality, altogether the heart of the matter. In the possibility of the clerics, in the Hindu case the Brahmin, in the Buddhist case the monk, in minor matters some lesser pundit, prevailing upon the king, prince, lord, or local official to rein his passions and selflessly follow the path of *dharma,* lay as well the possibility of attaining a settled justice of principle rather than an arbitrary one of will.[52]

There were many ways of trying, against the grain of sovereign arrogance, to accomplish this, to make, as Derrett puts it, "the *dharma* king over even kings": clerical praise in court poetry, clerical withdrawal from court ritual,

gence," the second "will"; the court priest is "the brain of the king," and so on (Lingat, *Classical Law of India,* pp. 216, 217. For general reviews of the learned man/ruler relationship in India, see Lingat, *Classical Law of India,* pp. 215–22; Dumont, *Homo Hierarchus,* pp. 71–79; L. Dumont, "The Conception of Kingship in Ancient India," in *Religion/Politics and History in India* (The Hague, 1970), pp. 62–81. For Southeast Asia, Geertz, *Negara,* pp. 36–37, 125–27.

The distinction between the application of punishment, *daṇḍa* (literally, "mace," "scepter"), considered as a part of the king's *dharma,* and the effectuation of purification through penance, *prāyaścitta* (literally, "prime thought," "thought about finding"), considered as part of the man of learning's *dharma,* as well as the relation between the two ("The [Brahmins] prescribe the penance: [the king] must see that it is carried out and punish the recalcitrant" [Lingat, *Classical Law of India,* p. 66]; Buddhist formulations differ mainly in the conception of what penance and purification amount to), is central to an understanding of the legal dimensions of this relationship. "It would be vain to look in Indian tradition on the relations between the two powers for an analogy with the Christian theory of the Two Swords. True, the Brahmin is master when the question is one of ritual and . . . of penance. But his scope extends in reality over all the field of royal activity, as much on its political side as on its religious. There are not two powers here each functioning in its proper sphere, the sacred to one side, and the profane to the other. Secular power alone has the capacity to act, but it is a blind force which needs to be directed before its application can be effectual. If the king were to disdain the advice of his Brahmins he would not only fail in his duty, but even incur the risk of governing badly" (ibid, pp. 214–218; see also, pp. 50, 61–67, 232–37). For Java, see Hoadley and Hooker, *Introduction to Javanese Law,* pp. 227–28.

[52]The doctrine of self-interest (*artha,* not in itself an illegitimate sentiment, but only when its attractions obscure one's sense of duty), is, like that of sensuality *(kama),* nearly as developed in classical Indian thought as *dharma,* and there are entire treatises *(arthaśāstra)* devoted to its cultivation. See Dumont, *Homo Hierarchicus,* pp. 165–66, 196, 251–52; Derrett, *Legal Systems,* pp. 96–97; Lingat, *Classical Law in India,* pp. 5–6, 145–48, 156–57, and in relation to the adjudicative function of the king, 251–54. For a discussion of the role of self-interest—there, *pamrih*—in Javanese political theory, see B. R. O'G. Anderson, "The Idea of Power in Javanese Culture," in *Culture and Politics in Indonesia,* ed. C. Holt (Ithaca, 1972), pp. 1–69: ". . . the correct attitude of the official should be to refrain from personal motives, while working hard for the good of the state. . . . The pamrih [of the power wielder] is really a threat to his own ultimate interests, since indulgence of personal and therefore partial, passions or prejudices means interior imbalance and a diffusion of personal concentration and power." For Thailand, see O'Connor, "Law as Indigenous Social Theory," pp. 233–34: "The modern Thai . . . accept unbridled self-interest but see it as morally inferior to the cosmic and royal laws, customs, and lawlike discipline . . . that join a person to the larger order of society"; and Engel, *Law and Kingship,* pp. 7–8. Cf. L. Hanks, "Merit and Power in the Thai Social Order," *American Anthropologist* 64(1962):1246–61.

clerical shaming of court morality.[53] But so far as the administration of law is concerned, two devices were clearly the most important: the codification of royal *dharma* and the inclusion of learned advisors on royal tribunals.

Codification of the royal duty to maintain the behavioral order of society by punishing those who disturb it is found already in classical India, where Manu devotes three full chapters out of twelve to the subject. But it became even more explicitly developed in Southeast Asia, where perhaps the best example (or possibly only the best described) was the Thai *Thammasat.* [54] Setting forth the history of the world and man, the evolution of laws, and the origin of kings, the *Thammasat* "defined the relationship between the individual and the state and prescribed the norms by which the ruler should be governed in his actions."[55] In twenty-seven, or in some rescensions thirty-nine, titles, it covered everything from palace law, ordeal, fines, witnesses, and "the division of people [into ranks]" to debt, inheritance, theft, quarrels, and treason.[56] It was, as Engel has said, "the fundamental statement of royal law and legitimacy in traditional Thailand," and it was designed, like its Burmese, Cambodian, and Javanese counterparts, to justify the adjudicatory role of the king by describing the status ethic by which he was bound:

According . . . to the *Thammasat* [a modern Thai scholar, himself a prince, has written], the ideal monarch abides steadfastly in the ten kingly virtues, constantly upholding the five common precepts. . . . He takes pain to study the *Thammasat* and keep the four principles of justice, namely: to assess the right or wrong of all service or disservice rendered unto him, to uphold the righteous and truthful, to acquire riches through none but just means, and to maintain the prosperity of his state through none but just means.[57]

[53]Derrett, *Legal Systems,* p. 99.
[54]On Manu: Rocher, "Hindu Conceptions of Law," p. 1294; Lingat, *Classical Law in India,* pp. 222–32. On the *Thammasat* (the Thai rendering of Sanskrit *Dharmasastra*): Engel, *Law and Kingship,* pp. 1–8; Hooker, *Legal History,* pp. 25–35; Lingat, *Classical Law in India,* pp. 269–279; Lingat, "Evolution "Of the Conception of Law"; O'Connor, "Law as Indigenous Social Theory."
[55]Engel, *Law and Kingship,* p. 3.
[56]Hooker, *Legal History,* pp. 26–27.
[57]Engel, *Law and Kingship,* p. 5; Prince Dhani Nivat, "The old Siamese Conception of the Monarchy," *Journal of the Siam Society* 36(1947):91–106. As royal decrees were incorporated into the *Thammasat,* it may be said to contain elements of "positive law," but they were well contained within the general *dharma* conception of the whole and were considered but expressions of it. On this, and in partial correction of Lingat's ("Evolution of the Conception of Law") view that decree incorporation represented a genuine departure from "natural law" conceptions in Southeast Asia, see O'Connor, "Law as Indigenous Social Theory," especially

But, in the mysterious East as in the pellucid West, constitutions, however detailed, are no better than the institutions they are written into. It was in the composition of tribunals that whatever juristic check on executive will actually occurred—less than one would hope, more than one might imagine—was secured.

The sorts of tribunals found throughout the Indic world before colonial regimes attempted, with mixed success, to standardize them were as diverse and multitudinous as the rules they sought to apply, the groups they sought to apply them to, and the justifications they sought to give for them. But the principle that men of learning did the justifying and men of power did the applying seems to have been pervasive. In India, there was a vast hierarchy of caste and inter-caste councils, "dominant caste" mini-rajas of the so-called "little kingdoms," and grand maha-rajas of the great regional dynasties, served as needed by assorted pundits. In Thailand, there was a tangle of thirty sorts of ministerial courts, as jurisdictionally ill defined as the ministries themselves, advised by a consultative ministry of legal affairs manned, in this supposedly Buddhist country, by a dozen Brahmins. In Indonesia, there were hundreds of large and little palace-yard tribunals composed of legal experts of varying kind and competence under the immediate eye of the resident lord. Everywhere, the procedural *grundnorm,* again stated in Indian texts as early as the fourth century, "one [is] condemned by the judges [and] punished by the king according to [dharma]," was the animating ideal of adjudicative process.[58]

pp. 225–27, who rightly doubts the usefulness of the whole natural/positive distinction in this context.

[58]The *Nārada-Smṛti,* in *The Minor Law Books: Narada and Brihaspati,* trans. J. Jolly (Oxford, 1889), p. 35; quoted in M. C. Hoadley, "Continuity and Change in Javanese Legal Tradition: The Evidence of the Jayapattra," *Indonesia* 11:95–109, at p. 97.

For India, where "next to nothing is known about actual legal practice in [ancient] times," as Rocher ("Hindu Conceptions of Law," p. 1302) says, useful materials for more recent times can be found in B. S. Cohn, "Some Notes on Law and Change in North India," *Economic Development and Cultural Change* 8(1959):79–93 and especially in his "Anthropological Notes on Disputes and Law in India," *American Anthropologist* 67(1965):82–122, as well as from the fascinating eighteenth-century letter by a French Jesuit, Jean Venant Boucher, from "Pondicherry to a great man in France," ("Father Bouchet's Letter on the Administration of Hindu Law," trans. L. Rocher, in press). The fourth-century south Indian Sanskrit melodrama, *The Toy Cart,* attributed to one King Shudraka, but more likely composed by a (clerical?) poet at his court (trans. P. Lal, in *Traditional Asian Plays,* ed. J. R. Brandon, [New York, 1972], pp. 14–114) contains a trial scene in which the tension between royal power and legal learning is particularly well evoked. (See especially the speech, at p. 96, of the "judge"—that is, the presiding "assessor" or "counselor"—which opens the trial.) For some text-based remarks on traditional Indian procedure, see Lingat, *Classical Law in India,* pp. 69–70, 254–56. For Thailand, Engel, *Law and Kingship,* pp. 60–63. For Indonesia, Hoadley, "Continuity and Change"; Hoadley and Hooker, *Introduction to Javanese Law,* pp. 26–28; F. H. van Naerssen, "De Saptopatti: Naar Aanleiding

Whatever the particular institutional shape of that process, whatever the cases considered appropriate for its regard (also a highly variable matter, as "Regreg vs. The Village Council" suggests), and whatever its general impact on social life (more variable yet; not all kings are mighty, and none are mighty everywhere), the central evidentiary questions to which it addressed itself pertained neither to the occasions of acts nor to their consequences, but to their type. That is, they were questions of *dharma* and *adharma* brought down to a judiciable level, a matter of determining where in the local version of the grand taxonomy of dutiful behaviors a particular behavior fell. Where the classical Islamic court, to put the point comparatively and doubtless overdraw it, sought to establish fact by sorting out moral character and was obsessed with testimony, the Indic one sought to establish it by sorting out moral kind and was obsessed with verdicts. "The essence of [traditional Indic] justice is not the fairness of its procedures in sifting through the evidence of particular wrongs," Engel has said (this for Thailand, but the matter is general), "but rather the aptness of final judgments as to the total value of an individual's existence."[59] The final judgments were the king's, depicted on the royal judicial seal as Yama, the god of death, astride a lion.[60] Whether they were apt depended on whether jurists could locate universal obligation in local rule and bring the king to heed it.

This distinctive mode of, if you will, skeletonizing cases so as to render them decidable, can be seen with particular clarity in traditional law tales of legendary judges, which, in the absence of records of actual trials, are about all we have to go on so far as the as/therefore style of classical adjudication is concerned. Two such tales from south India, related by the seventeenth-century Jesuit missionary, Jean Bouchet, and concerning an archetypal Brahman jurist called Mariyātai-rāman, are especially telling.[61]

van een Tekstverbettering in den Nāgarakrtāgama," *Bijdragen tot Taal-, Land- en Volkenkunde* 90(1933):239–58; Th. G. Th. Pigeaud, "Decree Jaya Song, About 1350 A.D." in his *Java in the Fourteenth Century: A Cultural History,* 4 vols. (The Hague, 1960–63), 4:391–98 (original text at 1:104–7; translation at 3:151–55); Geertz, *Negara,* pp. 241–244. For Burma or Cambodia, even less is known, or anyway available, concerning procedure: for what there is, see Maung Htin Aung, *Burmese Law Tales* (London, 1962); and S. Sahai, *Les Institutions politiques et l'organisation administrative du Cambodge ancien VI–XIII siècles* (Paris, 1970).
[59]David Engel, *Code and Custom in a Thai Provincial Court* (Tucson, 1978), p. 5.
[60]Ibid, p. 4. "Yama has always been associated [in classical Hindu-Buddhist cosmology] with justice. Indeed, *thamma (dharma)* is said to be another name for the god of death: he personifies the concept of justice itself.
[61]Bouchet, "Letter on the Administration." The stories also appear, in slightly different version in P. Ramachandra Rao, *Tales of Mariada Raman, 21 Amusing Stories* (London [?], 1902), pp. 5–10, 43–47; cited (by Rocher), in ibid.

The first tale, which Bouchet says "has something in common with Solomon's judgment," but is in actuality almost inversely conceived, concerns two wives of a rich, polygamous man. The first, an ugly woman, had a son by the husband; the second was barren, but because of her great beauty was esteemed by the husband while the first was disdained. Wild with jealousy, the first wife plotted revenge. She went about persuading everyone by her acts and speech how exceedingly fond she was of her son, how he meant everything to her, and how envious the barren wife, for all her beauty, was of her. She then strangled the child and put the corpse by the bed of her sleeping rival. Next morning, pretending to look for her son, she ran to the second wife's room, "discovered" his body, and ran crying to the multitude, "O this wretched woman! Look what she has done out of wrath because I have a son and she does not." The crowd, aroused, turned on the second wife: "It is just not possible a woman would kill her own son," and especially one she so obviously adored.

Mariyātai-rāman was called and listened, questionless, to the two women and decreed, "the one who is innocent . . . shall walk around this assembly hall in the condition I shall prescribe," the condition being a grossly indecent one. The guilty wife agreed—"I shall do it a hundred times if necessary"; the innocent one refused—"I shall never [do it], I shall rather die a hundred times than consent to doing things . . . unworthy of a woman." Mariyātai-rāman declared the second wife innocent, the first guilty, on the grounds that a woman so conscious of her *dharma* as to subject herself to certain death rather than contravene it obviously could not have committed so adharmic an act as to murder a child, whereas one so indifferent to *dharma* obviously could have, even her own.

The second story, more fabulous in content (at least from our point of view), brings the ontological aspects of *dharma,* its engrainment in the warp of reality, more vividly forward. A man, known for his great strength, abandoned his wife in a fit of rage. A god then took his form and moved in with the wife. In a few months the real husband, his anger cooled, returned, and the case presented to Mariyātai-rāman (whom the king called in when his own jurists found themselves stymied) was to decide who was who. Mindful of the real husband's great strength, he commanded each man to lift an enormous stone. The real husband heaved and hauled and lifted it but a few inches. The false one lifted it over his head as though it were a feather, and the crowd cried out, "There is no doubt, this one is the real husband." The judge, however, decided in favor of the first, saying that he had done what was possible to humans, even those with extraordinary strength, while what the second had done only a god could do.

Again, however, not only deceiving gods and clerical judges but absolute kings—"all the golden grasshoppers and bees"—are, of course, gone, at least from the institutions of legal life if not entirely from its imagination. In India, one has first the odd amalgam of Western procedure and Hindu custom called Anglo-Indian law and then the somewhat desperate, half-reformist, half-restorative experimentation in codification of the Independence period. In Thailand, a throne-led reform movement (the seal was changed from a death-god king riding a lion to the Roman scales of justice enveloped in royal regalia) was completed by a parliamentary revolution. In Indonesia, the imposition by the Dutch of a racially pluralized state court system was followed by its unification under the culturalist ideology of Sukarno's Republic. All this has altered matters in fundamental ways, an issue I shall return to at some length in the concluding part of this essay.[62]

Yet, as Derrett remarks of India, but could as well of Southeast Asia, the legal system was in the hands of native jurists for two millennia and has been in those of European and Western-trained Indians for two centuries. So not everything is changed utterly, and most especially not the forms of legal sensibility.[63] Secular, or somewhat so, law may have become; even causidical. Placeless it has not.

The obstacles that lie in the way of an accurate understanding of what, to those who regard themselves as bound by it, *adat* means are rather different, if no less formidable, than those that hinder our comprehension of *ḥaqq* and *dharma;* for the difficulties here are largely Western-made: lawyers' dust thrown in lawyers' eyes. Whatever European and American students of comparative law may have thought of the governing ideas of Islamic or Indic jurisprudence—that they were immoral, archaic, or

[62]The literature on modern Indian and Southeast Asian law is, of course, extensive if uneven. For India, see, J. D. M. Derrett, *Introduction to Modern Hindu Law* (Bombay, 1963), as well as his *Religion, Law and the State;* for Thailand, Engel, *Code and Custom* and *Law and Kingship;* for Indonesia, D. S. Lev, "Judicial Institutions and Legal Culture in Indonesia," in Holt, *Culture and Politics,* pp. 246–318. Material on Burma and Cambodia is harder to find, but see Hooker, *Legal History,* pp. 150–52 (Burma) and 166–68 (Cambodia). For a general review, see M. B. Hooker, *Legal Pluralism: an Introduction to Colonial and Neo-Colonial Laws* (Oxford, 1975).

[63]Derrett, *Legal Systems,* p. 83.

magically profound—they have always realized that those ideas, emerging as they do from developed traditions of literate thought, are difficult to grasp in terms of either civilian or common-law conceptions of what adjudication is all about. But *adat,* discovered lying about amid the common routines of village life, they have found assuringly recognizable, comfortably familiar. A potpourri of vernacular rules, apparently artless and mostly unwritten, it was "custom."

The mischief done by the word "custom" in anthropology, where it reduced thought to habit, is perhaps only exceeded by that which it has done in legal history, where it reduced thought to practice. And when, as in the study of *adat,* the two mischiefs have been combined, the result has been to generate a view of the workings of popular justice perhaps best characterized as conventionalistic: usage is all. As *adat* was "custom," it was, for the legist-ethnographers who gave their attention to it, by definition at best quasi-legal, a set of traditional rules traditionally applied to traditional problems. The question was whether it ought to be set aside in favor of reasoned law imported from outside or to be made into reasoned law by rendering it capable of system and certainty. From about the middle of the last century until nearly the middle of this, the struggle between Westernizing Western jurists and anti-Westernizing Western jurists—the first pressing for the uniform imposition of English, Dutch, or American codes on one or another part of Malaysia, the second for the establishment of separate spheres of native law constructed out of one or another variety of native custom—dominated scholarly debate concerning, not so much the nature of *adat* (which was taken as, in a broad way, understood) as its future. Whatever the virtues of these positions (and there is much to be said for both, and more to be said against either), the outcome, most particularly in the heartland Indies, where the debate was the most intense and the anti-Westernizers the most articulate, was to turn *adat* from a term standing for a form of legal sensibility, a particular way of thinking about if/thens and as/therefores, into, as *adat-recht,* "customary law," one standing for a sort of homespun *corpus juris* (or rather a whole set of them) needing either to be imperially discarded and juridically ignored or to be officially researched, recorded, sorted, and, backed by the power of the colonial state, administered.[64]

---

[64]The major figures in the *adatrecht* movement, centered for the most part in the University of Leiden, were Cornelis van Vollenhoven, usually considered its founder, though the general view much preceded him (see especially his *Het Adatrecht van Nederlandsche Indië,* 3 vols. [Leiden, 1918, 1931, 1933]) and B. ter Haar (see his *Adat Law in Indonesia,* trans. E. A. Hoebel and A. A. Schiller [New York, 1948]). For a series of area-organized adat law handbooks,

The *adatrecht* movement and its counterparts elsewhere in the chopped-up quarter continent (roughly southern Thailand to southern Philippines) where the term *adat*—as mentioned, Arabic in origin—is to be found produced some of the best legal ethnography, in the simple, fact-gathering sense of category fixing and rule describing, we have yet had; marvelously detailed studies of inheritance principles here, marriage restrictions there, land rights in the other place.[65] But with its assumption that law, or anyway "folk law," was custom, custom was usage, and usage was king—a collapsed circle of ought and is—it represented, that is, misrepresented, an indigenous sense of what justice is, social consonance, in terms of an imported one of what order is, a *Rechtsstaat.*[66] Since Independence, the *adatrecht* persuasion, opposed now to headlong modernizers with very much the bit in their teeth, has continued with diminished vigor and waning influence, and there has been a turn toward less exterior views, but, nationalism being what nationalism is, accompanied by a certain idealization, the romantic apologetics of the culturally defensive.[67] Though coming more

of a generally civil law sort, produced by "The Commission for Adat Law," under the general stimulus, not to say domination, of the Leiden School, see *Adatrecht Bundels* (The Hague, 1910–55). The Westernizing opposition was more diffuse (and less academic) but I. A. Nederburgh, *Wet en Adat* (Batavia, 1896–98), provides a representative example. For a general review, see M. B. Hooker, *Adat Law in Modern Indonesia,* (Kuala Lumpur, 1978). For an anthropological critique, from within the Leiden ambiance, of the *adatrecht* idea, see J. P. B. de Josselin de Jong, "Customary Law, A Confusing Fiction," Koninklijke Vereeniging Indisch Instituut Mededeling, 80, Afd. Volkenkunde, no. 20, Amsterdam (1948).

[65]Among the more notable examples, G. D. Willinck, *Het Rechtsleven der Minangkabau Maleirs* (Leiden, 1909); J. C. Vergouwen, *The Social Organization and Customary Law of the Toba Batak of North Sumatra,* trans. Scott-Kemball (The Hague, 1964); R. Soepomo, *Het Adatprivaatrecht van West-Java* (Batavia, 1933); M. M. Djojodigoeno and R. Tirtawinata, *Het Adatprivaatrecht van Middel-Java* (Batavia, 1940); V. E. Korn, *Het Adatrecht van Bali,* 2nd ed. (The Hague, 1932).

Though *adat* is Arabic derived (*ᶜada),* and is indeed normally translated "wont," "custom," "usage," "practice," the root from which it derives, *ᶜ-w-d,* has the force of "return," "come back," "recur," "revert," "reiterate" (*ᶜaud* means "again"), which actually catches the Indonesian sense more closely. The commonest word for custom in the central Islamic lands is, in any case, not *ᶜāda* but *ᶜurf,* from the root, *ᶜ-r-f,* meaning "to know," "to be aware of," "to recognize," "to be acquainted with."

[66]ter Haar, *Adat Law,* developed, in his notion of *beslissingsrecht* (roughly, "judge made" or "precedential" law) a slightly common-lawish version of adat law theory (he even hoped for law reports and case citations), as opposed to van Vollenhoven's more orthodox handbook approach, though the departure from civilian rule-and-sanction, "administrationalist" ideas was never very great. For the continuation of the *Rechtsstaat* conception, under the "Negara Hukum" rubric, in independent Indonesia, see Lev, "Judicial Institutions," p. 258.

[67]For the best, most reflective, and most sustained of the postwar discussions, only somewhat marred by a rather utopian view of village life, the nostalgia, perhaps, of the urban intellectual for an "organic" society that never was, see Moh. Koesnoe, *Introduction Into Indonesian Adat Law* (Nijmegen, 1971); idem, *Report Concerning a Research of Adat Law on the Islands of Bali and Lombok, 1971–73* (Nijmegen, 1977); idem, *Opstellen over Hedendaagse Adat, Adat-*

clearly into view, the realization that *adat* is not custom but outlook, *volksgedachte* not *volksgebruik,* is not quite here.[68]

Adat, writes one of the best of the more recent commentators, Mohamed Koesnoe, with a diffuseness wholly appropriate to the subject, "is the form of life of the Indonesian people as founded in their sense of propriety"—and the key word is "propriety."[69] For the whole effort of *adat* adjudication (and, despite some claims to the contrary, it is adjudication) is to translate a definitional conception of justice as spiritual harmony, a sort of universal calm, into a decisionary one of it as consensual procedure, publicly exhibited social agreement. Judgment, here, as we saw with Regreg, is less a question of sorting claims than of normalizing conduct.

At the definitional level, the vision of a just order of things as being one in which a quiet hum of agreement prevails in the outer realms of life and a fixed tranquility of mind in the inner finds a whole range of behavioral, institutional, and imaginative expressions. A cloud of negligent near-synonyms—*patut* ("proper"), *pantas* ("suitable"), *layak* ("seemly"), *cocok* ("fitting"), *biasa* ("normal"), *laras* ("harmonious"), *tepat* ("apt"), *halus* ("smooth"), *luwes* ("supple"), *enak* ("pleasant"), each running off along semantic gradients of their own to provide the discriminant overtones (*laras* is a musical term; *enak* is a gustatory one)—envelops the discourse

---

recht, en Rechts Ontwikkeling van Indonesië (Nijmegen, 1977); idem, *Musjawarah, Een Wijze van Volksbesluitvorming Volgens Adatrecht* (Nijmegen, 1969). For other valuable discussions, also not without a certain tendency toward idealization of "the Eastern Way" and a certain amount of reactive ethnocentrism, see M. M. Djojodigoeno, *Wat is Recht? Over de Aard van het Recht als Sociaal Proces van Normeringen* (Nijmegen, 1969), where the sociological foundations of "normmaking" are clearly recognized; R. Soepomo, *Kedudukan Adat Dikumudian Hari* (Plakata, 1947), where the future of adat law in a would-be modern state is reflectively considered. The concentration of postwar adat law studies at Nijmegen (see also, M. A. Jaspan, *The Redjang Village Tribunal* [Nijmegen, 1968]; G. van den Steenhoven, *The Land of Karenda* [Nijmegan, 1969]; H. W. J. Sonius, *Over Mr. Cornelis van Vollenhoven en het Adatrecht van Nederlands-Indië* [Nijmegen, 1976]) has nothing to do with Christian evangelism (though it may with resistance to Islamic hegemony) but is the result of the move of interest there from Leiden, apparently under the stimulus of van den Steenhoven.

[68]Except, again, for von Benda-Beckmann, *Property in Social Continuity:* "*Adat* is the symbolic universe by which the people of the Indonesian archipelago have constructed their world . . . *adat* does not mean custom. . . ." pp. 113, 114. In his glossary the word is "defined" as "tradition, custom, law, morality, political system, legal system," which, except for the omission of "etiquette" and "ritual," is about the size of it. My dependence on this work (and on Koesnoe; see footnote 66) in the formulations that follow is great, though those formulations are, of course, my own. For a general view of "customary law" similar to mine, there applied to East Africa, see Fallers, *Law Without Precedent.*

[69]". . . 'Adat' adalah tatanan hidup rakjat Indonesia jang bersumber pada rasa susilanja." Koesnoe, *Indonesian Adat Law,* p.A9. (I have altered the English translation—ibid, p. A8—because it seems to me a bit loose and introduces notions like "ethics" I think rather too academic to catch colloquial meanings.)

of everyday life in a softening moral haze.[70] An enormous inventory of highly specific and often quite intricate institutions for effecting cooperation in work, politics, and personal relationships alike, vaguely gathered under culturally charged and fairly well indefinable value-images—*rukun* ("mutual adjustment"), *gotong royong* ("joint bearing of burdens"), *tolong-menolong* ("reciprocal assistance")—governs social interaction with a force as sovereign as it is subdued.[71] And popular ritual life everywhere in the region is studded with prosy symbols of the deep interfusion of things: rice marriages, village cleansings, communal meals.[72] "Ought," here, the if/then vision of general coherence, is neither the universal execution of absolute command nor the punctilious performance of cosmic duty; it is the noiseless perfection of communal accord.

Such an ideal state of affairs is, of course, no more expected to obtain in fact than are others elsewhere; man is born to trouble, and to ill-use, as the sparks fly upward. The practical task of at least moving toward social harmony and individual composure rather than away from them toward dissonance and vertigo is what *adat* as judgment, the disposition of issues, is all about. It is the mechanisms of decisionmaking, procedure in the most procedural sense, that occupy the center of attention, rather than techniques for determining what actually happened or methods for containing magistral will. As Regreg's case, untypical only in the severity of its outcome (and not entirely even in that), shows, *adat* adjudication is a matter of what one can only call high etiquette, of patient, precise, and unexcited going through the elaborate forms of local consensus making. What matters finally is that unanimity of mind is demonstrated, not so much in the verdict itself, which is mere dénouement, the afterclap of accord, but in the public processes by which it has been generated. Propriety to be preserved must be seen being preserved.

The processes involved are mainly discussion processes, the propriety

[70]Such terms vary from place to place in "Malaysia." The above are rather Javanistic. For an interesting discussion of some of them, see Koesnoe, "Over de Operationele Beginselen voor het Oplossen van Adatrechtsgeschillen," in his *Opstellen,* pp. 39–80.

[71]The mistaking of such generalized normative ideas for specific institutions rather than moral covering notions for such institutions has sometimes led to rather scholastic efforts to distinguish among them in terms of some theory of "*adat* law principles," and thus to fix their meaning. For sociologically more realistic discussions, see R. R. Jay, *Javanese Villagers: Social Relations in Rural Modjokuto* (Cambridge, Mass. 1969); and R. M. Koentjaraningrat, "Some Social-Anthropological Observations on Gotong Rojong Practices in Two Villages of Central Java," (Ithaca, 1961).

[72]The literature on such matters is, of course, vast. For a particular example, see my *The Religion of Java* (Glencoe, Ill., 1960), part 1., pp. 11–118.

mainly discoursive propriety. Unanimity, or at least the appearance of it, is to be gained by talking everything through, in hard cases over and over again and in a grand variety of contexts, in a set and settled manner. Law here is truly the sententious science—a flow of admonitory proverbs, moral slogans, stereotyped Polonious speeches, recitations from one or another sort of didactic literature, and fixed metaphors of vice and virtue, all delivered in a manner designed at once to soothe and persuade. A passage from a long, thirty-five-hundred line, West Sumatran (that is, Minangkabau) poem, in which a mother instructs her son on how to behave when he is admitted, after his forthcoming marriage, to the various local councils in which *adat* decisions are taken, gives, its particular cultural accents notwithstanding, a fair sample of the manner:

> . . . O my dear son
> if you are sent for by the council, you must answer;
> if invited you must come.
> If it happens you are sent for,
> invited to attend a council feast,
> eat sufficiently before going,
> and drink something too;
> for at a feast or banquet
> eating and drinking have a strict form,
> sitting and standing have their place.
> There you must use all your politeness,
> never forgetting where you are.
> Be polite in everything
> and remember all the rules,
> even in passing betel or cigarettes.
>
> Then when it comes to the speeches,
> always be careful what you say:
> sweet speech is a quality of goodness.
> Always speak truthfully
> observing all the forms of politeness,
> taking care to understand people's feelings.
> When you speak, speak humbly,
> always deprecating yourself.
> Be sure you behave correctly
> and control all your passions.
> A council member should live by his principles,
> his speech should be of the *adat*
> following the line of the right path
> —calm as a waveless sea,

> settled as a plain without wind,
> his knowledge firm in his heart,
> ever mindful of his elders' counsel.[73]

The settings in which this sort of process takes place are multiple, ranging, as they did in Regreg's case, from household encounters to village conclaves, and the end toward which they reach, publically demonstrated unanimity of view, a right meeting of right minds, has as many names as there are settings.[74] Nor is it unconnected (as is also evident from Regreg's case) with images of natural and spiritual disaster if its requirements are neglected or its conclusions ignored. But the heart of the matter is a conception of truth finding—truth at once of circumstance and of principle—as a rhetorical enterprise, a bringing together of views through the suasive use of sanctioned words; the phrases, idioms, and tropes of . . . well, of *adat*. Or as another Minangkabau formula, a sort of proverb poem, succinctly puts it:

> Water circulates in bamboo pipes;
> Consensus circulates in accordant discussions.
> Water flows through bamboo;
> Truth flows through man.[75]

[73]A. H. Johns, ed. and trans., *Rantjak Dilabueh: A Minangkabau Kaba, A Specimen of the Traditional Literature of Central Sumatra* (Ithaca, 1958), pp. 113–16. I have altered Johns's translation somewhat in order to avoid having to explain ethnographic details or to describe the place of the passage in the overall narrative. On the central role of proverbs, maxims, and other sorts of "set sayings," "formalized speeches," and so forth—that is, of rhetoric—in *adat* adjudication, see (again, for the Minangkabau, but the phenomenon is general) von Benda-Beckmann, *Property in Social Continuity,* pp. 114–15, 132–33.

[74]The most prominent in independent Indonesia is the Arabic borrowed *musjawarah,* "communal discussion," "collective deliberation," (see Koesnoe, *Musjawarah*), but it is rather abstract and ideologized, and words such as *mupakat* (also Arabic-borrowed, but more deeply assimilated), "agreement," "consensus"; *setuju,* "of one direction"; *setahu,* "of one mind"; *bulat,* "unanimous," "perfect"; *rukun,* "peaceful accommodation," and a large number of local vernacular terms (see, for example, ibid, pp. 9–15, on Sasak *begundum,* "thorough discussion"; von Benda-Beckmann, *Property in Social Continuity,* p. 193, on Minangkabau, *seizin,* "consent") are, in one place or another, more current.

[75]von Benda-Beckmann, *Property in Social Continuity,* p. 115; original quoted from M. Nasroen, *Dasar Filsafah Adat Minangkabau* (Jakarta, 1957), p. 56. Again, I have altered the translation, here in the interests of a (somewhat) more natural idiom in English. The poem depends on a pun on *bulek,* "round," which means "circulate," in the sense of "go around," "be distributed," when applied to water *(bulek aie),* and "unanimous agreement," when applied to discourse *(bulek kato; kato—* "word[s]"). Von Benda-Beckmann's translation is: "The water gets around in the bamboo-pipe/The words (decision) get round through the *mupakat* (the unanimous decision)/The water is led through the bamboo/truth is revealed (bridged) by man." The original is: *Bulek aie dek pambuluah/ Bulek kato dek mupakat/Aie batitisan batuang/ Bana batitisan urang."* As *urang,* like Austronesian nouns generally, is unmarked for number or gender, it could as well be rendered "men" or "human being(s)."

Again, what the future of such a mode of skeletonizing cases by forming them within a ceremonialized vocabulary of collective discourse and resolving them by drowning them in unisonant voice will be in a world with a different sense of forensic style is a large question. Centered so firmly in the mechanics of procedure, the *adat* sort of legal sensibility is perhaps even more vulnerable to external disruption than either the *ḥaqq* or the *dharma,* where at least partial accommodations between local substance and foreign machinery are somewhat easier to effect. But for the meantime, anchored in local social organization, watched over by local guardians, adapted to local circumstances, and cast in local symbols, it maintains itself about as well as they. And like many other things supposed to go away—mullahs, caste, and the Emperor of Japan—now that modernity has at last arrived, it has, somehow, an odd tenacity.

So much, then, for distant ideas. Not that there isn't more to be said about them; there is virtually everything. But my intent has not been, as I mentioned earlier, to compress Islamic, Indic, and Malaysian notions about the interconnections of norms and happenings into some handbook for *ex patria* litigants but to demonstrate that they *are* notions. The main approaches to comparative law—that which sees its task as one of contrasting rule structures one to the next and that which sees it as one of contrasting different processes of dispute resolution in different societies—both seem to me rather to miss this point: the first through an overautonomous view of law as a separate and self-contained "legal system" struggling to defend its analytic integrity in the face of the conceptual and moral sloppiness of ordinary life; the second through an overpolitical view of it as an undifferentiated, pragmatically ordered collection of social devices for advancing interests and managing power conflicts.[76] Whether the adjudicative styles that gather around the *Anschauungen* projected by *ḥaqq, dharma,* and *adat* are properly to be called "law" or not (the rule buffs will find them too informal, the dispute buffs too abstract) is of minor importance; though I, myself,

[76]For an excellent critical discussion of these two, as they call them, paradigms, which ends however by adopting a too little modified version of the second, see J. L. Comoroff and S. Roberts, *Rules and Processes: The Cultural Logic of Dispute in an African Context* (Chicago, 1981), pp. 5–21. For an example of the "rule centered" paradigm, see L. Pospisil, *Kapauku Papuans and their Laws* (New Haven, 1958); for one of the "process centered," see Malinowski, *Crime and Custom in a Savage Society.*

would want to do so. What matters is that their imaginative power not be obscured. They do not just regulate behavior, they construe it.

It is this imaginative, or constructive, or interpretive power, a power rooted in the collective resources of culture rather than in the separate capacities of individuals (which I would think in such matters to be, intrinsically anyway, about the same everywhere; I rather doubt there is a legal gene), upon which the comparative study of law, or justice, or forensics, or adjudication should, in my view, train its attention. It is there—in the method and manner of conceiving decision situations so that settled rules can be applied to decide them (as well, of course, of conceiving the rules), in what I have been calling legal sensibility—that the informing contrasts lie. And it is there, too, that the passion of the anthropologist to set local views in local contexts and that of the jurist to set instant cases in determinate frames can meet and reinforce each other. I will try in my conclusion to this essay, in connection with the general question of legal imminglement (I can think of no exacter a word) in the modern world, not so much to demonstrate that this is so but to see what comes of assuming that it is.

III

Law, I have been saying, somewhat against the pretensions encoded in woolsack rhetoric, is local knowledge; local not just as to place, time, class, and variety of issue, but as to accent—vernacular characterizations of what happens connected to vernacular imaginings of what can. It is this complex of characterizations and imaginings, stories about events cast in imagery about principles, that I have been calling a legal sensibility. This is doubtless more than a little vague, but as Wittgenstein, the patron saint of what is going on here, remarked, a veridical picture of an indistinct object is not after all a clear one but an indistinct one. Better to paint the sea like Turner than attempt to make of it a Constable cow.

Elusive or not, such a view has a number of much less shadowy implications. One is that the comparative study of law cannot be a matter of reducing concrete differences to abstract commonalities. Another is that it cannot be a matter of locating identical phenomena masquerading under different names. And a third is that whatever conclusions it comes to must relate to the management of difference not to the abolition of it. Whatever the ultimate future holds—the universal reign of *gulag* justice or the final triumph of the market-mind—the proximate will be one not of a rising curve of legal uniformity, either across traditions or (something I have, so far, had rather to neglect here) within them, but their further particularization. The legal universe is not collapsing to a ball but expanding to a manifold; and we are headed rather more toward the convulsions of alpha than the resolutions of omega.

This view that things look more like flying apart than they do like coming together (one I would apply to the direction of social change generally these days, not just to law), opposes, of course, some of the leading doctrines in contemporary social science: that the world is growing more drearily modern—McDonald's on the Champs Elysées, punk rock in China; that there is an intrinsic evolution from *Gemeinschaft* to *Gesellschaft*, traditionalism to rationalism, mechanical solidarity to organic solidarity, status to contract; that post capitalist infrastructure in the form of multinational corporations and computer technology will soon shape the minds of Tongans and Yemenis to a common pattern. But it opposes as well, or at least raises doubts about, a leading view concerning the social potency of law: namely that it depends upon normative consensus. Grant Gilmore, in his deliverance from the Storrs pulpit seven years ago, put the point with characteristic economy and force. "The function of law, in a society like our own," he said,

. . . is to provide a mechanism for the settlement of disputes on whose soundness, it must be assumed, there is a general consensus among us. If the assumption is wrong, if there is no consensus, then we are headed for war, civil strife, and revolution, and the orderly administration of justice will become an irrelevant, nostalgic whimsy until the social fabric has been stitched together again and a new consensus has emerged. But, so long as the consensus exists, the mechanism which the law provides is designed to insure that our institutions adjust to change, which is inevitable, in a continuing process which will be orderly, gradual, and to the extent such a thing is possible in human affairs, rational.[77]

My problem with this is not, of course, the hope for order, reason, steadiness and so on, nor the un-American skepticism as to how much can be accomplished through the working of law. No more than he do I get a lump

[77]Gilmore, *The Ages of American Law*, pp. 109–10.

in my throat at the mention of the Rule of Law, imagine that World Court adjudication of international disputes—"Arafat vs. The State of Israel"—is the wave of the future, or think that setting out to build a general theory of law is any more likely a venture than setting out to build a perpetual motion machine. The problem is that so drastic a contrast, cleaving the world into what, if he were a Muslim, he would be calling the House of Observance and the House of War, not only leaves law the most powerful where the least needed, a sprinkler system that turns off when the fire gets too hot, but more importantly, leaves it, given the way things are on the consensus front these days, wholly marginal to the main disturbances of modern life. If law needs, even "in a society like our own," a well-stitched social fabric in order to function, it is not just a nostalgic whimsy, it is through altogether.

Fortunately or unfortunately, however, the legal mind, in whatever sort of society, seems to feed as much on muddle as it does on order. It operates increasingly not just in relatively settled waters—criminal offense, marital discord, property transfer—but in highly roiled ones where (to remain for the moment in immediate contexts) plaintiffs are shapeless crowds, claims moral resentments, and verdicts social programs, or where the seizing and release of diplomats is countered by the seizing and release of bank accounts. That it operates less well in such waters is beyond much doubt. But it is beyond any doubt at all that it is in them that it is more and more going to operate, as both social grievances on the domestic side and political ones on the international get more and more cast in idioms of entitlement and equity, legitimacy and justice, or right and obligation. Like just about every other long-standing institution—religion, art, science, the state, the family—law is in the process of learning to survive without the certitudes that launched it.

The notion that the mechanisms of law have serious application only where prior consensus guarantees their social force comes, I think, from a view of law, which, as Professor Gilmore acknowledges, derives from that excited stoic, Justice Holmes, as passively reflective of the community in which it exists: "Law reflects [this from Gilmore] but in no sense determines the moral wisdom of a society. The values of a reasonably just society will reflect themselves in a reasonably just law. . . . The values of an unjust society will reflect themselves in an unjust law."[78]

[78]Ibid, pp. 110–11. The Holmes quotation, "all of jurisprudence [reduced] to a single, frightening statement," that Gilmore says he is paraphrasing is at p. 49: "The first requirement of

There is doubtless more than a grain of truth in this rather lunar view of legal things, and it is certainly helpful to magistrate consciences. But it rather neglects the even more critical truth that law, rather than a mere technical add-on to a morally (or immorally) finished society, is, along of course with a whole range of other cultural realities from the symbolics of faith to the means of production, an active part of it. *Ḥaqq, dharma,* and *adat . . . ius, recht,* and *right, . . .* animate the communities in which they are found (that is, the sensibilities they represent do): make them—again along with a great many other things and to different degrees in different places—what juristically, if you will permit it, humanly, if you will not, they are.

Law, even so technocratized a variety as our own, is, in a word, constructive; in another, constitutive; in a third, formational. A notion, however derived, that adjudication consists in a willed disciplining of wills, a dutiful systematization of duties, or an harmonious harmonizing of behaviors—or that it consists in articulating public values tacitly resident in precedents, statutes, and constitutions—contributes to a definition of a style of social existence (a culture, shall we say?) in the same way that the idea that *virtūs* is the glory of man, that money makes the world go round, or that above the forest of parakeets a parakeet of parakeets prevails do. They are, such notions, part of what order means; visions of community, not echoes of it.

Taken together, these two propositions, that law is local knowledge not placeless principle and that it is constructive of social life not reflective, or anyway not just reflective, of it, lead on to a rather unorthodox view of what the comparative study of it should consist in: cultural translation. Rather than an exercise in institutional taxonomy, a celebration of tribal instruments of social control, or a search for *quod semper aequum et bonum est* (all of them defensible enough activities as such, though I do not have much hope for the last myself), a comparative approach to law becomes an attempt, as it has become here, to formulate the presuppositions, the preoccupations, and the frames of action characteristic of one sort of legal sensibility in terms of those characteristic of another. Or, slightly more practically,

---

a sound body of law is, that it should correspond with the actual feelings and demands of the community, whether right or wrong," and is taken from O. W. Holmes, Jr., *The Common Law,* ed. M. de W. Howe (Cambridge, Mass., 1963), p. 36. The degree to which this dictum assumes the prior, independent existence of "feelings and demands" to the "body of law" (and that "right and wrong" are some self-standing third things), so that "soundness" can be measured by the degree that the latter, as constructed, conforms to the former, as given, seems to go unnoticed by Gilmore and his illustrious predecessor alike.

to bring off this hermeneutic *grand jeté* with respect to some more focused problem, like the relation between the grounding of norms and the representation of fact (or: the representation of norms and the grounding of fact). This is, of course, like Englishing Dante or demathematizing quantum theory for general consumption, an imperfect enterprise, approximate and makeshift, as I trust I have proved. But, aside from resigning ourselves to the fixity of our own horizons or retreating into mindless wonder at fabulous objects, it is all there is, and it has its uses.

Among those uses is that, in such an approach, law is rejoined to the other great cultural formations of human life—morals, art, technology, science, religion, the division of labor, history (categories themselves no more unitary, or definite, or universal than law is)—without either disappearing into them or becoming a kind of servant adjunct of their constructive power. For it, as for them, the dispersions and discontinuities of modern life are the realities that, if it is to retain its force, it must somehow fathom. Whether or not it will so fathom them, in this place or that, with respect to this matter or that, employing these conceptions or those, is of course very much up in the air, and there is cause enough for even Holmesian pessimism, if not perhaps for such satisfaction in it. But the problem in any case is no different than for any other cultural institution: it will prosper if it can compass dissensus—"war, civil strife, and revolution"; not if it cannot. The sure fatality is to imagine variance not there or wait for it to go away.

As I say, it is not hard to find dissensus, legal or any other, these days; difference is too much with us late and soon. But one of the better places to look for it is surely in the international realm; particularly in that part of it that has come, a bit tendentiously in my opinion, to be called the Third World; more particularly yet in the interactions between the Third World and what is, in this headline taxonomy, I suppose still at least nominally the First: that is, the West. The lawyer attracted to hard cases and bad law and the anthropologist attracted to disturbed traditions and cultural incoherence can both find here more than enough to satisfy their deviant tastes.

So far as law is concerned, this inviting disorder derives from two main sources: the persistence of legal sensibilities formed in times not necessarily simpler but certainly more self-contained, and the confrontation of those sensibilities by others not necessarily more admirable or more deeply conceived but certainly more world-successful. In every Third World country—even Volta, even Singapore—the tension between established notions of what justice . . . *ḥaqq* . . . *dharma* . . . *adat* . . . is and how it gets done and imported ones more reflective of the forms and pressures of modern life animates whatever there is of judicial process. Nor is this confusion of legal tongues but mere transition, a passing derangement soon to yield to historical correction. It is the hardening condition of things.

As it has hardened, throwing up all sorts of curiosities, it has come to be discussed under all sorts of rubrics—"legal pluralism," "legal transplants," "legal migrations," "legal syncretism," "external law (versus 'internal')," "lawyer's law (versus 'folk' or 'customary')"; the multiplicity being but testimony to the improvisory quality of the discussions.[79] I will myself use "legal pluralism," mainly because it seems to commit one to less, hardly more than the mere fact of variance itself; and particularly not to the notion that the whole phenomenon is reducible to but another chapter in the history of oppression: who swindles whom, when, where, and how. Whatever the purposes driving the introduction of Western law-ways into non-Western contexts, and I have no quarrel with the view that they have not generally been philanthropic, what is happening to legal sensibilities in the Third World is not much elucidated by the opinionative categories of postcolonial polemic.

It is also not much elucidated by the more equable (or anyway, more

[79]See, inter alia, M. B. Hooker, *Legal Pluralism: An Introduction to Colonial and Neo-colonial Laws* (Oxford, 1975); S. B. Burman and B. E. Harrel-Bond, eds., *The Imposition of Law* (New York, 1979); M. Galanter, "The Modernization of Law," in *Modernization,* ed. M. Weiner, (New York, 1966), pp. 153–65; idem, "The Displacement of Traditional Law in Modern India," *Journal of Social Issues* 24 (1968): 65–91; idem, "Hinduism, Secularism and the Indian Judiciary," *Philosophy East and West* 21 (1971): 467–87; B. Cohn, "Some Notes on Law and Change in North India," *Economic Development and Cultural Change* 8 (1959): 79–93; R. S. Khare, "Indigenous Culture and Lawyer's Law in India," *Comparative Studies in Society and History* 14 (1972): 71–96; A. St. J. Hannigan, "The Imposition of Western Law Forms on Primitive Societies," *Comparative Studies in Society and History* 4 (1961–2): 1–9; V. Rose, "The Migration of the Common Law: India," *Law Quarterly Review* 76 (1960): 59–63; J. N. D. Anderson, "Conflict of Laws in Northern Nigeria," *International and Comparative Law Quarterly* 8 (1959): 44–56; M. Rheinstein, "Problems of Law in the New Nations of Africa," in *Old Societies and New States,* ed. C. Geertz (New York, 1963), pp. 220–46; A. Watson, *Legal Transplants: An Approach to Comparative Law* (Edinburgh, 1974); J. H. Beckstrom, "Transplantation of Legal Systems: An Early Report on the Reception of Western Laws in Ethiopia," *American Journal of Comparative Law* 21 (1973): 557–83; M. A. Jaspan, "In Quest of New Law: The Perplexity of Legal Syncretism in Indonesia," *Comparative Studies in Society and History* 7 (1964–65): 252–66; S. Hatanaka, "Conflict of Laws in a New Guinea Highlands Society," *Man* 8 (1973): 59–73; A. A. Schiller, "Conflict of Laws in Indonesia," *Far Eastern Quarterly* 2 (1942–43): 31–47.

equable-sounding) ones of international law. Whatever the uses certain features of such law—rules of embassy, freedom of the seas doctrines, prisoner of war codes—may or may not sometimes have in ordering relations between states, they are, those features, neither lowest common denominators of the world's catalogue of legal outlooks nor universal premises underlying all of them, but projections of aspects of our own onto the world stage. This is as such no bad thing (better, by my local lights, Jeffersonian notions of human rights than Leninist ones), except perhaps as it leads us to imagine there is more commonality of mind in the world than there is or to mistake convergence of vocabularies for convergence of views. But the central issue posed by the florescence of legal pluralism in the modern world—namely, how ought we to understand the office of law now that its varieties have become so wildly immingled—largely escapes its rather classroom formulae.

"Florescence," in any case, is not too strong a word, though it is a somewhat ironic one. Not every Third World country is perhaps in the position of Ethiopia, which by the 1960s (before the military simplified things in some ways and complicated them in others) boasted not only a host of sharply contrasting tribal legal traditions, from pastoral Galla to agrarian Amhara, some of them operating in a Christian context, some in a Muslim, some in a pagan, but a Caesaro-Papist imperial code dating from the seventeenth century, Mālikī and Shāfi'ī versions of the šarī͜ca introduced about the tenth, a Swiss penal code, French civil, maritime, commercial, and criminal procedure codes, and an English civil procedure code, as well as parliamentary legislation administered by a civil High Court (staffed until 1957 by English judges) and royal decree administered by a Supreme Imperial Court (staffed, if that's the word, until 1974, by the Lion of Judah).[80] But in less extravagant form, legal eclecticism—something from abroad, something from home; something secular, something religious; something statutory, something traditional—is general in that world.

[80]Hooker, *Legal Pluralism*, pp. 393–94. What the situation is since the 1974 takeover is obscure, save that there are now a lot of military courts as well. The civil code, drafted by continental scholars, who apparently had a marvellous time, contained 3,367 articles, making it one of the largest in the contemporary world (ibid, p. 399). I, of course, have no wish to argue that "legal eclecticism" is confined to the Third World or that it does not have a long historical existence (cf. Watson, *Legal Transplants*); merely that it is right now especially prominent there and looks like it is becoming even more so. Nor do I wish to suggest that it is, as such, pathological; it is, in fact, part of the usual process of legal change. ("History of a system of law is largely a history of borrowing of legal materials from other legal systems . . . ," R. Pound, quoted in Watson, *Legal Transplants*, p. 22.)

The initial instinct of the Western-trained lawyer to this sort of situation is, I think, to deplore it as an affront to juristic decency, as the initial instinct of the Western-trained anthropologist is to explain it away as cultural posturing. The degree to which adjudication worthy of the name can proceed in such a nomistic din and the degree to which, so far as it does, its operations carry much social weight are, of course, empirical questions with different answers in different cases. But an affliction so prevalent, if affliction it is, would seem unlikely to be merely factitious or trivial. However difficult it may be to assimilate to received categories and standard ideals, it is not dismissable as the senseless product of spoiled societies.

It is, indeed, just this difficulty that, for me anyway, makes it interesting, for it suggests that the inability of the Western polarization of applicable law and pertinent fact—the never-the-twain confrontment of pictures of "what is right" and stories of "what is so"—to describe effectively how adjudication proceeds in other traditions is only increased when those traditions become embroiled with one another and with those of the West itself. To rely on that polarization is now not just to distort the law elsewhere, it is to be left without anything, save mockery and lamentation, to say about it at all. We need, to put the thing in a way that will seem excitingly avant-garde to some and to others merely fashionable ("trendy" is the trendy epithet), a novel system of discourse, a new way of talking if you will, not only to grasp what is going on, legal-wise, in the Ethiopias of the world, but, as this sort of thing is always reflexive, redescribing the describer as it redescribes the described, among ourselves.

Richard Rorty, in his recent *Philosophy and the Mirror of Nature*—a full-scale assault on the sort of neutral framework epistemology I am, under the local knowledge battle cry, sectorially harassing here for law—makes a distinction useful in this regard between what he calls, not altogether fortunately, normal and abnormal discourse.[81] "Normal" (or, as I would prefer, to avoid unwanted echoes, "standard") discourse is discourse that proceeds under a set of rules, assumptions, conventions, criteria, beliefs, which, in principle anyway, tell us how to go about settling issues and resolving disagreements "on every point where statements seem to conflict."[82] It is

[81]R. Rorty, *Philosophy and the Mirror of Nature* (Princeton, 1979). The normal/abnormal discussions are at, inter alia, pp. 11, 315–22, 332–33, 357–65. As Rorty acknowledges, the distinction is taken, and rotated a bit, from Thomas Kuhn's between normal and revolutionary science: see T. Kuhn, *The Structure of Scientific Revolutions,* 2nd ed. (Chicago, 1970); idem, *The Essential Tension,* (Chicago, 1977).

[82]Rorty, *Philosophy and the Mirror of Nature* p. 316. My preference for standard/nonstandard

the sort of discourse scientists usually imagine themselves to have (and over great ranges of inquiry actually do) and literary critics perennially think themselves tantalizingly near at long last more or less to achieving (and in certain moments and particular circumstances actually are). But it is the sort, also, that governs Professor Gilmore's "rational" settlement of disputes under "sound," that is, consensual, procedures—a condition that also indubitably obtains, except, as he notes, where it does not. Normal discourse, Rorty writes, is "any discourse (scientific, political, theological, or whatever) which embodies agreed-upon criteria for reaching agreement."[83] It projects a situation

. . . in which all residual disagreements [are] seen to be "non-cognitive" or merely verbal, or else temporary—capable of being resolved by doing something further. What matters is that there should be agreement about what would have to be done if a resolution *were* to be achieved. In the meantime, the interlocutors can agree to differ—being satisfied of each other's rationality the while.[84]

"Abnormal" (or "nonstandard") discourse is, then, discourse in which "agreed-upon criteria for reaching agreement" are not the axis upon which communication turns and the evaluation of disparate views in terms of some accepted framework within which they can be objectively assessed and commensurated one with the other is not the organizing aim. Hope for agreement is not abandoned. People occasionally do change their minds or halve their differences as the result of intelligence concerning what individuals or groups of individuals whose minds run on other tracks believe. But "exciting and fruitful disagreement"—how do I know what I think until I see what you say—is recognized as a no less rational process.[85]

Normal discourse [thus Rorty] is that which is conducted within an agreed-upon set of conventions as to what counts as a relevant contribution, what counts as answering a question, what counts as having a good argument for that answer or a good criticism of it. Abnormal discourse is what happens when someone joins in the discourse who is ignorant of these conventions or who sets them aside. . . . The product of normal discourse [is] the sort of statement which can be agreed to be true by all participants whom the other participants count as "rational." The

stems from a dislike of the pathology overtones of normal/abnormal (itself a revision of Kuhn's rather too political-sounding normal/revolutionary) and from a dislike of pure types, dichotomous dualisms, and absolute contrasts.
[83]Ibid, p. 11.
[84]Ibid, p. 316.
[85]Ibid, p. 318.

product of abnormal discourse can be anything from nonsense to intellectual revolution. . . .[86]

It can also be, less dramatically, a practicable method for living in a situation where dissensus is chronic, probably worsening, and not soon to be removed. I do not want to pursue the philosophical issues here, themselves hardly settled into the world of the acclaimed and the obvious, any further. We can leave the vexed to vex the vexing. My concern is with what law is like when what most lawyers, and most anthropologists too, would probably regard as the *sine qua non* of its existence—"agreement about the things that are fundamental" (to quote this time the peroration of another Storrs lecturer than Professor Gilmore as foil, namely Justice Cardozo)—is rather spectacularly absent.[87]

So far as we, anthropologically-minded lawyers or law-minded anthropologists, are concerned, the issue that faces us is, as I say, how to describe such situations in a usefully informative way; informative both as to them and as to the implications they have for how we need to think about legal process as a general phenomenon in the world, now that the pieties of natural law, the simplicities of legal positivism, or the evasions of legal realism no longer seem of very much help. It is a matter of talking about irregular things in regular terms without destroying thereby the irregular quality that drew us to them in the first place; as noted before, a most irregular business.

It is this irregular business, "the study of abnormal discourse from the point of view of some normal discourse," as Rorty puts it, "the attempt to make some sense of what is going on at a stage where we are still too unsure about it to [know how, exactly, properly to] describe it and thereby to begin [a systematic] account of it," that has come to be called hermeneutics—a term whose Greek looks, theological past, and Herr Professor pretentiousness ought not to put us off because, under the homelier and less fussy name of interpretation, it is what many of us at least have been talking all the time.[88] Indeed, it is here that the ant-hill level conversation between

[86]Ibid, p. 320.
[87]B. N. Cardozo, *The Growth of Law* (New Haven, 1924), p. 145.
[88]Rorty, *Philosophy and the Mirror of Nature,* p. 320. Rorty's use of "hermeneutics" for normal discourse about abnormal discourse (and "epistemology" for normal discourse about normal discourse) is itself not altogether normal, and I am myself not completely ready to endorse it. Quite standard legal or anthropological (or literary, or theological . . .) commentary seems to me also properly to be termed hermeneutic, and epistemology, though I share Rorty's distaste for it in its traditional form, seems to me not its opposite but merely something else—namely, theory of knowledge. This, as I see it, terminological quirk is not however of

anthropologists, absorbed with the peculiarities of ethnographic cases, and lawyers, absorbed with those of legal ones, that I proposed in the first part of this essay as the most practical way for these dissimilar aficionados of the local to assist one another with, if not precisely common problems, anyway cognate ones, is most urgently needed. Legal pluralism, attracting the lawyer because it is legal and the anthropologist because it is plural, would seem to be just the sort of phenomenon neither could leave safely to the care of the other.

An hermeneutics of legal pluralism—an attempt to represent Ethiopic situations, whether in the Third World, the Second, or, now that challenges to one-state, one-law ideas are turning up closer to home, the First, in a reasonably intelligible fashion—does not imply, therefore, the construction of some miraculous Esperanto in which everything counter, original, spare, strange, can be blankly and neutrally said; the sort of thing Rebecca West once dispatched by remarking of a U.N. publication that, in deference to the dove of peace, it was written in pidgin English. (A leading anthropologist of law, Paul Bohannan, despairing, as well he might, of the long debate concerning whether African law ought to be analyzed in terms of African concepts or Western ones, once suggested, in apparent seriousness, that we all write about such things in FORTRAN.) What it implies, revolution enough for most academics, is an expansion of established modes of discourse, in the case at hand those of anthropology and comparative law, in such a way as to make possible cogent remarks about matters normally foreign to them, in the case at hand cultural heterogeneity and normative dissensus. The standards of cogency must needs be our own—Whose else could they be?—but they need not be such that everything that goes on in the world beyond the ordered talk of federal appeals courts or tribal ethnographies fails to meet them.

This effort, half-quixotic, half-Sisyphean (the implausible takes a little longer), to render anomalous things in not too anomalous words is especially illuminating in the case of legal pluralism because it is not just observers of Third World complexities who find themselves drawn inexorably into

any particular importance in the present connection. For my views of what interpretation in anthropology comes to, see my "Thick Description: Toward an Interpretive Theory of Culture," in *The Interpretation of Cultures,* pp. 3–30.

it but the subjects of those complexities as well. They, too, oscillate unsteadily between trying to comprehend their legal world in terms far too integral—revivalist-traditional, radical-revolutionary, law-code Western—to represent it realistically and abandoning much hope of comprehending it, save opportunistically, at all. Things do not look that much clearer from within than they do from without. And what from the one side is an hermeneutic challenge, what can we say about so polyglot a discourse, is from the other a practical one, what can we say *in* it.

Take Indonesia, and most especially Java, which I know somewhat more about than I do Ethiopia. Settled by Austronesians coming, in God knows how many waves, by God knows how many routes, out of what is now south China and north Vietnam a millennium or two before Christ; scene of elaborate Indic state building, Borobudur and all that, from about the fifth century to about the fifteenth; progressively honeycombed with rather single-minded Chinese settler-traders from the Han on; subject to intense Islamic missionization, some orthodox, some less, from the twelfth century; colonized inchmeal, region by region, by the Dutch from 1598 to 1942 (with an English interlude, bringing eminent domain and leftside driving, around the time of the Napoleonic wars); occupied, and rather generally manhandled, by the Japanese Army from 1942 to 1945; and now variously intruded upon by American, East Asian, Australian, European, Soviet, and Middle Eastern political and economic interests—there is hardly a form of legal sensibility (African, perhaps, and Eskimo) to which it has not been exposed.

I have already alluded to the general nature of legal arrangements in the Netherlands East Indies in connection with my discussion of *adat* as against *adatrecht.* Basically, it was a to-each-his-own sort of system ("like over like is grace," the homily-slogan went), with the Netherlands government as the final arbiter as to who the each-es were and what was their own.[89] The fundamental distinction was straight-forward enough: it was between Europeans and non-Europeans. But there were too many sorts of non-Europeans, too much disagreement between resolute modernizers, resolute orientalizers, and resolute temporizers among the Europeans, and too

---

[89]For general descriptions of Netherland East Indies legal development, see J. S. Furnivall, *Netherlands India: A Study of Plural Economy* (Cambridge, England, 1944); Supomo, *Sistim Hukum di Indonesia Sebelum Perang Dunia II* (Jakarta, 1957); M. B. Hooker, *A Concise Legal History of Southeast Asia* (Oxford, 1978), chap. 7; Hooker, *Legal Pluralism,* chap. 5; M. B. Hooker, *Adat Law in Modern Indonesia* (Kuala Lumpur, 1978), chap. 4; D. Lev, "Judicial Institutions and Legal Culture in Indonesia," in *Culture and Politics in Indonesia,* ed. C. Holt (Ithaca, 1972), pp. 246–318.

many ways in which individuals on opposite sides of the divide were caught up in one another's lives to make this straightforwardness more than the frame for grand indirection.

The history of this indirection is, of course, a long and changeful one, full of wistful codifications and policy turnarounds. But by the early part of this century it had more or less reached the form, or nonform, in which the Republic finally inherited it: three major legal classes—Europeans, Natives, and Foreign Orientals; two major court hierarchies—one *Rechtsstaat* administrative, full of jural bureaucrats, one colonial administrative, full of native affairs experts; and a horde of special cases, particular arrangements, and unassimilable practices blurring the classes and scrambling the hierarchies.[90]

On the classificatory side, the main complicating factors were the porous quality of the Foreign Orientals category, from which all sorts of socially interstitial types were always leaking into quasi-European status, the ambiguous position of "educated" Indonesians, who were sometimes Natives and sometimes not, and a vast set of elaborate rules for bending the rules when they got in the way of the business of imperialism. On the hierarchy side, they were a developed *šarī͗a* court system only half controlled, and less than half understood, by the colonial administration, and a great host of *adatrecht* tribunals grouped by *adatrecht* jurists into nineteen *adatrecht* jurisdictions on diffusely, and sometimes rather notional, culture-area grounds. Details aside, however piquant (that the Japanese were honorary Europeans; that a Native who lived sufficiently like a Dutchman could apply to the Governor General to become legally treated as one; that intermarriage made Dutch women into Indonesian or Chinese, and vice versa; that you could be a European for purposes of a particular transaction, like bank borrowing, and a Native for everything else), whatever one has here it is certainly a great deal of law and not very much consensus.

In any case, after first, the rigors of the Japanese occupation, when for about three years law came out of the barrel of a gun, and second, the dislocations of the miscarried Dutch return, when for about five it came out of a desperate effort to restore at least the semblance of the prewar social order, the various components of this collage were rudely pried apart and, some

---

[90]For a brief systematic review of all this, see E. A. Hoebel and A. A. Schiller, "Introduction," in ter Haar, *Adat Law*. Cf. J. H. A. Logemann, *Het Staatsrecht van Indonesië, Het Formeel System* (The Hague and Bandung, 1955), pp. 17–30. The court system was actually rather more complicated than this, given the somewhat different arrangements in the "directly" and "indirectly" administered parts of the colony; see Hooker, *Legal Pluralism*, pp. 275–77.

discarded, some added, some reworked, about as rudely glued back together again.

As Daniel Lev, the foremost student of these matters, has repeatedly pointed out, what the coming of Indonesian independence (declared in 1945, achieved in 1950) meant for legal institutions there was their engulfment by a suddenly much more active political life, a phenomenon usually misperceived, inside the country and out, as that most feared of tropical diseases, the Decline of Law.[91] The tension between religious, regional, racial, economic, and cultural groupings that in the colonial period was prevented, save now and again and then in mainly outlaw fashion, from breaking into open political expression came, under Sukarno, who was nothing if not eclectic, not just to expression but to uproar. Everyone from soldiers and civil servants to schoolboys and sharecroppers splintered into contending factions, fixedly embittered; a fate from which judges, lawyers, law scholars, legislators, and policemen did not escape. Rather than disappearing with the disappearance of the Dutch, legal pluralism burst the high-wrought institutional structure that, however inequitably, previously contained it.

The irony, largely unperceived at the time, glaring now that its human price is known, was that this efflorescence of disagreement about everything and anything took place in the accents of a radically unitary nationalism that denied the legitimacy, indeed sometimes the very existence, of such disagreement in the name of pervasive, exceptionless social integration. So far as law was concerned, this took the form of trying to subordinate the established legal sensibilities—Muslim, adat, Indic, Western, or whatever—to a novel, visional one, called "revolutionary," whose animus was a great deal clearer than its content. The initial reaction to the simultaneous discrediting of colonial legal arrangements and the accentuation of the problem to which they were a response—incommensurable notions of what justice is—was to regard the arrangements as having caused the problem. Remove the one and you remove the other.

[91]Lev, "Judicial Institutions," (on "the decline of law," pp. 257 ff., 316 ff.); idem, *Islamic Courts in Indonesia* Berkeley, 1972; idem, "The Politics of Judicial Development in Indonesia," *Comparative Studies in Society and History* 8 (1964–65):173–99. Lev himself occasionally writes (for example, "Judicial Institutions," pp. 316–17; "Politics of Judicial Development," p. 189) as though the intensity of political conflict and the social weight of legal institutions were in inverse correlation, the advance of the one leading *pari passu* to the retreat of the other. But this is, I think, but the result of taking consensus theories of Western, and especially Anglo-American law, which he represents as "impersonal," "formal," and "unitary," rather more seriously than the facts of its legal life, now or in the past, warrant.

This did not turn out to be so. Rather than a grand coming together in the name of a recovered national identity, there was, in its name, a grand falling out. So far as law is concerned, this in part occurred (as, again, Daniel Lev has shown) in the form of a three-cornered struggle between judges, prosecutors, and police for dominance within the Western-without-Westerners, thus "national," legal apparatus that emerged with the disestablishment of racial categories and segregated courts. Judges, seeking to inherit the elevated status of their Dutch predecessors without the colonial odor associated with it, looked to Common Law models, and especially to the American one, to shore up their position (they even sought, unsuccessfully, to institute judicial review). Prosecutors, seeking to correct the lowly status of their "native justice officer" predecessors, who were hardly more than exalted law clerks, looked to continental Civilian models, the *juge d'instruction* sort of thing, to upgrade theirs. And the police, seeking independence not only from judges and prosecutors, but from ministers of justice and army chiefs of staff, and the end thereby of their running-dog image in the popular mind, looked to their vanguard role in the Revolution to refurbish theirs.[92] In part, the falling out occurred in the form of a reinvigoration of the šarīⁱa court system—organized pressure from the pious (and organized resistance from the secular) for its expansion, centralization, and "officialization"; for broadened jurisdiction, increased authority, and indeed, in extreme "Islamic State" notions, constitutional status.[93] And in part, it occurred in the form of a renewal, under local management, of the *adatrecht* movement, represented as an authentically Indonesian, "law of the people" bulwark against foreign impurities of whatever sort: Western "positivist," Middle Eastern "dogmatist," or Indic "feudalist" alike.[94]

Leaving aside the question of how all these struggles have come out (they have not come out; they have merely continued, and will probably do so, in some fashion or other, more or less indefinitely), the upheavals attendant upon invasion, reaction, and revolution in a single decade—and Putsch,

[92]Lev, "Politics of Judicial Development"; "Judicial Institutions."

[93]Lev, *Islamic Courts.*

[94]On *adatrecht* (or now, *hukum adat*) in the Republic, see Jaspan, "In Quest of New Law." The issues here are complicated by the fact that open attacks on "Islam" are more or less impossible in Indonesia, which is self-defined as a Muslim society, polity, and population, so that the strong anti-šarīⁱa sentiments of *adat* law theorists have to be somewhat indirectly expressed, by the fact that even the most headlong Westernizers (Capitalist or Communist) or Islamizers must give at least lip service to *adat* and "The Indonesian Spirit," and by the fact that, explictly in Bali, implicitly in many parts of Java, much of what is taken to be *adat* is in fact Indic in character and origin. The politics of more-authentic-than-thou can get, in such a context, both extremely elaborate and extraordinarily delicate.

mass murder, and military rule in the following—hardly caused either thought about the law or the practice of it to become peripheral to the mainstream of social development. If anything, they pushed them even more toward the middle of it.[95] The effort to connect if/then views of how life coheres and as/therefore formulae for rendering cases decidable does not lessen when the views proliferate and the formulae clash. It merely takes on a more determined tone.

What I called the constructional role of law is indeed especially clear here. For what is at issue is not, after all, whether property is to devolve according to *adat, šarīca,* or Roman Dutch principles; whether secular marriage is going to be recognized or financial institutions may charge interest; nor even whether Balinese Hinduism or Javanese Indic mysticism should be admitted by the state to legal standing—all perduring controversies in independent Indonesia. What is at issue, and what these specific disputes in one way or another evoke and symbolize, is the sort of society, what counts and what does not, this ex-East Indies is now going to be. Law, with its power to place particular things that happen—this promise, that injury—in a general frame in such a way that rules for the principled management of them seem to arise naturally from the essentials of their character, is rather more than a reflection of received wisdom or a technology of dispute settlement. Small wonder that it draws toward it the same sorts of passions those other begetters of meanings and proposers of worlds—religion, art, ideology, science, history, ethics, and commonsense—draw toward them.

The passions are intense because what is at risk, or anyway is felt to be, is not just agreement as to how fact is to be found and law instituted. If that were all there was to the problem it could be well enough negotiated: a little moral witnessing here, a little status legislating there; some verdicts

[95]Even amidst the massacres of 1965, where probably somewhere between a quarter and three-quarter million Indonesians were killed by other Indonesians, a perverse kind of justice doing persisted. In the area of Java where, thirteen years earlier, I had worked, the army assembled village populations in the district capital square, asked each to indicate who the "Communists" among them were, and then assigned the condemned of one village to the condemners of another, and vice versa, to take home and execute. Under the Suharto regime, when the presumed subversives who had escaped fates of this sort, perhaps as many as a hundred thousand, were interned in prison camps, legal activity centered around human rights issues conceived in largely Western, due process terms and around the formation of a Western sort of client-centered advocacy profession, something Indonesia had barely had to that point, to pursue them. And finally, since the general resurgence of Islamic political activity, stimulated by the Iranian "legists to power" revolution, the role of *šarīca* adjudication has become an even livelier focus of dispute than it had been previously.

designed to quiet village disharmonies, some fictions concocted to enable commercial banking. Hardly anyone, even a marriage closer or a probate judge, is ready to die for pure procedure. What is at risk, or felt to be, are the conceptions of fact and law themselves and of the relations they bear the one to the other—the sense, without which human beings can hardly live at all, much less adjudicate anything, that truth, vice, falsehood, and virtue are real, distinguishable, and appropriately aligned.

The struggle over how adjudication is to be conducted—the sort of thing that set the bureaucrat god-king of Bali and the citizens of my village at odds—is, in short, part of a much wider, deeper struggle, as it was there, to evolve a practible form of life, to patch together what, in reference to Anglo-Indian law, an even more jigsaw affair than Dutch-Indonesian, has been called a working misunderstanding. The prospective parties to such a misunderstanding have, of course, changed somewhat in recent years, and their relative power has changed even more. And there is, also, of course, at least the possibility that one of the parties will so triumph politically as to be able to fasten their views on the others, though I myself rather doubt it. It may even be that a genuine Hobbesean moment will appear where nothing matters save the economy of violence (something that, to a degree, has already occurred in October and November of 1965); but if it does, it will be followed (as has also occurred, under Suharto) by yet another attempt to force the pieces of the collage into some tolerable arrangement. But one thing is surely clear: an instrumental view of law as having to do only with means not with ends, a pure agency for realizing social values set some place else—in religion maybe, or philosophy, or by that famous man at the back of the Clapham bus—will simply not do.[96] "Never place confidence in a man you see flying until you know whether he obeys the *sarīᶜa,*" wrote the great Egyptian enemy of Muslim ecstaticism, Rashid Rida, who, whatever one may think of his legalism, at least saw law as casting its own shadow.[97]

[96]Such a view is, of course, characteristic of legal positivism in general, but it seems particularly attractive to students of comparative law, where facing up to the life-defining character of law is especially nervous-making: "The trend of the foregoing [discussion of Indonesian legal pluralism] tends to the view that law may usefully be considered not as an ultimate value in itself but as a means of realizing other values, including a variety of social and political goals. The law may be regarded as a medium or instrument of social and political worth which need not necessarily have intrinsic value. It should be obvious that this view clearly distinguishes the instrumental value of law, on the one hand, from the value intrinsic goals that law is used to serve on the other." Hooker, *Adat Law,* p. 7.

[97]Quoted in A. Hourani, *The Emergence of the Modern Middle East,* (Berkeley and Los Angeles, 1981), p. 97.

⟨⟨

What will do? That, of course, is hard to say. But it will surely involve a shift away from functionalist thinking about law—as a clever device to keep people from tearing one another limb from limb, advance the interests of the dominant classes, defend the rights of the weak against the predations of the strong, or render social life a bit more predictable at its fuzzy edges (all of which it quite clearly is, to varying extents at different times in different places); and a shift toward hermeneutic thinking about it—as a mode of giving particular sense to particular things in particular places (things that happen, things that fail to, things that might), such that these noble, sinister, or merely expedient appliances take particular form and have particular impact. Meaning, in short, not machinery.

Such, anyhow, is my view, and the governing themes of this discussion, coming into and out of sight as this or that matter has been breathlessly addressed, have all been designed with an intent to advance it. The local knowledge, *Anschauung* and instant case, view of the law; the disaggregation of "law" and "anthropology" as disciplines so as to connect them through specific intersections rather than hybrid fusions; the relativization of the law/fact opposition into a various play of coherence images and consequence formulae; the conception of the comparative study of law as an exercise in intercultural translation; the notion that legal thought is constructive of social realities rather than merely reflective of them; the stress on the historical tenacity of legal sensibilities; the rejection of a social consensus account of the practical force of law in favor of a sense-seeking one; the conviction that legal pluralism is not a passing aberration but a central feature of the modern scene; and the argument that self-understanding and other-understanding are as internally connected in law as they are in the other realms of culture—all these are products of a certain cast of thought, one rather entranced with the diversity of things. Taken together they do not so much cohere into a systematic position, "hermeneuticism" or something equally barbaric, as bounce off one another, insofar as themes may properly be said to do such a thing, and to do so with enough regularity to suggest that, although it is doubtless going rather too far to rework Shelley's line and proclaim lawyers the unacknowledged poets of the world, to conceive of law as a species of social imagination may have something to be said for it.

One thing to be said for it is that analytical resources from somewhere else than behavioralist psychology, neoclassical economics, utilitarian sociology, or functionalist anthropology—hard-edge social science—can be brought to bear in understanding it. The move of social theory toward seeing social action as configuring meaning and conveying it, a move that begins in earnest with Weber and Freud (or, in some readings, Durkheim, Saussure, and G. H. Mead) and that has now become massive, opens up a range of possibilities for explaining why we do the things we do in the way that we do them far wider than that offered by the pulls and pushes imagery of more standard views.

Although this "interpretive turn," as it has been called, the conceiving of human behavior and the products of human behavior as "saying something of something—" which something needs to be drawn out and explicated—has touched virtually every domain of cultural study, reaching even to such positivist strongholds as social psychology and the philosophy of science, it has not as yet had very much influence in legal studies. The strong "how-to" bias of practiced law—how to keep out of court if you can, how to prevail there if you cannot, to echo again Holmes's sardonic summary—has kept it at bay. But it is doubtful whether the history, sociology, and philosophy of a field are well advised to adopt as their own the sense of it held by its practitioners, caught up, as those practitioners are, in the immediate necessities of craft. We need, in the end, something rather more than local knowledge. We need a way of turning its varieties into commentaries one upon another, the one lighting what the other darkens.

There is no ready method for this, and for myself I rather doubt there ever will be. But there is by now some accumulated cunning. We are learning—more I think in anthropology than in law, and within anthropology more in connection with exchange, ritual, or political symbology than with law—something about bringing incommensurable perspectives on things, dissimilar ways of registering experiences and phrasing lives, into conceptual proximity such that, though our sense of their distinctiveness is not reduced (normally, it is deepened), they seem somehow less enigmatical than they do when they are looked at apart. Santayana's famous dictum that one compares only when one is unable to get to the heart of the matter seems to me, here at least, the precise reverse of the truth: it is through comparison, and of incomparables, that whatever heart we can actually get to is to be reached.

I apologize for this Zen koan ("What is the sound of two hands not meeting?") way of putting the matter. But when it is considered that this, comparing incomparables—Milton and Shakespeare, Rembrandt and Reubens, Plato and Kant, Newton and Einstein—is what the disciplines devoted to the descriptive explication of imaginative forms spend a large proportion of their time doing, the sense of outrageous paradox evaporates. And it is for that reason, too, that those disciplines, literary criticism and art history, moral philosophy and the history of science, *inter* a great many *alia,* may have more to offer us in making our way through such perplexities as the shape-shifting nature of the fact/law distinction across cultural traditions and historical phases than supposedly more "scientific" enterprises, where everything that arises must converge. If there is any message in what I have been saying here, it is that the world is a various place, various between lawyers and anthropologists, various between Muslims and Hindus, various between little traditions and great, various between colonial thens and nationalist nows; and much is to be gained, scientifically and otherwise, by confronting that grand actuality rather than wishing it away in a haze of forceless generalities and false comforts.

Phrased thus, it of course all sounds very bracing. We like to think that the reality principle is good for us, except perhaps when it finally kills us. But a serious effort to define ourselves by locating ourselves among different others—others neither distanced as Martians, discredited as Primitives, nor disarmed as universal Everypersons, bent like us on sex and survival—involves quite genuine perils, not the least of which are intellectual entropy and moral paralysis. The double perception that ours is but one voice among many and that, as it is the only one we have, we must needs speak with it, is very difficult to maintain. What has been well called the long conversation of mankind may be growing so cacophonous that ordered thought of any sort, much less the turning of local forms of legal sensibility into reciprocal commentaries, mutually deepening, may become impossible. But however that may be, there is, so it seems to me, no choice. The primary question, for any cultural institution anywhere, now that nobody is leaving anybody else alone and isn't ever again going to, is not whether everything is going to come seamlessly together or whether, contrariwise, we are all going to persist sequestered in our separate prejudices. It is whether human beings are going to continue to be able, in Java or Connecticut, through law, anthropology, or anything else, to imagine principled lives they can practicably lead.

Acknowledgments

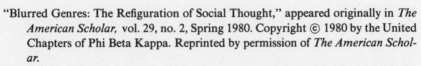

"Blurred Genres: The Refiguration of Social Thought," appeared originally in *The American Scholar,* vol. 29, no. 2, Spring 1980. Copyright © 1980 by the United Chapters of Phi Beta Kappa. Reprinted by permission of *The American Scholar.*

"Found in Translation: On the Social History of the Moral Imagination," appeared originally in *The Georgia Review,* vol. 31, no. 4, Winter 1977. Copyright © 1977 by the University of Georgia. Reprinted by permission of *The Georgia Review.*

" 'From the Native's Point of View': On the Nature of Anthropological Understanding," appeared originally in the *Bulletin of the American Academy of Arts and Sciences,* vol. 28, no. 1, 1974. Copyright © 1974 by the *Bulletin of the American Academy of Arts and Sciences.* Reprinted by permission of the American Academy of Arts and Sciences.

"Common Sense as a Cultural System," appeared originally in *The Antioch Review,* vol. 33, no. 1, Spring 1975. Copyright © 1975 by The Antioch Review, Inc. Reprinted by permission of the editors.

"Art as a Cultural System," appeared originally in *MLN,* vol. 91, 1976. Copyright © 1976 by The Johns Hopkins University Press. Reprinted by permission of The Johns Hopkins University Press.

"Centers, Kings, and Charisma: Reflections on the Symbolics of Power," reprinted from *Culture and Its Creators,* ed. Joseph Ben-David and T. N. Clark (Chicago: University of Chicago Press, 1977). Copyright © 1977 by the University of Chicago. All rights reserved. Reprinted by permission of the University of Chicago Press.

"The Way We Think Now: Toward an Ethnography of Modern Thought," appeared originally in the *Bulletin of the American Academy of Arts and Sciences,* vol. 35, no. 5, February 1982. Copyright © 1982 by the *Bulletin of the American Academy of Arts and Sciences.* Reprinted by permission of the American Academy of Arts and Sciences.

Index